ALAN SUTTON

MY JOURNEY

PAVEMENT TO PREMIER LEAGUE
WITH LEEDS UNITED

To ALAN ~ BERYL.

WHO WILL EVER FORGET THEM GREAT
TIMES BACK IN THE 70s WHEN WE
WERE LIVING NEXT DOOR TO EACH OTHER.
AND OF COURSE THAT GREAT SONG.
FROM YOUR PARTY "SWEET CAROLINE"
HOPE YOU ENJOY THE BOOK.
LOVE ~ BEST WISHES.

Alan Shirley xx

ALAN SUTTON

MY JOURNEY

PAVEMENT TO PREMIER LEAGUE WITH LEEDS UNITED

DB
PUBLISHING

To Shirley, Adele and Miles with all my love

First published 2022 by DB Publishing, an imprint of JMD Media Ltd,
Nottingham, United Kingdom.

ISBN 9781780916279

Printed in the UK

CONTENTS

ACKNOWLEDGEMENTS

There have been many people who have played a part in helping me to write this book, all of whom have been pivotal.

I want to start by thanking my niece Wendy Whitaker for her unending patience, dedication and for the numerous hours she spent helping me with this book. She had the unenviable task and challenge of putting my words and memories to paper and ensuring my thoughts were transcribed into a more reader friendly format! I am forever in her debt.

My nephew, Philip Whitaker also provided a great input and guidance with his wonderful memory regarding facts and events in my life and I would like to thank him too.

I am grateful to the journalist Jon Howe, whose advice and experience of the book writing world was invaluable. I would also like to thank David Conn of *The Guardian* for his early input and encouragement.

One of the unfortunate aspects of writing a book which covers many decades is that some of the people mentioned are no longer with us. They were an influence and inspiration throughout my career and I will never forget their support.

FOREWORD

Do you ever think about the first time you met one of your best friends?

March 1989 and I was doing afternoon training on a Thursday, two days before a Leeds home game, supervised by the one and only Alan Sutton physio.

A brutally hard session which I thought was totally unnecessary, so I told Mr Sutton what I thought of his session and he didn't bat an eyelid; he didn't get involved in an argument and it kinda unnerved me.

Throughout our time together absolutely nothing bothered or upset him, he just ploughed on and did his job.

He became an integral part of the Leeds success, not only as our physio but as our - or maybe just mine - psychologist and he did it, most importantly, with a smile.

Nothing was too much work for Alan, he saved my Sundays many a time by travelling miles to treat my chronic back pains.

And in the darker moments when I thought I would have to retire through my back problems, he was always there to help me believe I could carry on.

Gordon Strachan

PS he always made me laugh, great medicine for the injured.

INTRODUCTION

I began writing this book in March 2020 as football vanished from our stadia and screens almost overnight when the coronavirus pandemic took hold. The word 'unprecedented' has been used many times since then, but a period without football in my life was indeed a new and unwelcome experience. However, the suspension of the sport gave me the opportunity to answer the question I had been asked many times over the years – how I went from working as a builder to becoming part of the wider team that won the First Division championship with Leeds United, the pinnacle of the domestic game.

Like countless others, my dream as a youngster was to become a professional footballer, but sadly those ambitions were never fully achieved. I had limitless amounts of drive and dedication but despite spending all my spare time training and playing with local amateur teams, I knew that I did not have that missing ingredient, the natural talent or genetic advantage to make it as a professional player.

But football was my sustenance, my lifeblood. It was my way of making friends, keeping fit, educating myself and a distraction from the thoughts of the conventional future that failing the 11-plus in 1950s industrial Bradford had in store for me. And although I learned a trade and forged a career outside of the game, football was always there, and I knew it would continue to be a major part of my life in some form or another.

In my spare time I worked as a part-time coach, until one day I witnessed an incident that made me change direction. It was the start of a career lasting over four decades as a sports physio, working with teams in football and rugby league and travelling all over the world.

We all have our up and downs, but I have been fortunate to have met some great people from all walks of life, who have supported me and have been there when I have most needed them. Many of them have been kind enough to share their own stories with me for this book, for which I am very grateful.

I am sure that many people will relate to this story. Life does not always follow a straight path and is often more interesting and fulfilling as a result, but it is what you make it. As a young teenager, I remember reading this quote from the late, great Bill Shankly, 'It's the greatest thing in the world, natural enthusiasm. You're nothing without it.' His words have always stayed with me.

Alan Sutton May 2021

1

HOME, AWAY AND HOME AGAIN

I was born the year after World War Two ended, and it is fair to say that life was not luxurious. I lived with my mum and dad, Winnie and Alf, and my elder sister Joan in a rented back-to-back house in Bradford. It was a typical mill worker's home, like many thousands in the city, with a passage on to the street at the front and a toilet at the end of a small back garden. Inside, there was a cellar and an attic, a tiny scullery kitchen, a living room, and two bedrooms. It was a northern working-class life of coal fires, cobbled streets, smog and gas lamps. The smell of lanolin and smoke hung heavy in the air.

My family was never out of work. Dad was a foundryman and Mum worked in the mills. With two wages coming in, we were better off than many. We had plenty to eat; in fact, I was a bit of a chubby kid for a while, and my mum and dad enjoyed a good social life. Everyone in the street knew each other, and it was a great atmosphere in which to grow up.

As a child with two loving but busy parents, I had a lot of freedom, and like all young kids I enjoyed being outdoors. I always felt like I was an only child; my sister Joan was seven years older than me, an age gap too big for us to seek each other's company, so often I was left to my own devices, but I was never on my own.

My best friends were the Rhodes twins, Alan and Chris, and we played outside all day, in all weathers. We played football all year round, as well as cricket in the summer. We roamed the local streets and nearby woods, and their dad used to take us to the local recreation ground to play football on Sunday mornings. I also loved swimming at the pool at Lapage School, where our Joan was deputy head girl.

Aged five, I went to Barkerend Junior School, where I was more enamoured with talking than working, and when I was seven it was discovered that I was deaf in my left ear. My hearing loss, compounded by my obsession with playing football, had a detrimental effect on my schoolwork. It has been a lifelong regret that I did not spend as much time learning English and maths in my early years as I should have done.

While I was at Barkerend I was picked for the school football team, but being short and stocky, I could not believe it when the teacher put me in goal. We won two of our first three matches, but when we played Bowling Back Lane School we lost 3-1. Their last goal was a penalty taken by Barrie Wright, who later captained England Schoolboys. When the ball flew past me, I was gutted as I felt I had let everyone down. Thankfully, after that the teacher put me on the left wing as I had a half-decent left foot.

When I was not playing football, I read, talked, and dreamed about the game. One of our neighbours, 'Uncle' Arthur, started taking me to Valley Parade to watch Bradford City, who became the team I supported for years. We stood above the tunnel, which in those days was next to the Spion Kop. As a ten-year-old, cheering my idols and soaking up the banter from Arthur and his pals as they complained about the ref and jeered at the opposition, it was the most exciting place in the world. I was also renowned for my good memory. Arthur would buy the Saturday night 'Pink' sports newspaper, with that day's football results, and I could look at them for just a few seconds and remember the scores. My dad's friends would challenge me to recall them for a few pennies, and I always won.

As well as local teams, I followed the big names of the day and I hero-worshipped many of the Manchester United players, especially the imperious Duncan Edwards. On 6 February 1958, I cried when I heard about the plane crash in Munich. I shared a birthday with Edwards, and he was only ten years older than me; I had lost my hero. I was also an avid John Charles fan, and I was in my element when my mum and dad took me to Elland Road to watch his last game for Leeds United before he left for Juventus.

Like many people, I failed the 11-plus, so I did not go to the local grammar school but instead to Barkerend Seniors Boys School. Along with hundreds of thousands of other kids, my life prospects were mapped out at this early age. The Ken Loach film, *Kes*, with its harsh commentary on the limited expectations and narrow options for its young charges could have been filmed at my school. According to the world of education my future would be, at best, skilled manual work. It was up to me to prove otherwise.

My main interest was still football and, at that time, it was possibly my only route out of the mills. When we had our first football practice, the sports teacher Mr Stapleton said he had heard good things about me from junior school, and after a while playing on the left wing he put me at left-back. He did not think I was quick enough to be a winger and to be honest, left-back did suit me better. A full-back never crossed the halfway line; all the teams played with five forwards.

I was still following Bradford City with Uncle Arthur and a local team from Seymour Street, who played on Saturdays, called Albion Rovers. They were from the Albion pub in Leeds Road and had some excellent players, and I got to know everybody, including their trainer, George. When Albion went through to the semi-final of the local league cup against Bradford Telephones, they played at Manningham Mills on Easter Monday. I made my way to the game on my own, which took three buses. Determined to play my part, I remember saying to Arthur's wife, Auntie Nellie, 'What if George forgets something for the game?' She helped me put together a supply of bandages, plasters, and scissors in a small case to take with me.

When I arrived, purposefully clutching my carefully crafted medical bag, with a prescience I can now acknowledge, there were over 1,000 people at the ground, and I did not get near George nor put the kit to use. Albion Rovers lost 3-2 on the day but they got to another final, at Bradford Park Avenue, where they won 4-0 against Low Moor Alloys. This time, we had a bus to take us there and back and I can remember sitting at the front of the bus with their captain Alfie Mahon, holding the trophy as if we had just won the World Cup Final.

Apart from becoming a professional footballer, I did not have a clue what else I might do if my ambition was not realised. I was captain of the school's under-13 football team and trained with Bradford Boys for a short while. But I also tried to pay more attention in lessons; maths and English were still my weakest subjects, and I had to work hard to catch up.

By the time I was due to leave aged 15, I was glad to say there had been a good improvement in my schoolwork. Everyone who was leaving school had a meeting with the youth employment people. I was given an apprenticeship at Airedale Electrics, assembling wired panels, which I was due to start on 1 January 1962. Little did I know that it would be the start of possibly the worst three months of my life.

* * *

My working life did not start well. In three months I had three different jobs, and I was sacked from them all. It was a low point. By this time I think the people at the youth employment centre were sick of seeing me. When I went in for the fourth time, the guy looked through his file without much enthusiasm. He told me that a job had come in for an apprentice street mason with Bradford Corporation. At the interview, I discovered that the superintendent knew my mum and dad and my Uncle Arthur. Thankfully he offered me the job, and I knew it would suit me better than factory work.

On my first day, the depot was busy with wagons hurrying in and out all day. They put me in the workshop to learn how to use a hammer and chisel by chipping away on pieces of stone. I kept hitting my left hand with the hammer and drawing blood, so I went to ask the foreman for some plasters. His reply was, 'Nay lad, we don't have plasters. Go to the toilet and piss on your hands. That will harden them!' It did the trick, although I still have a few tiny scars from my battered hands. Over the next few months I went out on the road with different gangs, and they taught me how to lay stone flags. I was about nine stone wet through, and some of the flags were nearly as tall as me, but I was determined to work hard, get a bit of confidence back, and put the first three months of my working life behind me.

My apprenticeship lasted for four years, but I had not let go of my ambitions to become a professional footballer. My friends Alan and Chris Rhodes were training with Salts FC at Saltaire, a village on the outskirts of Bradford, and they suggested that I joined them. Salts were in the open-age Yorkshire Football League and although they put me in the reserves, I would be playing against adults for the first time in my life. The coach, George Hinsley, had been a centre-half for Bradford City before the war, and he helped me improve my right-footed technique. We trained twice a week on their well-maintained pitch; they also had good facilities with showers and a bath, which was a big bonus given our sanitary arrangements at home.

Shortly after, Bradford FA Minors set up a training squad at the Salts ground on Sunday mornings, and Chris, Alan, and I began training with them. Their coach, Maurice Conroy, who also worked at Bradford City, invited the three of us to play in the under-17 West Riding Cup. Then I was asked if I fancied playing for Glenwood Rovers in the Shipley league on Sunday afternoons; they were looking for a left-back. I met the committee, who all worked at Butterfields Engineering at Baildon Bottom, and agreed to play. So now I was training and playing with three teams, usually with three matches each weekend. All three teams were doing well in their respective leagues and I was getting some good experience.

That year, Bradford Minors got through to the final of the West Riding FA Cup against Leeds FA at Farsley Celtic's ground. I was at left-back alongside Chris Rhodes. We knew that Leeds would have a strong team as every player was already on Leeds United's books. Peter Lorimer, a first-team player, and Jim McCalliog, who later went on to play for Scotland, were there that day. As Scottish players they were classed as amateurs, so they were permitted to play. Only Bruce Bannister from our team was assigned to a club, and fortunately for us it was Leeds. He had some inside knowledge which gave us a bit of hope and surprisingly we managed to win 4-2. The next day, when I showed my dad the medal, he said proudly, 'That will be the best medal you will ever win.' In terms of my playing career he turned out to be correct.

In the pre-season of 1963/64 I had a trial for the West Riding FA team at the Leeds United training ground at Fullerton Park, adjacent to Elland Road. Alan and Chris were invited, along with Bruce. They picked us to play against Yorkshire Grammar Schools under-18s in a friendly at Harrogate Town on 19 October 1963, which we won 3-1. When I got home and told my dad, he went to the pub and had a couple of extra pints in celebration.

In February 1964, after a Glenwood Rovers match, an elderly gentleman stopped me for a word. He introduced himself as Albert Bartlett, the chief scout for Fourth Division side Bradford Park Avenue. He had spoken to Salts FC, who had permitted him to invite me to train with them the following Thursday.

The training went well. Avenue's manager was the legendary Jimmy Scoular, the captain of Newcastle United when they had won the FA Cup in 1955. At the end of the session they told me to bring my boots and pads and report at 2pm on Saturday to play against Middlesbrough juniors. In the end I had to wait a bit longer before I made it on to the pitch, and I watched the game from the stands. But the following Monday, when I got home from work, there was a telegram waiting for me from Albert. It confirmed that I would be playing against Huddersfield Town juniors and to report to the ground at 6.45pm for a 7.30pm kick-off.

On the night, we won 2-0. I thought I had played reasonably well and hoped I might get another game. Nothing was said at the time, but I knew the manager was watching, so it was just a matter of wait and see.

The next day the club secretary at Salts told me, 'Avenue have been in touch. They want to sign you.' They asked me to go to their training session the following night and to meet Scoular. I went on my own as my dad was on the night shift; I remember feeling apprehensive. Scoular was one of the hardest men in football when he was at Portsmouth and Newcastle. When I arrived at the ground, I was shown to the manager's office and there he was, not intimidating in the slightest. He told me that he thought I had done very well on the Tuesday evening and they would like to sign me as an apprentice. When I explained that I was midway through an apprenticeship with Bradford Corporation, he told me, 'If you sign with us, we will find you some building work to do.' He told me to think it over and speak with my dad. I had realised my dream, whatever way I decided to take it forward.

The offer had been a big confidence boost, but I resisted my natural impulsiveness for once in my life and took the time to think things over and discuss them with my mum and dad. There were other things to consider now I was working. I had lost three jobs before securing my apprenticeship with Bradford Corporation, which had been tough. Having a trade was a big deal in those days; I was learning skills that would last me for the rest of my life. An offer from Avenue was great but it was not necessarily going to change my life. At that time, players in the lower divisions still needed to have another income. I had spent a lot of time in the reserves at Salts, so I knew I would be up against a lot of competition to convert an apprenticeship into a professional contract.

After speaking with my dad, the bottom line was that I wanted to keep working, but at the same time sign for the Avenue if that arrangement would work for them. I was also offered a semi-pro contract at £5 a week, but in those days, if you signed professional forms you could not play amateur football afterwards, and I wanted to continue playing for Bradford FA and Glenwood Rovers. Over the next week everything was arranged. I signed as an amateur and we would see how I got on.

I trained with Avenue two nights a week, and shortly after signing I was picked for a midweek reserve game away at Doncaster Rovers. With no home telephones in those days, a representative from the club had knocked on Uncle Arthur's door to ask him to let me know. Arthur tracked me down by calling at the depot and then taking two buses to find me; I was working on the other side of Bradford. Doncaster had the biggest pitch in the league, and as a 17-year-old, I was thrilled to be there.

That summer, Alan Fiddler, the secretary of the West Riding FA, chose Bruce Bannister and me to attend a coaching course at Crystal Palace. Their new athletic stadium had just opened and I think we were the first group to use it. The coaches were Charles Hughes, who became director of coaching for the FA, and George Curtis, who had worked abroad coaching football. Once again, Bruce and I found it helpful to have a week of dedicated training. Towards the end of the week I rang the Avenue to check in. They told me that they needed me to play on Saturday afternoon in a pre-season game, the first team versus the reserves; I had to be at the club at 2pm.

We finished on the Friday afternoon and I had not given much thought to the match the next day. I caught the bus back to central London, which seemed to take forever, and discovered the next steam train to Bradford was not until 9pm and it took over six hours.

By the time I got to bed it was almost 5am. I woke around lunchtime and made my way to Avenue's ground at Horton Park. The new season had brought a few new players, including Bobby Ham, who had played for Avenue in the past. I was in the reserves, playing against the likes of Kevin Hector, Jim Fryatt and John Hardie. As the game went on I think I did okay. We lost 2-1, but that week of training at Crystal Palace had helped a lot.

For the next three seasons I continued playing in the reserves at Bradford Park Avenue; I also had a short spell with Halifax Town's reserves. When I reached my 20th birthday on 1 October 1966 I had worked on assignments all over Bradford and completed my four-year apprenticeship as a street mason. It was a good job I had decided not to give it up; the writing had been on the wall for some time that I would not be good enough to become a professional footballer.

I was doing the odd private job, including some work for my cousin Ann and her husband; I was at their place every Sunday for weeks. Ann toured the east coast of America for a few months, paid for by her mum and dad, for her 21st birthday. During lunch she would get out the maps and show me the places she had visited. I had already been thinking of doing something similar myself, although America was out of the question with the war in Vietnam.

I had been on bonuses for a few years and had a bit of money saved, so I started to make plans. My friend Chris was home from university; he had spent time in Canada through school, and I went round to his house to pick his brains about his trip. He gave me the thumbs-up and agreed to go with me to the immigration office in Leeds. At the interview they told me that a ship was sailing on 21 February 1967, and offered me the papers to sign straight away. Their next question was where did I want to go? The only place I had heard of was Toronto in Ontario. So that was it and without discussing it with anyone but Chris, I signed up there and then to sail in four months' time.

* * *

When I arrived home and told my mum and dad what I had done, to say my mum was upset was an understatement. I had signed up for a one-way ticket and I think she was convinced that she would never see me again. Life in Bradford was not bad by any means, and I had lots of friends and a loving family, but I needed a new purpose especially now my football career had reached a standstill. My dad was more measured; I think he understood my reasons.

In February 1967 I was crossing the Atlantic bound for Halifax, Nova Scotia. I met a few people on the boat. Everyone seemed to have jobs sorted out and somewhere to stay. When I told them that I was going to arrive in Toronto and take it from there, they thought I was crazy.

A week later, in the early hours of 28 February 1967, we docked in Halifax. We had breakfast and made our way to the immigration shed. It took a few hours to process the paperwork for the 800 passengers who had just arrived, so it was later that afternoon before we were permitted to enter the country. It had been snowing heavily and was bitterly cold.

I had a 27-hour train journey to Montreal and then another five hours to Toronto, so it was late the next day before I arrived at my destination. I realised I might have a problem with my Yorkshire accent when the ticket collector lost his temper when I could not make myself understood, but thankfully a guy from Wales came to my rescue. He said to me, 'It's your accent. It's quite strong. I have to listen hard, too.' Talking to him helped to pass the time until we arrived in Toronto.

I found some accommodation for the night and reported to the employment office. The only work available was measuring land, and I knew that it was not for me. When I went to a diner around 5pm to have something to eat, the enormity of what I had done began to hit me. I'd been swept along by the excitement of the journey but now I was feeling deflated and homesick. But I told myself there was no turning back; I just had to get on with it.

From what I had seen of Toronto on my first day and the fact that there was little work, I was not impressed. I knew that my school friend David Brock had emigrated to Canada, and I had his address; he was living in Guelph, about 60 miles west of Toronto. I decided that I would try my luck there, but first I would need to check if there was any work. By lunchtime I was at the bus station for the 1pm departure to Guelph. The guy at the employment centre had rung through to the Guelph office. There was only one job in a factory, but it was better than nothing. I just said, 'Tell them I will take it.'

When I arrived, I booked into the Royal Hotel, bought a paper to look for somewhere to live, and then found David Brock's place. It was great to see a familiar face after the last few days. The next day I found myself somewhere to stay within easy walking distance of the centre; a few other guys were renting rooms there. We were not allowed to use the kitchen area, so I had to eat out or make sandwiches in my room. On the plus side there was a bathroom, which we all had to share, but it was one more than we had at home.

For five weeks I worked at Dayton Steel of Ohio, a couple of miles outside Guelph, where they manufactured truck wheels. I discovered that the foreman was not a fan of English people. When he spoke to me, he always addressed me as 'Limey'. Most of the other Canadian workers had a similar attitude, and they often gave me the cold shoulder when I tried to be friendly. I just got my head down and got on with the job.

After five miserable weeks I decided to move on again, this time to Kitchener, where thankfully the weather was warming up, and I got a job working outside on building sites.

If I thought I had worked hard in Bradford, I had another think coming – these guys were on a completely different level.

After a few months I had an invitation to stay with a family in Edmonton, Alberta, 2,000 miles north-west of Kitchener. Their nephew, Kenny Riley, was a friend of mine from Bradford. I decided to take them up on their kind offer, so I got in touch and bought a train ticket for the two-day journey, leaving on 20 June. I was moving even further away from home.

When I arrived, Joan Bartkus, Kenny's aunt, met me at the station. She took me to their lovely modern house in North Beverley, where I met the rest of the family: Joan's husband Walt, sons Peter, aged 12, Michael, aged five, and their daughter Janet, who was 11. Walt had been born in Lithuania and had emigrated to Bradford from Germany after the war, where he met Joan. They made me feel welcome; it was good at last to have some friendly company.

Walt was a plasterer, and he got me sorted out with a job as a labourer. I had to run between the plasterers with a barrow, keeping up the mud supplies they used to plaster the walls. The new road we were working on was about half a mile long, with new houses on either side, and we had to do four houses each day. If I had any doubts about how hard the work was in Canada compared to England, I would soon find out it was like playing a football match for eight hours in temperatures of 80°F.

If I had thought I was fit, my body was telling me something different. When I woke up the next day, at about 6am, I could not move. My whole body had completely seized up. I had to fall out of bed to try and stand up; every muscle in my body ached. Joan had kindly made me some breakfast, and somehow I climbed into Walt's truck and got through another eight hours. During that first week Walt even did a private job after work, and I helped him. Joan felt sorry for me; she said to Walt, 'Do you have to finish him off in the first week?' It was very much welcome to the real world.

When the work began to dry up as winter approached, I decided to fly back home for Christmas. After hugging everyone and tears from my mum, their main concern was that I looked thinner. I had lost over a stone in weight, but my dad understood. No matter how much I ate, running with the barrow all day long through the summer, I was burning it all off.

It was great to see everyone, but in early January I flew back to Canada. There had been a lot of snow in Edmonton while I had been away, and there was still little work to be had, so I spent the time reading books, ice skating and swimming. I tried to find other work, but once employers knew I had been working outdoors they were not interested; they assumed that I would return to the building sites when the weather improved.

By the beginning of April 1968 I decided to make my way back home via the States. The winters had convinced me that I did not want to be hanging around for months without work. I had been in touch with a family friend named George Wignall, who was now living in Los Angeles, and George had agreed that I could visit him. So I sat down with Joan and Walter and told them of my plans; I would always be grateful for their kindness and for letting me stay.

On 14 May 1968 I caught the first train for my long journey to Los Angeles via Vancouver, Seattle, Portland, and Sacramento. I slept in my seat to save money and passed the time by chatting with my fellow travellers, many of whom were young men on their way to Vietnam. We shared some beers; it was hard to get my head around the thought that most of these lads were going to war while I was going back to safety in England.

I spent a pleasant few days with George, sightseeing in Los Angeles and Hollywood. George took us in his car around Beverley Hills and Bel Air. There were lots of guided tour buses pointing out the homes of stars and other landmarks. It was another world. When we arrived at Elvis Presley's mansion, I tried to climb over the wall for a better look. I spent my last evening in the States watching baseball and talking with George and his friends.

My PanAm 707 flight from Los Angeles landed at Heathrow early in the morning of 21 May 1968. My old life was waiting for me again.

2

THE ROAD TO LEEDS

I had to start somewhere, so I got my old job back at Bradford Corporation. On my first day, it seemed strange that just a week before I had been in Hollywood and Beverley Hills, touring the homes of movie stars, and now I was back raking tarmac again. But after a few months a job offer came out of the blue. While chatting with Allan Ham, he told me that he and his brother Bob were setting up their own building company. They thought that my skills in flagging and tarmacking would give them an extra string to their bow. It was the break I was looking for; I would be their first employee. At the time, Bob was Bradford City's striker. I knew he could open a few doors so I gave in my notice at the council. I was looking forward to a new challenge.

That summer, one of the Bradford City players, Bruce Stowell, gave us a hand at work. On his first day we were doing a job across the road from the house of City manager Jimmy Wheeler. Allan put Bruce in charge of the dumper, filling it with building materials and transporting them across to us. The dumper had a rear-wheel drive and could take a while to master. Bruce was getting on okay, and Allan and I were heads down, getting on with the job when suddenly we heard a shout behind us. We turned to see Bruce frantically grappling with the dumper as he yelled, 'Help! Help!' in panic. We stood and watched in alarm as he lost control, hurtled down the incline with the dumper, and crashed through a neighbour's fence before coming to a halt in the garden. Allan and I didn't know whether to laugh or cry. We ran across to help, but Bruce was okay. However the fence, which the neighbours had only put up the week before, was flattened. We had to spend the rest of the day replacing it. Bob was quite chilled; he said, 'No worries Bruce, we will find you another job to do.' Bruce turned out to be a good worker. Happy days.

There was another incident that Allan, Bob, and I still talk about whenever we get together. It happened one day when we were pebble-dashing a wall in Fagley. Bob was playing for Bradford City at Valley Parade that afternoon, but he came to give us a hand for a few hours before the match. Later that morning he set off with the wagon to take it back to their workshop at Chapel Green Works in Little Horton Lane. Bob had put the ladders in the back, hanging over the cabin's front on the passenger seat side. As he was driving, one or two fans were already making their way to the ground. In a queue of traffic he pulled the wagon up behind a bus full of City supporters, and as the bus stopped to drop people off he pulled out to overtake. Unfortunately, Bob got a bit too close, and the ladder went straight through the back of the bus window. The driver got out, ready to read the riot act, and did a double-take when he saw it was no other than Bobby Ham driving the wagon. Luckily for Bob, the bus driver was a City supporter, and he said, 'Bloody hell, Bobby, what are you doing?! Listen, you'd better get a move on; we need the points this afternoon. You get going, and I'll sort this out.'

Bob dashed home, had a quick shower, and got to the ground just in time; the other lads knew he had been on the building site. I don't think it would ever happen today. They were great times and memories. Early the following season, Bradford transferred Bob to Preston North End, where Alan Ball Snr was the manager and won the Third Division championship. I was very happy for him.

I worked for the Hams for three years. One evening, while I was laying some flags, I was rushed to Bradford Royal Infirmary with an infection in my leg. There I met my future wife Shirley, who was one of the nurses looking after me, and on 31 July 1971 we were married in Sowerby Bridge.

By May 1972 I thought that a change might be in order, so I started working for myself. After a couple of years I went into partnership with a lad I knew named Ian Cooper, a full-back at Bradford City. We built up the business and set on more men, including bricklayers and casual labourers. One of them was Graham Oates, who was a player at City with Ian. Graham and I had played together at East Bowling Unity on Sundays years before. While he was working with us, there was a rumour that he might be getting a transfer from City. One afternoon we were in the wagon, and we stopped at a newsagent to buy the *Telegraph and Argus*, the local evening newspaper. While looking through the paper, Graham suddenly shouted out, 'Bloody hell! I have been sold to Blackburn Rovers!' There were no agents at the lower-league level in those days, and sometimes reading the paper was the only way you found out what was happening to you in football. He went on to win the Third Division championship with Blackburn, just like Bobby Ham had with Preston a few years before.

On 16 December 1974 our daughter Adele Jane was born, followed by our son Miles Richard three years later, on 8 September 1977. By 1979 things were not good in the building trade, and our business was struggling, so Ian and I decided to go our separate ways. After visiting Shirley's cousin one weekend in the beautiful village of Pateley Bridge in Nidderdale, we felt a change was in order, and we moved there from Bradford.

I had decided that I wanted to resume football coaching and use the preliminary coaching badge I had obtained years before to have an outlet from work pressures, so I did a bit here and there in the community. In 1980 I had a call from my friend, Malcolm Cook. We had played at Bradford Park Avenue together, and when I passed my coaching badge in 1970 we had coached together for a few years. He got in touch with me to say that he was in charge of a new setup at Bradford City. He provided evening coaching sessions for young players while trying to spot those with the potential to become apprentices. He asked me if I wanted to become involved, and I jumped at the chance. Ernest Womersley and a lad called Peter Jones were also part of the setup. Over time, I got to know a lot of people at Bradford City.

I had also decided I would like to have some medical training, like Shirley. I had witnessed a car accident while Shirley and I visited our friends Steve and Jenny Fisher. It happened just outside their home and four people were severely injured. Shirley and Jenny immediately began to assist while I just stood there helpless, and it was the worst feeling ever. If I had been the only person on the scene I would not have been able to help the people involved. That incident made up my mind. I had also experienced a lot of injuries while I was playing, and medical training interested me.

I talked to Bryan Edwards, the first team physio at Bradford City, and Bernard Ellison, who looked after the juniors and the reserves. I had also spent time with Colin Kaye, the physio at Bradford Park Avenue, who now had a private practice. He advised me to read about the subject and talk to as many people as possible, which I did.

Eventually, alongside the coaching, I was given some physio work to do. I had a bag with a first aid kit and began looking after one or two rudimentary injuries. It was great to get some practice running on the pitch and giving treatment, and I always asked for advice when I needed it. I must have been doing okay because when Bernard Ellison had to miss a reserve game at Sunderland, Bryan asked me if I could cover the game for him. It was a fantastic experience running on the pitch at Roker Park.

I had become good friends with quite a few City players, including Mick Wood. Mick was also keen to go down the sports injury route, so in early July 1981 we attended the first part of the three-year FA Management and Treatment of Sports Injuries Diploma at Lilleshall. It was an intense week but I enjoyed every moment.

Just after I got back from Lilleshall, I was at Andrew Fielders, the builders' merchants. Little did I know but what happened that day would result in a dramatic change to the rest of my life. The sales manager, David Sharp, asked if I had got a minute; I had always got on well with David. He explained that he and a guy called Sam Rourke had gone on to the board at Halifax Town. He asked if I was still doing physio as well as the building work. I told him what I had done so far, and then he said, 'We are looking for a physio at the Shay. Do you fancy having a chat with our new manager Micky Bullock?' Knowing how difficult things were with the building trade, I said that I would love to, so he told me he would arrange a meeting with the manager. I got the call a couple of days later and went across to Halifax.

* * *

When I met the Halifax Town manager Micky Bullock, I told him that I had just completed my first year at Lilleshall, had been a part-time physio at Bradford City, and had some coaching experience. Micky said, 'That's great, but money is very tight here to pay for a physio.' I later discovered that Micky had been doing the physio work himself alongside the coaching. I secured a deal which would just about cover the weekly bills plus some petrol money. Because of my lack of experience, Micky told me that I would be working with the club doctor, David Lord. As it turned out, Dr Lord was a great guy to work with, but I knew that I had to be my own man as well.

I went to see David Sharp to thank him and tell him that I was starting the following Monday. The last word belonged to him. David's reply was, 'I have opened the door for you; now it is up to you what you do with this opportunity.' Little did David know, or myself for that matter, but what he said to me that day would completely transform the rest of my life.

On 27 July 1981 I began my new career as a physio at Halifax Town. I cannot recall who I treated on my first day, but I did meet the Doc, and we hit it off straight away. I also got to know Brian Hendry; he ran on the pitch on home matchdays. To start with, we agreed that he would continue with the home games as I needed as much help as possible.

Within a few days of starting the job we signed a new striker, Bobby Davison, from Huddersfield Town. I soon found out from Bobby that he was late starting his career as a professional footballer as he had done an apprenticeship as a welder in the shipyards in the north-east. I got to know the rest of the players; one of them was Paul Hendrie, who as a youngster had been the boot boy for Kenny Dalglish at Celtic. I also got to know Paul's six-year-old son Lee, who later had a great career at Aston Villa. Another great player was Billy Ayre, the captain. Billy was a larger-than-life character and became a valued friend for several years. He went on to have a good career as a manager at Blackpool and Cardiff.

My first season seemed to go well, although the club had to apply for re-election to the Football League. During the summer, Mick Wood and I went to Lilleshall to complete our second year of the FA diploma. The lecturer was Geoff Ladley, the Leeds United physio. I had met Geoff a few months before when Halifax played Leeds in a friendly behind closed doors during the winter.

The course was challenging but Geoff was a good lecturer. We were in our rooms revising, some nights until 9pm. I was constantly asking Mick, 'What does that mean? How do you pronounce that?' He was the salt of the earth for putting up with me. At the end of the second week, we had to sit a written exam. The only other formal written exam I had taken before was my City and Guilds at the end of my apprenticeship, and I passed the practical but not the theory. I had always struggled with writing, but to my relief I passed the exam, along with Mick and everyone else. Geoff did point out that it would help if I improved my English, which was fair enough.

After what seemed like a whirlwind of a summer it was back to work as a physio at Halifax. On the playing front, the new signings included my pal Mick Wood, and Dave Staniforth, whom I knew slightly; both had come from Bradford City. Dave was appointed the player-coach as Billy Ayre had moved on to Mansfield Town. I was gutted that he had left.

In November 1982 we went to Plough Lane to play Wimbledon. It was a game that I will never forget, nor would many others at the club, especially Bobby Davison. Wimbledon were near the top of the league and we were almost at the bottom but to everyone's surprise, we played brilliantly and won 4-2. Bobby scored a hat-trick. The happiest person on the coach on the way home was the driver; he always put a fiver on Halifax to win. He got odds of 7/1 that day so he won £35 plus his bet, which was good money in those days.

Wilf Dixon, the chief scout from Arsenal, watched the game that day, and the following week there was no sign of Bobby at training. I have subsequently spoken to Micky Bullock and Bobby about that era. Bobby told me that Halifax had done a deal with Arsenal for him to train with them the following week. At the end of the week, Terry Neill, the Arsenal manager, told Bobby, 'I can tell you are a class player, but I can only offer you a year's contract. I also understand that Halifax are in talks with Derby County, who want to sign you.'

Micky told me that the week after, he had a call from Roy McFarland of Derby County, inviting him to a Derby reserves game that evening. Micky drove down in thick fog, and within two minutes of getting to his seat, there was a tap on his shoulder; it was Roy. He said to Micky, 'Can you come up to the board room for a meeting with me and Peter Taylor [Derby's manager at the time]?' After hours of talking, around midnight, Micky rang Jack Turner, the new Halifax chairman. Mr Turner was not too happy about being disturbed from his bed and warned, 'This had better be good.' Micky told him, 'Derby County are prepared to pay a six-figure sum for Bobby Davison.' So the chairman told him to do the deal.

That summer, I had a year off Lilleshall but I spent a lot of time reading up on anatomy and physiology. I was gradually improving and getting more experience, and the following year I went back for the last part of the diploma. That year, Paddy Armour was the course leader, while Geoff Ladley lectured on the second-year course. I had spent a few months working hard on my thesis and I sent it to the FA with my fingers crossed. My subject had been the treatment and rehabilitation of the ankle. When the letter arrived a few weeks later, telling me I had passed, it was a great relief.

During pre-season in 1984, I found out about a newly formed rugby league team called Mansfield Marksmen. Their players came from all over Yorkshire and Lancashire and they used Siddall Rugby Club in Halifax as their base. I met with their general manager, David Parker, and agreed to physio for them. Halifax Town had no problem with me working for Mansfield, so long as football remained my number one priority. It meant I would be spending even less time at home with Shirley, Adele, and Miles, but I needed to earn some extra money. With rugby league, I was entering into another world.

By the end of October 1984 I received the sad news that Micky Bullock had lost his job as Halifax manager due to a run of poor results. I will always be grateful to Micky and David Sharp for giving me the chance to start a new life. Mick Jones, who was the assistant to Roy McFarland at Derby County, was appointed as his replacement a few weeks later, and for the rest of the season we picked up some decent results. Under the new manager, Halifax continued to improve in form into the 1985/86 season.

For their first season in rugby league, Mansfield Marksmen had a good run and finished well up the table. But after a chance meeting with the Australian Chris Anderson, the top-division Halifax RL coach, I decided to leave Mansfield to work for Chris. To make sure I did not leave the club in the lurch, Brian Hendry agreed to take over my role.

After a poor start, Halifax RL started to pick up some great results, and by the end of the season, due to great man-management and coaching by Chris, on the final day we needed one point to win the RFL Championship from Wigan. On 20 April 1986 we had a home game against Featherstone Rovers. It was a one I will never forget because of the dramatic finish.

I sat on the bench with Jack Scroby, the legendary ex-Halifax RL player, who was now a coach. As always, I set the stopwatch on my wristwatch when the game began. At half-time we were in the lead by ten points, but the second half was a different story and Featherstone came back into it. With a few minutes to go the score was 13-13. We were trying everything to grab another point from somewhere. According to my watch, we had two and a half minutes to go when suddenly the hooter sounded for the end of the game. Jack Scroby and I looked at each other in confusion. The fans stormed the pitch, and the players hugged each other in celebration. We had won the championship. I took a little while to get into the spirit as I was still concerned about the time discrepancy. I spoke to the timekeeper Andy Hardcastle and said, 'Andrew, by my reckoning, there were still over two minutes left to play?' He replied, 'No, there was four minutes left to play'. It turned out that the chairmen of the two clubs had sat together to watch the game. We needed a point to win, and they needed a point to stay up. The rest is history, as they say. We had been 200/1 outsiders to win the Championship at the start of the season. It was a brilliant achievement by Chris Anderson.

After a family holiday to America, pre-season was just around the corner, and I thought I might spend more time working within rugby and doing more private physio work. I had already spoken to Halifax RL and the wheels were beginning to turn, but a telephone call out of the blue a few weeks later was to change everything.

Around the middle of August, Geoff Ladley rang me. He told me that he was leaving his position at Leeds United to return to lecturing at Pinderfields Hospital. Geoff asked if I would like him to arrange an interview for me with the manager, Billy Bremner, with a view to taking over from him. My answer was, 'Yes, please.'

Although it might sound crazy, especially to Leeds supporters, I had some concerns about whether I was doing the right thing, and that must have come across in the interview with Billy. Whether it was because of the recent success in rugby league the season before, I'm not sure, but when I got back to The Shay and Mick Jones asked me how it had gone, I told him of my doubts. Mick said to me, 'Alan, there is no way you can turn down a job at Leeds United if they ask you.' So I rang Geoff and asked if I could meet Billy again, keeping my fingers crossed. Billy agreed to see me, and this time I went along with a better attitude and was offered the job. I would start on Friday, 22 August 1986, a day before the new season. Now my problem was telling Chris Anderson I was leaving.

The meeting with Chris did not go well. He had been trying to put together a deal with the board to get me there on better terms, and he felt that I had let him down. It would be a long time before he would be okay with me again, but many years later, he did say that he could understand my decision. It was only a couple of years after my move that he went back to Sydney to coach the Canterbury Bulldogs, however our paths were to cross many times in the future.

Before I left I had one more pre-season game to do for Halifax Town; I think it was at Farsley Celtic. Everyone at the club was pleased for me. It would also be an easier commute from Pateley Bridge. On Thursday, 21 August I said my farewells to Halifax Town and a big thank you for giving me the chance which had changed my life. I would never forget my time and my friends at The Shay.

3

THE EARLY ELLAND ROAD YEARS

On 22 August 1986 I arrived in the car park at Elland Road. I looked up at the famous facade, with 'Leeds United AFC' in large blue letters above the reception. I knew that once I stepped through that door one thing was certain, I had to make sure that I conducted myself every day as if it was my first day; in a place like that, it could also be my last day.

I met Geoff Ladley and he introduced me to the rest of the staff. Billy Bremner was there, along with David Bentley, his number two, and Dave Blakey, the chief scout. I had watched Dave play for Chesterfield against my team Bradford City; he was an old-fashioned uncompromising centre-half who did not take many prisoners. I soon found out that Dave ran most of the show for Billy. The youth team coach was Peter Gunby, whom I knew through coaching courses we had taken together over the years, as far back as 1966. I also met the laundry staff, Elaine and Liz. All the apprentices had various duties, and the one assigned to clean my room out every day was Gary Speed. We formed a friendship from that first day. The other apprentices included David Batty and Simon Grayson. Batts was a bit older than Gary and Simon; I discovered that he was a favourite with the manager. I also met the club doctor, John Berridge, and his assistant, Stuart Manning.

Billy had not given much thought to my wages, and to be honest, neither had I. Doing the job well was my primary consideration. He told me to see David Dowes, the club secretary, who asked me, 'What are you looking for?' I did not have a clue, so I worked out what I earned doing the football and rugby at Halifax, and we agreed on a rate.

The first game was the next day, away against Blackburn Rovers. Geoff covered it while I helped with the kit. Brendan Ormsby, the captain and centre-half, came off injured, so I had to take him to hospital for an x-ray. We got a taxi back to the ground only to discover that Ian Snodin had been sent off, and we went on to lose the game 2-1.

The next day, I worked with the injured players, and then on bank holiday Monday I did the physio alongside Geoff when we played Stoke City at home and got our first win of the season, 2-1. From then on I was on my own.

The thought of working at a large city club like Leeds had not fazed me, but after a few days I began to understand what Mick Jones meant when he had said that it was a special place. In the reception area, photographs of the great players of the much-celebrated Don Revie era of the 1960s and early '70s were still proudly displayed on the walls. The backroom areas were compact, although the facilities were impressive compared to Halifax Town. With a large table in the centre, the home dressing room was the same size as the adjacent bathroom, and there was only one toilet off the main corridor to be used by both the home and the away team. Another room housed a sauna, a sunbed and a massage table. The medical room led directly into the tunnel and included a large room with two beds and ice-making machines; there was also a smaller room with equipment for rehab work and the doctor's consulting room. Barbara and her assistant Pauline managed the players' lounge, where we could have something to eat, and it was the venue for the pre-match meal when we had a home game. The training pitches were across the road from the stadium at Fullerton Park. They were also well kitted out with their own dressing rooms used for the junior games.

Despite their drop in form in recent years, there was always a buzz and energy around the club. It was a much larger setup than I was accustomed to; I now had around 40 players to look after, including many apprentices. I knew I was operating at a different level.

On 20 September we played Bradford City at Odsal Stadium. Valley Parade, City's ground, was being rebuilt after the fire in 1985. I knew Odsal well as Shirley and I had lived just down the road in Low Moor when we were first married. Bradford were the better team on the day. We lost Ian Snodin when he had to come off with a suspected knee injury, and when Bradford scored their first goal the Leeds crowd made their displeasure heard. Then, when another goal went in, things began to turn very ugly.

The Leeds fans pushed a burger van, situated at the top of the terraces, on to its side, and we watched in dismay as it caught fire. Later there were frightening scenes as they hurled rocks on to the pitch to get the match abandoned. The referee stopped the game, took the players off, and the ground was cleared. It finished in an empty stadium and we lost 2-0. To say it was not a good day for Leeds United is an understatement.

In those days, the Leeds fans had a poor reputation, and a local derby always brought out the worst in the substantial minority who were complete idiots. It was particularly shameful because it happened just over a year after the Valley Parade fire. I felt for the City players and supporters, many of whom had been at the ground on that terrible day. Years later, I remember talking to City player Stuart McCall, whom I had worked with during my coaching days with Malcolm Cook. I asked Stuart whether he had ever wanted to play for Leeds, his home city. He told me that while he was at Glasgow Rangers, Leeds had put in an offer for him. However, being present on that shameful day at Odsal, he had vowed that he would never play for the Leeds supporters.

It was a bad day all round as we also lost Ian Snodin for six to eight weeks. I contacted Dr Berridge about Ian's injury, and he referred him to a new orthopaedic surgeon at the Leeds General Infirmary named Mr John Lawton. John eventually became our club surgeon, a post he held for many years. He also became a good friend.

In those early weeks I also got to know the groundsman, John Reynolds. Although we didn't hit it off straight away, over time we became great friends. John had come from South Wales as a 15-year-old apprentice at the same time as the legendary John Charles. His playing career was cut short through injury in his early 20s, so he became a groundsman. One of John's tasks was to climb the 260ft-high floodlights to check the bulbs; at that time, our lights were the highest in Europe. I don't know how often John had to climb up there, but it was not a job anyone could do. John did eventually warm to me and allowed me to use the main pitch if there was no space spare at Fullerton Park to work with the injured players.

John had a few assistants: Brian Cartwright, Barry Endeacott, and a guy named Trevor. Brian had worked in rugby league so we had a bit in common. Hunslet RL played their matches at Elland Road that season, so rugby was still a presence in my life at Leeds.

In between games, I got to know quite a few players as they came for treatment. John Sheridan, known as Shez, Ian Baird, Andy Ritchie, Brendan Ormsby, Ian Snodin (Snods) and John Stiles, were working-class lads off the street, just like me. Snods could be a bit of a character, along with one or two of the others. There was always a mad couple of hours every day, strapping and sorting out other bits and pieces before training. I worked my way as quickly as I could through the line of players patiently waiting outside my door, as I repeatedly said to those in the queue, 'I'll see you in two minutes,' which became a standing joke.

I started to get some stick from some of the jokers, and I worked out who I needed to keep an eye on. John Stiles, son of the legendary Nobby Stiles and the nephew of another great at Leeds, Johnny Giles, was one of the main culprits. One day, I was carrying out an ultrasound treatment when suddenly the machine stopped. I immediately thought it had packed in until I discovered Stilesy had somehow turned it off. I said, 'Don't worry, John, I hope you don't get injured any time soon, as payback time might be just around the corner when I get my fingers into you!' I was eventually nicknamed 'Sausage Fingers' because of my short stubby digits. The pranks were always lighthearted and good-natured.

A few days after my 40th birthday, we went to Plymouth. It was a different setup to the away trips with Halifax Town. We travelled in some style with TV sets, tables and a microwave oven; it was luxury compared to some of the coaches I had been on before. The non-playing staff sat at the front and the players at the back, and there was often a game of cards to pass the time on the journey; Billy Bremner was an excellent player. At least three directors and the chairman, Leslie Silver, also accompanied us, as did members of the press, usually Don Waters of the *Yorkshire Evening Post*, John Wray of Bradford's *Telegraph and Argus*, and sometimes, Barry Foster of the *Yorkshire Post*.

I discovered that John Wray and I had been born on the same day but he looked ten years younger than me, with his well-groomed wavy hair and his smart business suit. I said to the other guys on the coach, 'I put it down to when we had our paper rounds as kids. You can tell who did the 30-storey flats and who did the bungalows!' Everyone just laughed.

We stayed at the Hilton Hotel in Plymouth, and after our meal everyone gathered in a meeting room. When I asked what was happening, one of the lads told me that they had organised a game of carpet bowls. It was a Revie-era tradition intended as a bit of relaxation before a match and included a knock-out competition with bets on the winner. Billy's friend Herbie Warner, also a familiar face at the club during the Revie days, oversaw the stakes. Eventually they would have me running the 'book' but I never knew how to work out the odds, although as John Sheridan won nearly every game it didn't really matter.

As for the match, we drew 1-1 with Ian Baird scoring. Bairdy was a good lad but one Monday morning I made the mistake of asking him how his weekend had gone; he just told me to f**k off and walked out of my room. He was not a Monday person.

There was another surprise on our journey home from Plymouth. A guy was sitting at the back of the coach, so I went to say hello. His name was Jim and he worked for British Rail in the restaurant car. It transpired that when Leeds played away from home, he would make his way to our opponents' ground then travel back with us on the team coach and make a meal for the players and staff. So as we headed back up north, playing cards, after about an hour, everything stopped and he served us steak, chips and peas, followed by gateau. In time, the manager changed it to steak sandwiches for our table so the card games could continue. At Halifax our food had been a plastic box with some sandwiches and fruit. It was an excellent first trip, apart from not winning.

I had got into a routine with treatment, and we would follow with circuit training at the multi-gym and running drills outside for the lads who were almost match fit. In

October, Andy Ritchie, one of our top players, had a problem with his knee. Two days before our home game with Portsmouth on Saturday, we decided that he needed to see an orthopaedic surgeon so we took him to Middlesbrough to for an appointment with David Muckle, who had worked with the England team. At the end of the examination, Mr Muckle was unsure whether Andy might need surgery but suggested that he carry on for a while and see how it went. Andy was happy with this; it meant that he would be good for the game on Saturday, and of course, the boss was pleased that Andy would be playing.

The match could not have gone any better. Portsmouth were at the top of the division and had only let in three or four goals all season, but Andy scored a 25-yarder into the top corner and we won 3-1. Afterwards, the boss said, 'I don't think Andy needs to go for that op.' I spoke to Mr Muckle, who had read that Andy had scored a spectacular goal, and he thought it would help us make a decision. Andy was also a lot happier after his performance.

The day before the match I had been talking to Shez. He had been playing well, and I congratulated him on being picked for the Republic of Ireland squad. I also asked him about his plans for that weekend. He told me that after our game he was going to Manchester to watch 'our Daz', his younger brother Darren, play in a pub team match on Sunday morning. Darren also went on to become a professional footballer.

Shez was our star player that Saturday and had scored from a penalty. But on Monday morning there was no sign of him at training. Billy usually turned a blind eye when it had happened before as, in those days, Shez liked a drink. The following morning when he walked into the treatment room, I asked him, 'What happened to you yesterday?' He grimaced and replied, 'I didn't wake up until about three o'clock.' I remembered about his planned weekend in Manchester. He said, 'I walked to the ground with our Daz for his match, and when we met the other team, they started giving us some stick saying, "Hey, we've not lost a match for two years, so prepare to get your backsides kicked."' To Shez, that was like a red rag to a bull. He continued, 'I said to our Daz, "Pass me that number eight shirt, we'll show them who's going to get their backsides kicked."' He played the full 90 minutes for his brother's team; I think they were from the Dog and Duck. When I asked him how they had done he said, 'We won 6-2.' I asked him, already prepared for the reply, 'Did you manage to score?' 'Yes,' he offered with a grin. 'Four.' He told me that he finished off his weekend watching the Manchester United versus Manchester City derby and then went on to Bernard Manning's club in the evening. I thought that was the end of the story, but there was more.

Some years later, when Shez had left Leeds, he returned to Elland Road to say hello and asked if I could look at his knee. I told him I would never forget that tale of when he had turned out for the Dog and Duck. He smiled, 'Ah, but I didn't tell you the whole story. After the game one of the lads said, "Shez, the ref wants to see you in his room." I thought that I had been rumbled, and if so, I was in big trouble; my football career might be over. I knocked on the door, and the ref said, "Come in and sit down, son." With my heart in my mouth, I did as I was told. The ref looked at me for a moment, then he said, "I was watching you, and you're not a bad player. How would you like to play for Manchester FA against Ashton-Under-Lyne next week?"' John smiled, 'I had to say, "Sorry ref, I've got a lot on next weekend." Then I legged it out of his dressing room ASAP.' Fortunately for Shez, in those days there was not as much TV coverage so no one had recognised him, although I often wonder if that referee ever saw him play for the Republic of Ireland and think, 'I know that face from somewhere.'

As we moved towards Christmas and new year, I was beginning to feel that Leeds was a bit like Halifax Town. It was a real family club and everybody knew each other. I got to know the admin staff, too; Mandy Ward in the ticket office was joined by Katie Holmes a few years later. Andrea and Jane worked on the front desk, and Maureen Holdsworth was Billy's secretary.

I talked to Simon Grayson recently about when he, Gary Speed, David Batty, and another good lad from Scotland, Vinny Brockie, were apprentices. Everyone had their chores to do, and Simon's were to clean and mop the corridor by the players' lounge and the multi-gym. He would get his jobs done, and then the boss would say, 'Okay lads, let's have a game of keep-ball.' Everyone formed a circle, with someone in the centre. In my day, it was called 'piggy in the middle'. Sometimes I joined in, although if I was in the middle, I was sure to get nutmegged a few times and I never got out again. It put a smile on a few faces and plenty of 'Olés!' While we were playing, David Blakey, the chief scout, would often come down and tell Billy he was needed on the phone. All you would get from the boss was, 'Tell them I'll call them back in ten minutes.' It was the longest ten minutes ever. The lads loved it; the problem was, as Simon said, they had to mop everything again, and depending on where the apprentices' digs were, it could be after 7pm before they got home on the bus.

When I talked to Simon, we laughed about my first couple of seasons with the boss. Simon told me about the day Billy was watching the apprentices over at Fullerton Park. Pete Gunby set up a practice game, and all of a sudden Billy decided to join in with the lads while wearing his business suit and shoes. It was great to watch. I had seen the boss go out on a heavy training pitch in an old pair of trainers with the first team and get stuck in. The lads said his balance was so good that he never slipped once.

Simon and I also talked about Pete Gunby, our great friend and colleague. Every season we had a new group of apprentices, and of course, they all wanted to show us how good they were. Pete got them out on the track around Elland Road, ready for his famous party trick. He would say, 'Is there anybody here who thinks they can beat me on one lap of the track?' Of course, everyone put their hand up. Then Pete would say, 'The only rule is that when I say "Go," you have to drink a cup of water.' So the first lad goes up, mouthing cockily under his breath, 'Right you are, Grandad.' Pete would ask one of the older lads to get the cup of water and then shout, 'Go!' The unwitting apprentice was then handed a cup of boiling water. Pete set off at a steady pace, shouting, 'Make sure he drinks it all.' The other lads just fell around laughing. Welcome to Leeds United, lads.

After being 5-0 down at half-time, we lost 7-2 away at Stoke just before Christmas. I felt for our goalkeeper, Mervyn Day, who was just getting back on track with his career. When we got back to Elland Road, the boss said to Don Waters and John Wray, 'I want to see you in my office.' Dave Bentley and I were also there. Billy got the whiskey out and then said, 'Right lads, this is the headline I want in your papers. I want to apologise to the fans for that first-half display.' He gave them some other snippets, but the message was that we had let the fans down.

The next big turning point was our game away to Ipswich Town on New Year's Day 1987. A few clubs, including Everton, had been showing an interest in Ian Snodin but unfortunately events were to turn sour. The game was going okay until John Sheridan was sent off. I got involved with one of the stewards who was having a go at Shez. Things went from bad to worse; we were 2-0 down and the boss was telling Snods, our captain, to get something sorted out on the pitch. Snods reacted with a bit of dissent, and Billy was having none of it. Straight away, he said to Dave Bentley, 'Ring Everton and tell them they can have him.' When things calmed down after the game, Snods and the boss were great friends again, but the decision had been made. It seemed a shame for everything to finish that way.

A few days later, Ian was ready to leave the club, but there was another twist in the tale as Liverpool matched Everton's offer of around £820,000. Ian told me that when it became known that two clubs were vying for him, a newspaper offered him £2,000 to say who he was signing for; he turned them down. He signed for Everton and won the league championship with them at the end of the season.

The boss bought four new players with the fee: Mickey Adams from Coventry, Bobby McDonald from Oxford United, and John Pearson and Mark Aizlewood from Charlton Athletic. Those signings made a real difference to the season. The next big test for us was a third-round FA Cup tie away against Telford United. Because the Leeds fans had a troubled reputation at the time, the FA refused to allow the game to take place at Telford's small stadium. They stipulated that it would kick off at lunchtime on Sunday, 11 January at West Bromwich Albion's ground, The Hawthorns.

When we arrived in Birmingham the temperature was -11°C. The boss, David Bentley and I planned to view the pitch and meet the referee early in the day. The coach wouldn't start, and Duncan Jackson, our driver, told us it had frozen up. So we got a taxi, and when we looked at the pitch it was covered with frost. We met the groundsman and asked him when the referee was coming to inspect it. 'He has already been and has passed it fit to play,' was his reply. But there wasn't a footprint to be seen on the pristine white surface; the FA must have decreed that the game had to go ahead. Often, a bone-hard surface is a great leveller.

Back at the hotel, another coach had turned up to take us to the ground. At the game, Ian Baird got a couple of goals and we won 2-1. The referee was Vic Callow from Solihull, just down the road. The last time I had spoken to Vic was at Torquay when I was with Halifax. Vic was not the only reminder of my Halifax Town days; ready for home, we discovered that the second coach had broken down.

Talking about transport, the next time we played Ipswich away, our coach driver became ill and was admitted to hospital in Ipswich while the match was under way. We appealed over the tannoy to ask the Leeds supporters if anyone was a qualified coach driver. Thankfully one came forward, and as you can imagine he was delighted to drive the team back home. No doubt he would enjoy telling his kids about his unusual journey back to Leeds.

During that first season, I worked flat out and did my best to get the players fit as quickly as possible and back on the pitch for the manager and the much-needed points. In time, we sent some of the longer-term injuries to the Lilleshall Rehabilitation Centre for treatment by Graham Smith, Grant Downie and Phil Newton, all of whom I got to know well. It also allowed me to concentrate on working with the lads who just needed week-to-week treatment. One player who went to Lilleshall was getting towards the end of his career. At the end of the week, he rang me to ask if he could have a few days off as he had the chance of a player-coach job in Malta. Being a little bit naïve at the time and always trying to help where I could, I said, 'Yes, that should be okay for a few days.' I never thought any more about it. At the end of the next week, I had a telephone call from Graham Smith. He usually rang me every week with an update. This time he asked me if

I knew where the player had gone. I said, 'Graham, it's okay; he has the chance of a job in Malta, so I said he could have a few days off.' It was then he hit me with the bombshell, 'Sorry to tell you, pal, he and a few mates have gone off to Spain for a week.' My heart sank. Of course, I had to tell Billy what had happened. When I went into his office, Dave Blakey was there, and at best I expected a roasting from them both. At worst I thought I might be out of the door. But after I apologised, to my great surprise, Billy said, 'Don't worry, Dave and I had been thinking of ways how we could move him on. Now you have given us an opening.' I breathed a sigh of relief; I had got away with my mistake, but I would not do it again. I learned that I could be friends with the players but I had to be careful how close I got to them while they were at the club. I always made sure that I remembered I was working for the manager.

We were doing okay in the league and even better in the FA Cup. In our fourth-round midweek tie away to Swindon Town, we had a tight game and won 2-1. We were then drawn against First Division Queens Park Rangers at home in the fifth round. Their manager was Jim Smith; I had heard all about Jim when I was at Halifax as he had been a player there years before.

There was a larger crowd than our usual 12-13,000 supporters and a brilliant atmosphere. Bairdy opened the scoring, and then an own goal from David Rennie made it 1-1. With six minutes to go we got one of our most celebrated winners for years. Shez's corner was met at the far post with a brilliant header by the captain, Brendan Ormsby, at the Kop end to make it 2-1. The place went wild. A famous photograph of Brendan jumping on to the fence with the supporters reaching out to hug him is now part of the club's history. Afterwards, when Bairdy came out of the shower, he had a nasty cut on his head; he had not noticed it during the celebrations. The doctor had already left so I took him to the hospital to get it stitched. It gave the A&E department a big lift seeing him come in after that superb win.

We were drawn away to Wigan Athletic in the quarter-final, but the club had rearranged an away fixture at Portsmouth beforehand. Brendan Ormsby had a one-match suspension and Billy wanted him to play in the FA Cup. However, the FA were having none of it and decreed that he remained suspended for the quarter-final but could play against Portsmouth. That match took place just five days before the quarter-final, and we knew it was going to be tough; they had some players who took no prisoners, and the same could be said for our team. It was good to catch up with John Dickens, Portsmouth's physio. I also met a young referee named David Elleray for the first time. I found out later that David was a housemaster at Harrow School.

David and I became good friends over the years, but there was a fierce contest on the pitch that night, and we disagreed with some of his decisions. By half-time he'd booked five of our players and only one of Portsmouth's. Walking to the dressing room, I said to David, 'How the hell do you get five bookings for us and one booking for them?' He was not happy about the stick he was getting.

In the second half, there was an incident that kicked everything off. Mick Kennedy, whom I knew slightly from my Halifax days, hit Neil Aspin, and he went down. I ran on to the pitch to treat Neil but Mick was on the floor, holding his face as if Neil had hit him. Neil immediately jumped up to go and sort him out, so I grabbed hold of him. In the heat of the moment he shrugged me off with his elbow to get free and, in doing so, hit me in the mouth. John Stiles saw what happened and exclaimed, 'Neil, you have just hit Sutty in the gob!' I could see the referee was heading over to send Neil off for hitting me, so I stood in front of Neil, put my hands up and said, 'Ref, it's okay, I am fine,' so David let it go. Neil was immediately contrite, 'Sutty, I can't believe what I just did!' But for me, that was the end of the issue. The game finished 1-1; Mickey Adams got a late goal for us. In the second half, David booked four Portsmouth players and one of ours.

In the FA Cup quarter-final against Wigan, we got a great result with John Stiles and Mickey Adams scoring to win 2-0. After the match, Billy's best friend Alex Smith, the St Mirren manager, and his number two, Jimmy Bone, were in the dressing room. They had travelled down from Scotland to watch the game. That season they went on to win the Scottish Cup Final with St Mirren.

So now we were in the semi-final against Coventry City. We were still doing well in the league and everyone was clamouring for tickets. I managed to get a couple for my son Miles and my friend Terry Burden, who lived on our estate.

Dealing with Billy Bremner every day, you never knew who might walk through the doors at Elland Road. Leeds legends, players from the past and Billy's friends from the footballing world would often pop into the club. A regular visitor was the famous player Cyril Knowles, who had worked for Billy as a coach in his Doncaster Rovers days. Cyril had a song named after him, 'Nice One, Cyril', adapted from a TV advertisement, and the crowds would sing it to him whenever he was on the pitch. Cyril could take the mickey with people. It may have been the boss or Dave Bentley who told me a story about Cyril when he was a player-coach at Middlesbrough. He was a bit late with a tackle during a game and joked to the ref, 'Sorry, Ref, I got there as quick as I could!' The young referee got his notebook out and barked at Cyril, 'NAME?!' Cyril replied, 'Oh, you want my name? Well, my name is Cyril Knowles. I've won the League Cup, the FA Cup, the UEFA

Cup and I've got four international caps.' As he rattled off his achievements, he looked the young ref up and down and, pushing his luck, asked cheekily, 'By the way, son, who might you be?' By this time, both teams were laughing at Cyril's antics.

Cyril always had a sense of fun. One evening after a reserve game, we walked out to the car park at Elland Road together. When Cyril spotted my car, one of my many old bangers, he remarked on the licence plate, teasing, 'Oh, I see you've got a new car, Al? Looking good!' It was a D reg, which was the new registration for 1986, but the trouble was that mine was a D reg from the last time round in 1966 and Cyril could see it was ready for the scrapyard. It was one of his usual piss-takes. I was sorry when Cyril died in 1991 at an early age; he was one hell of a player and a true gentleman.

The FA Cup semi-final was a noon kick-off on Sunday, 12 April 1987 at Hillsborough against Coventry City. Neil Aspin should have been getting married that day, but he cancelled his wedding. I went to the ground early doors to put the kit out, and once again the coach broke down, so we hired another to bring the players from the hotel. I had a chat with Coventry's physio, George Dalton. Before kick-off, the referee came into our dressing room to say that the game was delayed for 15 minutes as the stadium was still filling up. After the game I asked Miles what had happened. He told me there had been barriers across the road leading into the stadium for ticket checks which had held everyone up. On the day, we lost 3-2 in extra time. There would be no Wembley that year, and as I write this in 2021, Leeds have never since made an FA Cup semi-final.

In our away game on 2 May 1987, Derby County needed a win to secure promotion to the First Division. The last time I had been at the Baseball Ground was with Halifax Town in 1982. I had always kept in touch with Bobby Davison by phone after his move to Derby, and he was one of the first to ring me when I got the physio job at Leeds. It was Derby's day, and we lost 2-1, but I was pleased for Bobby.

On the same day, Halifax RL were in the Challenge Cup Final at Wembley against St Helens. After our game, I was sat in the big bath on my own when I saw Herbie Warner, the boss's pal. I said, 'Herbie, do you know how Halifax went on in the final at Wembley?' He went to find out and returned with the news that they had won 19-18. I was delighted for Chris and the boys, but it was a bittersweet moment, made even more so by the loud celebrations of the Derby players in the dressing room next door. But as history will show, I made the right move.

We were through to the play-offs, and the last match of the season was away at Brighton. Billy's main concern was that we did not pick up any injuries. In the team meeting he said to the lads, 'Enjoy the game. Anyone with the slightest knock, you must let us know straight away.' As the players went out, he turned to me and said, 'If anyone so much as breaks a fingernail, get them off.' The one thing he was hoping to avoid was having to play Oldham Athletic as they had become a bogey team for us. If we did not get a win, we had more chance of avoiding them. Five minutes from the end of the game, Keith Edwards, who had come on as a sub, struck the ball from 20 yards out. It bounced five times, went over the goalkeeper's body and into the net, to the delight of the Leeds fans, many of whom had slept on the beach the night before. Usually we would have been delighted, but not the boss, 'What are you doing?!' he shouted from the touchline.

As it turned out, it did not make any difference; Oldham lost their game, so we had to play them with the first leg at home. We won 1-0 at Elland Road and in the second leg we lost 2-1 after extra time, so we qualified for the final on away goals. We lost 1-0 to Charlton Athletic in the first leg and won the second leg at home by the same score. The third and deciding game was played at Birmingham City, where we lost 2-1, so it was another season in the Second Division for Leeds.

I loved it when Billy talked about his days with Scotland, playing alongside one of my heroes, Denis Law. He told me about the time the national team's new manager held a training session the day before a Scotland match. Billy said, 'We all stood there, and he said, "Right lads, today, I just want you to do what you always do with your club team." When Denis started walking away, the manager called, "Hey Denis, where are you going?" Denis shouted back, "Matt [Busby] never likes me to train the day before a match. See you later, boss," and off he went.'

Talking of Sir Matt Busby, Billy told us about the time he almost signed for Manchester United. It was during the 1970 World Cup, which was also the year Billy won the Football Writers' Association Player of the Year award. While Billy was there watching some of the games, he bumped into Busby, who knew Billy's contract was coming up for renewal at Leeds. During their conversation, Billy said to Sir Matt that he might consider a move over the Pennines. But Don Revie was also at the World Cup, and in Billy's words, Revie never missed a trick. Billy said that when the time came for him to see Revie, he was seriously thinking of signing for Manchester United and knew that money to keep him at Leeds would be on the table. 'I had an idea what Leeds might offer me, but I had another figure in my head, which was more. I assumed that the gaffer would throw me out of his office when I went to see him, but before I could say a word, Revie put a piece of paper in front of me and said, "There's your contract, Billy." I looked at it, and there was half as much again on top of what I had hoped, so I just signed it. Then I had to tell Sir Matt I was staying. The gaffer had obviously read the signs.'

Towards the end of my first season, John Sheridan was becoming a big name. He was in the Republic of Ireland squad and had been a vital player for Leeds all year. The day before one of our Saturday home games, I was getting the dressing room ready and laying out the kit when Shez came in and handed me a pair of new boots. Shez usually played in boots with moulded studs. I asked him, 'What are these?' He told me, 'They're my boots. I've just signed a new deal.' I said, 'Oh, right. Fine. What are they like?' Shez replied, 'I don't know; I haven't tried them yet. I'll just wear them tomorrow.' I was surprised he had not tested them, but I put them out with the rest for the game the next day. During the game, we had been playing for about 20 minutes when Shez shouted to me, 'Hey Sutts, these boots feel like they have got concrete in them. Get me my usual ones.' He just threw them off. 'You can give them to Stilesy; they'll be okay for him!' Shez and Stilesy were always taking the p*** out of each other. I don't know what he told his new sponsor or whether he paid them the money back.

* * *

At the beginning of pre-season in 1987 a few players had left, including our top striker Ian Baird. He had moved to Portsmouth and would fit in well there.

We signed Gary Williams from Aston Villa and Glynn Snodin from Sheffield Wednesday. Glynn was the brother of Ian, who was by then at Everton. Billy Bremner had also worked with Glynn at Doncaster Rovers. Five years earlier, Gary had been part of the Villa side who had won the European Cup.

Some of the young players under Pete Gunby's wing were also coming on well. Along with Batts, Speedo, Simon Grayson and Vince Brockie, there was also a youngster called Bob Taylor. Bob was a striker and the boss had him training with the first team.

I was travelling with the first and second teams for all our pre-season games. Another good guy who gave us a hand and did the physio work for Pete with the juniors was Alan McIvor, known as 'Mac'. He had worked part-time with the boss at Doncaster.

Billy wanted to bring in another striker and was after Duncan Shearer at Huddersfield Town, but they wanted £500,000. To my surprise, the guy who walked through the door was Bobby Davison from Derby County. I think they paid about £350,000 for him. Years later, Bobby told me in a telephone conversation that I had made it happen for him. I had put his name forward to the boss. Like many of the lads, Bobby said that some of his best years were playing for Leeds.

Many people remember our home game against Swindon Town; not only did Bobby score on his debut, but Peter 'Fish' Haddock also got his only goal for Leeds. In that game, a young David Batty also made his debut in our 4-2 victory. I remember David that day. At half-time, while the boss was doing his team talk, Batts sat behind him engrossed in the matchday programme. Billy had to tell him, 'David, come around here, so I can see you.' In the second half, Batts got one hell of a tackle in on big Dave Bamber, Swindon's striker. Bamber grabbed him and David just looked at him as if to say, 'What's your problem?' The referee had a word with David, and with the angelic way he looked back at the ref you would have thought that Batts was a choir boy. I asked David a couple of days after why he was reading the programme; his answer was, 'I just wanted to know who they had playing for them.'

The boss recruited another member of the coaching staff. It was none other than another hero of mine from my teenage years, Norman Hunter. I admired him because he was left-footed and loved a tackle. I spent a lot of time with Norman; after midweek games I dropped him off at his house in Horsforth on my route home. We had some interesting conversations. I remember him saying that the game had become too fast, and he did not think he would be good enough to play modern-day football. I said, 'Are you kidding me, Norman? You would be just as good and would've easily adjusted to this era.' This was from the guy who was the first person to win the PFA Player of the Year award; all the best players of that time had voted for him. Norman said that he thought Ian Callaghan of Liverpool would take the trophy, but then Don Revie gave him the heads up two weeks before the award ceremony that he had won it hands down. I also remember telling Norman about when I was in Canada in 1967 and had seen in the local paper that the FA were sending a team to help develop Canada's football scene. Two of the players were from Leeds, Paul Madeley and Norman Hunter, but sadly, I did not see the game.

On New Year's Day 1988 we were at home against Bradford City. Shirley was bringing Miles to the match, and because it was a local derby with the possibility of crowd trouble I arranged for them to be there two hours before kick-off. It was the coldest day for weeks. When I got home I asked if they had enjoyed the game, which we had won 2-0. Shirley's response was not entirely unexpected, 'DON'T EVER ask me to go back there for another game! I was so cold stuck in that stand.' Football is not everyone's cup of tea.

In the 1950s, when I was around nine or ten years old, two of the game's greats were Duncan Edwards of Manchester United and the Leeds legend John Charles. On Fridays, when it was fish and chips day in the canteen at Leeds, Big John often joined us. I enjoyed chatting with him about his time in Italy. I told John the first time I had seen him play was when my mum and dad took me to watch his last game at Elland Road when Leeds beat Sunderland 3-1, and John scored two of the goals.

I also played in a charity match involving ex-Park Avenue and City players against ex-Leeds players, and John was on the team. John was a very modest man; when he talked about his time at Juventus, he was matter-of-fact about his achievements. In the five years John was there, they won three league titles and two Italian Cups. He was also the player of the season in his first year at the club. Before he went to Juventus, the club had finished second from bottom in the league. Then they signed John and an inside forward from Argentina named Omar Sivori, and the two of them helped to transform Juventus' fortunes.

John was so successful because he could play both centre-half and centre-forward. He would start as a forward and score a goal, then in the second half they would move him back to centre-half to stop the opposition. John always featured in the world's best XI lists compiled by experts. The Juventus fans also voted him their best foreign player, with over 100 goals in around 150 games. When Jimmy Greaves named his top 50 footballers, John was his number one choice. Jimmy knew how hard it was to play in Italy in that era. The referee, Ron Groves from Somerset, once told me he had been refereeing a match in northern Italy. Posters of John were displayed prominently in many shop windows, 40 years after he had played there. Peter Gunby also recounted the time he went to Italy with the ex-players, including John. There were thousands of people at the airport waiting to see him. The trip did not cost them a penny; every restaurant wanted to welcome John and the lads with open arms.

At that time, one of the things I loved doing was travelling with Norman Hunter and the reserve team. Norman had some great stories. On one away trip he told me about the time he played for England against Scotland. He said, 'Someone caught me with a bad tackle, and at that point I was seething. So, the next pair of Scottish socks I saw that was it, I was straight in. When I looked down it was Wee Billy Bremner, my teammate at Leeds. At the end of the game, going down the tunnel, I looked up and the boss, Don Revie, was waiting for me. His expression said it all. I don't think I need to tell you what he said to me.'

Billy Bremner was always a good storyteller. When recounting his Scotland days, he said it was great being with the other guys. One of the tales Billy told me involved Eddie McCready, the Chelsea player. He said, 'I was with Eddie one time, and as we were leaving after a Scotland game, I said to him, "See you again on Saturday up at our place," then in the same breath, I said, "Oh no, you won't be there will you? I forgot Gilesy still wants to have a word with you about what happened last time you met." I didn't see Eddie again for a while.'

During lunchtimes, in addition to carpet bowls in the canteen, a few of us listened to a music quiz on BBC Radio 1. One day, Glynn Snodin popped his head around the treatment room door and asked me, 'What were your favourite records when you were growing up?' I rattled off a few and thought no more of it.

One evening a few weeks later, I arrived home and Shirley said, 'Someone from the BBC rang today; they've left the number for you to call them back.' My initial reaction was it would be one of the lads at the club messing about, so I ignored it. The next day at work, Cath from the office stopped me, 'There's a call for you from the BBC,' she said. Mystified, I went into the office and picked up the phone, 'It's Alan Sutton.' I said, 'Are you sure it's me you want to talk to?' A female voice replied, 'Alan, you have been nominated to participate in the music quiz on the Gary Davies radio show at 1pm.' Still thinking it was wind up, I said something dismissive. She assured me it was not a joke; I was going to be on national radio. Then it dawned on me that the lads had set me up, and the culprits were probably the boss, Snods, Stilesy, Shez and Bobby Davison. Billy told me later that the whole club had been in on it.

Billy planned that everyone would listen in the room next door, and when they heard the question, they would run in and give me the answer. Just as I was about to go on, Billy said, 'Don't worry, there's probably only about 250,000 people listening to you.' The quiz took place over five days with an immediate knock-out for a wrong answer. I made it to day two. Before we said our goodbyes, Gary finished by saying, 'Alan, if we give you a Radio 1 bag, will you run on the pitch with it on Saturday?' 'Sure,' I agreed; anything to get me off the line! Within five minutes of being back in my room, the telephone rang again; it was the guy from Umbro, our sponsors. 'There is no way you are running on the pitch with anything other than our kit; your contract is with us,' he said. 'What could I have said with all those people listening?!' I replied. In the end, he laughed with me about it.

In April, we played in a tournament at Wembley to celebrate 100 years of league football in England. It was a knock-out competition with each team playing for 20 minutes. We stayed in a hotel near Watford along with Liverpool and Tranmere Rovers. After our evening meal, Kenny Dalglish, the Liverpool manager, joined us for a chat. I sat around the table with Billy, Norman Hunter, Dave Bentley and Kenny. Anybody would have paid money to be in their company. They discussed who they thought was the best winger of all time, and for Billy and Kenny there was only one contender, the Celtic legend Jimmy 'Jinky' Johnstone. It was a great night, and the next day I had breakfast with Kevin McDonald, the Liverpool double winner of 1986. As for the tournament itself, we lost to Nottingham Forest in the first round. Micky Adams had promised me a run on the pitch, so he went down with an 'injury' and I thanked him when I got there. That was one crossed off the bucket list.

That season I also met two 1966 World Cup winners. Billy arranged for Gordon Banks, who was now a coach, to visit Elland Road to work with the keepers, and we all had lunch together. He was a great guy and I enjoyed talking with him. We also had a game against West Bromwich Albion where Nobby Stiles was the reserve team coach. I had told John Stiles of my admiration for his dad. Before the game, I was in the West Brom dressing room talking to their player David Cork when the door to the dressing room opened and in walked Nobby with the words, 'Hello Alan, how are you? John has told me all about you,' I went from 5ft 6in to 10ft 6in in one fell swoop. Nobby went back to work at Manchester United in 1989 as the youth team coach, and we always shared a few words when we visited.

In 1988, the club organised a testimonial game for John Charles and Bobby Collins. Bobby had been the masterstroke signing from Everton by Don Revie in 1962, so it was fitting that Everton would send a full squad to play against Leeds and their guests. When Kenny Dalglish discovered who was playing, he rang Billy and asked if he could be part of the Leeds team, along with Ian Rush, who was now playing for Juventus. The former Juventus champions Gaetano Scirea and Michel Platini also came over together on Platini's private plane. It was also a big night for our apprentice Vinnie Brockie, who was playing at right-back.

I have since spoken to Glynn Snodin and Simon Grayson about that night. Glynn had started on the left and Simon came on as a substitute. When Platini arrived on the day, I was getting the kit sorted in the back. Simon said he could not believe it when he saw Platini walk through the dressing room door. He was wearing a *Columbo*-type raincoat and carrying his boots in a plastic bag as if he had just been to the supermarket. Glynn added that Platini got his boots out, still caked in mud, and while everyone was getting changed for the game, he coolly sat smoking a cigarette. When the players went out to warm up, Platini stayed behind in the dressing room with me. After a while he changed into his kit and asked for a massage. I took him into the back room and massaged his legs while he finished his cigarette. It was probably a first for the three-times Ballon d'Or winner to have his legs massaged with cooking oil from the local shop, which was our staple back then. But if he noticed then he did not complain, and was very talkative and friendly.

There was live coverage across Europe for the game, and it was a brilliant experience to see those superb players on the same team. Glynn remembered Platini's first strike of the ball. It was a 60-yarder down the left wing set up for him. Glynn said, 'I could not believe it; Platini was so good, I did not have to break my stride. I just took the ball straight on.' And that was without a warm-up.

Leeds won 3-2 in front of 13,000 fans, with Rushie scoring a hat-trick. These days we would have played to a full house with such illustrious names in the stadium. As kit man I managed to claim Platini's shirt on the night and four years later, Eric Cantona got Platini to sign it when Eric was playing for France and Platini was manager. Sadly, two years after the testimonial, Gaetano Scirea was in Poland scouting for Juventus and was killed in a car crash. There were 15,000 people at his funeral. It was a great honour that he had played in our game. I had not realised what a great player he had been in the sweeper position at Juventus and when winning the 1982 World Cup with Italy.

A month or so later, we held a tribute game for Don Revie, Leeds United versus the Soccer All-Stars. Mr Revie had been diagnosed with motor neurone disease. The team included, among others, Graeme Souness, Ray Wilkins, Mark Wright, Peter Shilton, Paul Gascoigne, Eddie Gray and Kevin Keegan. There was the old family atmosphere engendered by Mr Revie, with all the players and ex-players coming together to honour him and pay tribute for his contribution to the game. Derby County's manager, Arthur Cox, carried Mark Wright's and Peter Shilton's bags into the dressing room. Looking after both dressing rooms was a terrific experience. As we were going through the tunnel after the match, I was chatting with Kevin Keegan as he told me about when he had played at Elland Road and had scored twice for Liverpool.

I remember my early days at Leeds when Mr Revie had arranged to meet Kevin at Elland Road. He was doing a coaching course, and Kevin was helping him. When Billy arrived, everyone seemed to be good friends, unlike at the Charity Shield in 1974. I also remember going to Manchester City with Norman Hunter, and when we arrived the first person we met was the chairman Franny Lee. He and Norman were just like old friends, which was brilliant to see. For these guys, disputes on the pitch had been long forgotten.

During the rest of the season, there was only one match of note; it was at Shrewsbury, where an incident involving our centre-half Jackie Ashurst occurred. As Shrewsbury's striker went to hit the ball into the net, Jackie put out his foot to block it. Unfortunately the striker caught his foot under Jackie's. There was a big cheer from the crowd as the ball flew into the back of the net. Their player was delighted with himself and did a backflip to celebrate, but he landed on his back and stayed down. With the crowd singing and chanting his name, his pals came to congratulate him and help him up. The next thing we saw was the staff running on with a stretcher, and he was carried off to the dressing room.

4

CHANGES AND THE CHAMPIONSHIP

As usual, we had changes in the squad for the start of the 1988/89 season. Ian Baird came back to us, along with Noel Blake and Vince Hilaire from Portsmouth. I don't think Bairdy had the best of seasons at Portsmouth, who had been relegated and were back in our division. Our first game of the campaign was against Oxford United at home. Glynn Snodin scored a late equaliser; in celebration, he jumped up on the fence at the Kop end and pounded his chest with his fist wrapped around the bars. It was an iconic image that has stayed with a lot of Leeds supporters.

Our next match was away against Portsmouth, where we lost 4-0. Their top man, ex-Leeds player Terry Connor, scored two goals. After the match, he came into our dressing room to chat with Billy. 'Is there any chance of getting any lemonade around here for my whiskey?' Billy asked him. Terry replied, 'Leave it to me, boss,' and after battering us on the pitch he went running off again to try and purchase a bottle of lemonade. He still loved the manager and his old club. While we were there, I caught up with John Dickens, Portsmouth's physio. 'Your team is looking good,' I remarked. 'Yes,' he replied, 'but don't forget it's a marathon, not a sprint.' He was dead right.

At the end of September we were hit with a bombshell as the directors had decided to sack Billy. I had tears in my eyes; it had been a great place to work under his leadership. But football is all about results and we'd only had one win in the league, having finished in a poor position the previous season.

Later that day, I got another surprise. Something happened which would never take place today. I was called in to see the chairman, Leslie Silver; he wanted to explain why the board had decided to remove the manager. The club's family ethos included the directors and they knew everyone would be upset about Billy. Mr Silver will always be the number one chairman for me. When I first met him his ankle had been giving him some trouble, and he asked me to look at it. I think I was not the first person who had tried to treat him at the club; he'd had x-rays, the works. Then one day, I asked, 'Mr Chairman, how's the ankle?' 'Never been better,' he replied cheerfully. 'Oh, why, what have you done?' I asked him with interest; I was always keen to hear about new treatments. 'I've started taking cod liver oil tablets,' he told me. I had to scratch my head at that one.

When I spoke to Glynn Snodin, we shared some memories of the past season; there were many funny moments. He told me about the five-a-side games Billy and Norman had played with Glynn and Ian Baird. Billy always played in his trainers, and during one match, Bairdy had wiped him out with a tackle. At the next game, the boss came out wearing boots. 'These are for you, son,' Billy joked to Bairdy, showing him the studs.

I was at the receiving end of another prank. At home, our tumble dryer had packed in, so I ordered a new one from one of our sponsors who had an electrical company and arranged to have it delivered to our house in Pateley. Someone must have got their wires crossed as a few days later I had a message from the front desk at work to say that a tumble dryer had arrived for me. I told them I would collect it from reception when I had finished treatment. Later, there was no sign of the dryer; I searched all over the building. Then someone asked, 'Have you tried looking outside?' Sure enough, the usual suspects, Shez, Stilesy, Snods and Bobby D, had been at it again. I found the dryer perched on the flat roof of our ticket office, with a note, 'For sale: £50 ono'. I was more miffed about their price; the dryer had cost me over £200! But I just laughed and took it on the chin. People still rib me about that dryer to this day.

Norman Hunter and Pete Gunby were placed in charge until the club appointed a new manager. We lost the next three games, and at lunchtime Monday, 10 October the new manager arrived. As we had suspected, it was Howard Wilkinson with his assistant Mick Hennigan. I had seen Mick on the touchline when we played Sheffield Wednesday reserves; he was fiercely energetic and passionate, and I watched as he slammed his pen to the floor in frustration. I wondered what was in store for me.

That first afternoon, the new manager had a meeting in the first team dressing room with the players and some of the staff. I was there but someone was missing. Of course, it was John Sheridan. The new gaffer said, 'As I see it, you are near the bottom of the league, so as of now, that makes me one of the worst managers in this league, so we better do something about it. So, get your gear on; we are training in 30 minutes.' It was a new broom, and over the next few weeks the players were to experience a training regime like no other.

The other sad news was that Norman Hunter was told his services were no longer required. Only Pete Gunby and I remained from the old setup. I thought it would only be a matter of time before I would be on my way too. The new gaffer quizzed me about my experience and how the club doctor and I worked together. He wanted to know all about our current injury problems. Dr Berridge was delighted with the appointment; he thought he would work well with Howard Wilkinson on an intellectual level.

A few days later, the reserves played at Blackburn Rovers. I felt a bit sorry for some of the players as they had full training sessions that morning and afternoon, and then played the game in the evening. Mick Hennigan was now in charge of the reserves and the trip gave me a chance to learn a bit more about him. We had a bit in common; he had been a professional footballer and then worked for the Electricity Board while coaching and managing part-time. Maybe through him I would find out when the axe was going to fall.

It was not a good atmosphere at the club during those first few weeks. There was the usual tension when a new manager is appointed; the players did not know who would stay and who would be out of the door. One thing I knew was that Howard Wilkinson and I were as different as chalk and cheese. A player came to tell me that one of the junior coaches who knew the manager had been openly saying that I was on my way out. He had also told one of the players that the gaffer was going to replace him with a new full-back. I went to see Mick and told him what I had heard. Shortly afterwards, I was called to the manager's office. I explained what had been going on and asked him straight, 'Just tell me if I am going?' He did not enlighten me, but we saw less of that junior coach at the club.

Glynn Snodin told me that my friend Alan Smith, the physio at Sheffield Wednesday, had been in touch to say he would not be joining Howard Wilkinson at Leeds. I also found out through Mick that when our new gaffer had broken the news of his departure to the Sheffield Wednesday staff, he had said, 'Anyone who wants to join me at Leeds United, I will see you tomorrow lunchtime at Elland Road.' On the day, Mick was the only one who had turned up. Hopefully that meant I would be keeping my job for the time being.

Years later I spoke with John Sheridan about that time at Leeds. He said, 'With Billy Bremner, he knew what I was like and used to put his arm around me. So long as I kept putting in the performances, he was great. Whereas I knew with Howard Wilkinson that it was only a matter of time before I would be moved on. But I remember some great times.' Shez told me about the day he needed to collect his dry cleaning from the city centre. 'Batts and Speedo were apprentices at the time, and I told them whoever got it for me could use my XR3 for the weekend. It caused fights between them,' he laughed.

He also reminded me of when I had taken him to see John Lawton, the orthopaedic surgeon, to have an injection in his knee. 'Yes,' I replied, 'you had Taff, the night-watchman at Leeds, ring me at two o'clock in the morning to get you some paracetamol!' My answer was, 'Tell Shez to get f****d!' He laughed and protested. 'But I was in pain!' I continued. 'And do you remember the next morning when you sent Stilesy into my room to ask, "What's all this about Shez getting Taff to ring you?" As soon as I opened my mouth, you were straight in the room behind him!' It was another wind-up, but I think Shez had driven around looking for an all-night chemist in the end.

Three new players had joined the club: Andy Williams from Coventry and two young lads from Witton Albion, Mick Whitlow and Neil Parsley. I still keep in touch with Neil today.

At the end of the season, I was still at the club and working around the clock. We had some excellent results and had moved up the league table; Howard Wilkinson's fitness regime was paying off.

There were a couple of other incidents I remember that season. At Ipswich, we had a good 1-0 victory with a penalty from Shez. After the game, the manager asked if I would drive his car up to Sheffield while he travelled with the players. 'Sure, no problem,' I said, but we needed to stop for some petrol first. Just outside Ipswich, I pulled into a full garage. I spotted a free pump, moved over and parked up. As I was looking for the petrol cap, a body jumped over the bonnet, opened the door and flicked the catch. It was the gaffer. By the time I got out of the car, he already had the nozzle in his hand. It was then that I realised why it was an empty pump, 'Gaffer!' I said, 'You're putting diesel in your tank, not petrol!' To say he was not happy was an understatement, and of course, it was all my fault for stopping there. He even mentioned it in his book. But Mick Hennigan and I knew the truth. As Mick once said, 'He will not make that mistake again.'

Another time, we were away at Oxford United and by half-time we were 2-0 down. In the dressing room the gaffer got stuck into the players. While in full flow, he picked up my medical bag and said to one player, 'Can you head the ball?' To demonstrate, he headed my bag. He said to another, 'Can you kick the ball?' and did an imaginary kick. In his rant, he had not realised how close he was to the large solid table in the middle of the room and unwittingly kicked the table leg. Gritting his teeth, he said to everyone, 'Get back on the pitch!' When they had all left he turned to Mick and me and said, 'I think I might have just broken my toes.' We lost the game, 3-2. I hope Howard can laugh about that incident today.

When we had an away game at Watford, the legendary tennis player and Wimbledon champion Stefan Edberg was at the match and asked if he could meet the team. Stefan had been an avid Leeds fan since the Revie era and had watched them on TV as a child in Sweden. At 6ft 2in he looked in great shape. When the gaffer introduced Stefan to the team, he told him jokingly that we had a few players who played a mean game of tennis. Everyone laughed and looked at each other, wondering who he might mean.

At the end of March 1989, it was transfer deadline day and a busy time arranging medicals for the new players. Three signings we made at that time would make a massive impact on the club's fortunes. The first was Carl Shutt from Bristol City. The gaffer had sold Bob Taylor, our young striker, to Bristol City for £175,000, and Shutty was part of the deal. Mick had worked with Shutty at non-league Spalding United and then at Sheffield Wednesday. We also signed Gordon Strachan, who'd been a great player for Dundee, Aberdeen and Manchester United, to help with our bid for promotion. Most people thought it would be his last big move, but time would show that Gordon's transfer to Leeds was a masterstroke. At the 11th hour we signed Chris Fairclough from Spurs for around £500,000 on the recommendation of Paul Hart, who had played with him at Forest; it would also turn out to be another stroke of genius.

Bill Fotherby was the director heavily involved with facilitating these and other transfers. He was commercially very astute, always looking at ways to bring money into the club. We always said that he could sell coal to Newcastle. He and Howard Wilkinson formed a good working relationship. I enjoyed spending time on Friday evenings on away trips, listening to Bill and his stories.

Before the end of the 1988/89 season, there was an incident involving Shez and a few other players. It was a Thursday evening before our away game at Plymouth on Sunday. Some of the lads, including Shez, had a night out in Leeds; they got young Micky Whitlow to be the driver. One of them had been kissing a girl in a doorway when a police officer flashed his torch at them. The officer was told in no uncertain terms to leave them alone. Somehow Shez became involved in the altercation. The first we knew about the incident was the next day; the club received a phone call from a reporter asking if the gaffer knew that John Sheridan had been arrested for being drunk and disorderly. He was taken to the police station then released. The gaffer looked at me; I told him that I had done Shez's strapping that morning and there was no smell of alcohol on him. I could always tell when he had been on a bender. The gaffer had everybody in his office, along with poor Micky, who was only the driver.

One Thursday, I had been with Gordon Strachan and Bobby Davison at the ground, doing some running drills; the edict was we worked everyone hard at every session. Gordon and Bobby were two of the fittest guys at the club when it came to running. I thought the session had gone well. Two days later, on Saturday, 15 April 1989, we were at home to Brighton and Hove Albion and won 1-0. After the match, Gordon went on a rant in the dressing room, 'What a load of rubbish! What do you expect with all that running I had to do!' Mick just looked at him, but I said, 'It's not you he's having a go at; it's me.' At that moment the gaffer rushed through the door to tell us what had happened at Hillsborough. It stopped us in our tracks, and the heat was taken out of our exchange as we all listened to the terrible news at Sheffield Wednesday's ground. It was the worst day in footballing history.

Gordon's criticism stuck with me, though, and I decided to think about my running sessions so near to a game. Years later, when Gordon was the Coventry City manager, I spent time with him and his wife, Lesley, in Leeds after our game. I reminded him of that running session. Before I could say anything else he said, 'Listen, Alan that had nothing to do with you. It was me. On the day I had a s**t game, I had to blame someone, and you were the easy target.' In the years I spent with Strach, I always liked to think that we were honest with each other.

We had been third from the bottom of the Second Division when the gaffer arrived. We reached as high as sixth place under Howard Wilkinson's stewardship before finishing the season tenth in the table. It was a significant improvement.

* * *

In the run-up to the 1989/90 season, John Sheridan left us to join Brian Clough at Nottingham Forest. I think one person who was not too unhappy was our orthopaedic surgeon, John Lawton. The manager knew about Shez and his drinking, and if we were going to train on a Sunday for a midweek game, he had said to me on a few occasions, 'I want John Sheridan putting in hospital on Saturday night after the match, to make sure he is at training the next day.' The only one who could authorise the hospital stay was John Lawton. I met up with him a few years later in Australia, and he mentioned those days with Shez. He said it took him a while to work out what was going on, and when the nurses asked him why Mr Sheridan had been admitted, he would say, 'I don't know, but I'll call and examine him later.' We just laughed about those times.

Another player who lost out with our change of manager was Vince Hilaire. He had been a great player for Crystal Palace and stayed at Leeds for less than a year, but the gaffer wanted to move him on. He finished up playing in the reserves under Mick Hennigan. Vince was another joker. He could never sleep on away trips and would wander the corridors in the middle of the night. When I spoke to Dylan Kerr, Dylan reminded me of when Vince placed a row of dancing plastic flowers on a high ledge on the dressing room wall, they would start dancing in time to any noise that occurred. When Mick came in at half-time, unimpressed with the team's performance, he let rip with the players, oblivious to the flowers positioned behind him. The more he shouted, the more the flowers swayed and danced to his voice. Some of the players were smirking and laughing, and Mick could not work out why. When he found out, he could not see the funny side. The new management team wanted to move the jokers like Vince out of the club.

I recall in Vince's last game before he went on loan to Stoke, he was playing for the reserves on the right near the dugout. The manager came down from the stand, handed me a note and told me, 'Give that to Hilaire.' When the play stopped, I passed the message to Vince. He stopped and looked up into the West Stand. I found out afterwards the note said something along the lines of, 'I have got a dozen scouts here to watch you. Are you going to pull your finger out and start playing?'

We had many new players to assess during pre-season, and the gaffer decided that he did not want me doing both the physio and the kit man's jobs. He appointed a full-time kit man, Sean Hardy, whom Mick knew from Sheffield Wednesday. He had been an apprentice there and then had a spell at Barnsley.

The new players that year included Jim Beglin from Liverpool, Micky Thomas from Shrewsbury and John McClelland from Watford. But the big surprise was Vinnie Jones from Wimbledon; I think Mick had convinced the gaffer that we needed someone like him to sort the dressing room out. John Hendrie also joined us from Newcastle. I knew John from his Bradford City days, and his uncle Paul had played at Halifax Town when I was there. The gaffer also signed Mel Sterland from Glasgow Rangers. Mel had been at Sheffield Wednesday, so Howard Wilkinson knew all about him. When he signed Mel, I think his first words were, 'You might have to go to a health farm for a couple of weeks,' but Mel was a great lad and much fitter than he looked.

We also acquired Dylan Kerr. He was one of the season's lesser-known players, but we got to know each other and became friends. His journey to the club was quite unusual. He had been released as an apprentice from Sheffield Wednesday and then had played in South Africa. When he returned to the UK, Mick and the gaffer were at Leeds, and he asked to train with us. They were reluctant at first until he told them about a recent game he had played for Frickley Athletic, where he had made four goals and scored two. It had reached the local paper, so Howard and Mick changed their minds and invited him to train with us. One day the reserves were short of a left-back, so he played to help them out, and as they say, the rest is history. He played a few games for the first team and stayed at the club for a few years. Then I think Gordon recommended him to his pal Mark McGhee at Reading and Leeds got £75,000 for him. Dylan went on to win the Third Division with Reading and the Scottish Cup with Kilmarnock.

On the coaching side, Dick Bate was placed in charge of the juniors with Pete Gunby. We were looking good for the new season. The bookies had us as favourites to go up, although that kind of pressure was not welcome.

Pre-season training started about six weeks before the first game. We did bleep tests at the ground to test fitness levels; this was especially useful for those players coming back from injury. A good score was around 14 or 15, but two players were particularly impressive. At 32 years old, Gordon Strachan would consistently score more than 15, and Dylan, who had an unusual running action, would be beyond 16. We also used the Leeds University sports facilities at Weetwood and did the occasional run at Roundhay Park.

The lads soon found out what pre-season was all about under Howard Wilkinson. As Chris Fairclough said to me, 'The most we did at Forest and Spurs was play five-a-side and do a bit of running.' We had a real running club going; John Pearson, who had been at Sheffield Wednesday with the gaffer and Mick, told me if you did not play on a Saturday you had to be in to do a five-mile run on a Sunday. After a couple of weeks of intensive training, we played three 30-minute periods against a local team. Having Vinnie Jones and David Batty in the same midfield was interesting. Then the players were given a few days off; that was the carrot from the gaffer if they worked hard. When pre-season matches started for the first team and the reserves, I was hardly at home.

The first game of the season was away at St James' Park against Newcastle. We had some late injuries; Vinnie had to miss out so he sat on the bench with us, while Jim Beglin was a late call-up and had to miss a lot of training. John McClelland played, but a few weeks later he had to have an operation for a long-standing problem with both his heels. The game started okay and we were 2-1 up at half-time, but Newcastle's Mick Quinn scored four goals in the second half and we lost 5-2. The drama did not end there; going down the tunnel at the end of the match, I saw Vinnie and Jim Smith, the Newcastle manager, having a go at each other. Whether it concerned a past issue, I am not sure, but the manager and Jim were old friends from when they had been at Boston United together.

A few weeks later, we were away to Hull City. Before the game, the gaffer discovered that Billy Whitehurst was playing up front for Hull. Everybody knew that Billy did not take any prisoners, so Howard said to Peter Haddock, 'Sorry, son, but I am leaving you out for this one. I think Billy might eat you alive tomorrow, so I am playing big Noel Blake with Chris.' Peter and Chris Fairclough had been playing well together. The next day, Bairdy scored, and we won 1-0.

In early October our trip to West Ham was the top game in the league that day as there were no First Division fixtures because of internationals. I got to know West Ham's kit man, Eddie Gillam, who became a lifelong friend. There was a tense atmosphere in the dressing room. The gaffer wanted everyone to be on the front foot from the moment the whistle blew. When the players went out to look at the pitch, Howard said to Gordon Strachan, 'Today, I want you to take Vinnie for his warm-up.' Vinnie was a great guy, he always had a word with everybody and liked to have a chat with the disabled fans at the side of the pitch, but on this day the gaffer wanted him to focus on the game. We were there to do a job and get back up north with no distractions. I was interested to hear what Vinnie would have to say. On the way out, Gordon said, 'Vinnie, you are going to do your warm-up with me.' Vinnie's immediate reply was, 'Yes, Skip.' It was a testament to the respect that Gordon had built up in the dressing room. We won the match 1-0 from a Micky Whitlow cross, and Vinnie put the ball in the net. After the game, the London press had a go at the team and the manager, but as Bill Fotherby used to say, 'Winners can laugh, losers can please themselves.'

With only one loss so far, in November we had to go away to Leicester City. That day they had a class player who would come to us the next season; his name was Gary McAllister. At 2-1 down we got a penalty. Martin Hodge, Leicester's goalkeeper, was known by many people in football for his 'library of penalty takers'. In other words, he had an encyclopaedic knowledge of the opposition. Strach knew this; he casually placed the ball just beyond the penalty spot towards the goal and walked back as Hodge got ready. Just as Gordon was about to run up, Gary spotted what he had done with the ball and alerted the referee. Gordon said, 'Sorry, Ref,' and went back to put the ball on the right spot. Hodgie had relaxed while this was happening, so Gordon put the ball on the penalty spot and, in the same movement, kicked it into the bottom corner of the net. I was told afterwards that amid all the protests from the Leicester players, Gordon ran up to the goalkeeper, picked up the ball, and said, 'Put that one in your library, Hodgie.' As for the rest of the game, we were beaten 4-3 and had to carry our keeper Mervyn Day off on a stretcher with a shoulder injury.

We had been getting some great results at home and our crowds were creeping towards 30,000. In early December we played Newcastle at Elland Road on David Batty's 21st birthday. We won 1-0 from an Ian Baird header following a great cross by Mel Sterland six minutes from time. Mel was now known as 'Stan' after the great Stanley Matthews or 'Zico' after the Brazilian legend. So that was one of our rivals beaten.

On Boxing Day we travelled south to play Sheffield United. Most of our team had a connection with Sheffield Wednesday on the other side of the city, while United were up there with us trying to get into the First Division. The referee on the day was a good friend from my Halifax Town days, Trevor Simpson. Trevor was a massive Halifax supporter. Talking to Trevor about that game years afterwards, he told me that he had nearly missed out. The police had stopped him while he was in his car outside the stadium and when they asked him to produce his match ticket, Trevor replied, 'I don't have one. I am the referee.' The officer thought he was trying to pull a fast one and said, 'Oh yeah? You're the third referee for this game that I've stopped today.' Trevor replied, 'Listen, pal, I am the real McCoy. I'll show you my kit if you don't believe me!' Trevor jumped out of his car and showed the officer his gear so he could get on with his job.

The game finished 2-2, but from Leeds's perspective it would be remembered for Sterland's free kick from 35 yards out. It looked impossible, but Mel hit it so sweetly into the roof of the net. Afterwards, someone remarked that the ball would have landed on the M1 if the net had not been there. Carl Shutt, another ex-Wednesday player, scored our second goal. Carl had grabbed his chance a few matches earlier when Bobby Davison was out with a knee injury. The gaffer and Mick knew when to play him and when to leave him out, but there was no stopping him when he was on fire. For the trivia fans, Shutty had a unique record. On his debut for Wednesday he scored once, he scored two goals in his first match for Bristol City, and with Leeds he scored a hat-trick against Bournemouth on his debut.

Behind the scenes we had a few injuries I had to sort out. The competition between the recovering players in the gym was brilliant, each trying to out-perform the other. It was good for me, too, as I tapped into their rehab experience and their running sessions from their other clubs, and I picked up some good ideas.

Two injured players I worked with during that time were Jim Beglin and Micky Thomas. Jim came from Southport, and Micky from Colwyn Bay in North Wales, a 220-mile round trip. They met up every day at Birch Services on the M62 and drove in together. We had a telephone in the corridor opposite the coach's room, and a few times, Jim and Micky would call to say, 'Sutts, we are just running a bit late.' I would reply, 'Okay, but make sure you have got your wallet with you for the fine!' Then I would just hear a laugh.

In 1987, Jim had suffered a horrific fracture in his leg when playing against Everton at Goodison Park. When he came to us he was having problems with his right knee but was coping. Jim worked hard to get his fitness back and we needed everybody for the second half of the season. Working one-to-one with Jim was enjoyable as he told me tales of his Liverpool days. He was there when they won the double in 1986 and had been at the Heysel stadium disaster a year previously. He said everything was still done the Bill Shankly way, even though it was many years since Shankly had left the club. Their physio came in a couple of afternoons a week, and the remaining time they would sort themselves out. I was astonished to hear that this was the setup in the team that had won the league so often in recent years.

Jim told me, 'I went over on my ankle once, and it swelled up like a balloon. I told Ronnie Moran that I might be struggling for the weekend. Ronnie said, "You'll be okay, Jim." The day before our game with Ipswich, I saw Ronnie again, and he said to me, "You see that guy over there; he has been knocking on the manager's door for the last six months. If you don't play tomorrow, it might be six months before you wear that number three shirt again."' I asked Jim, 'What happened? Did you play?' He replied, 'Yes, and we won 3-1.' Jim made it into the team at Leeds by the end of the season after being on loan at Plymouth for a few games.

One player with a load of energy, who could never sit still for two minutes, was Welsh international Micky Thomas. I called him the 'Scarlet Pimpernel'. When he would ring me at home, even my kids would say, 'Dad, the Scarlet Pimpernel wants to talk to you.' John Lawton told me that when Micky was recovering from a knee operation in the BUPA hospital, the nurses could never find him. They would find him sitting with one of the elderly patients, watching TV and eating their grapes. He would often tell me about his antics at other clubs. When he was at Chelsea, Micky would think nothing of sleeping in the physio room the night before a match. When he signed for Brighton, he was ready for an interview with the press when he realised it might be challenging to get from Colwyn Bay to Brighton each day. I think Micky got a place down there but I don't think he lasted long. Neville Southall, who lived near Micky, once told me that every time he looked out of the window Micky would be running past, whatever the weather.

I had been working with the gaffer and Mick Hennigan for just over a year. Howard Wilkinson liked to keep everyone on their toes; you never knew if he might replace you the following week. I learned a lot from him about physiology as well as about his wine collection. Every day at 4pm I would go running with him and Mick, so I learned more about running and got fitter myself. The gaffer once asked me if I had ever won anything. I told him, 'Yes, at a local level as a player, and when I was the physio at Halifax RL, they won the 1986 Championship as 200/1 outsiders.' Another time I was at a function and Howard was at the top table. The next morning, he said to me, 'I was watching you last night sitting with people you had never met before, and the conversation seemed to be flowing. You were enjoying yourself talking to everyone. I have known people to pay good money to learn the confidence to do that.' It was not often that he threw me a bone, but I was happy to take it.

During the 1989/90 season I got to know Vinnie Jones. He had a huge personality, a reputation as a hard man and was immensely popular with the fans. The gaffer got the best out of him, and he had a successful, albeit short, career at Leeds and only got booked a few times. He told me that his dad had been a gamekeeper in Hertfordshire, so I said, 'If you are into shooting and fishing, I can arrange for you to meet some of the guys where I live in Pateley Bridge.' He came over to our place one Sunday afternoon and I introduced him to Shirley. She offered him a cuppa, but in the two minutes it took her to make it he had nodded off on the sofa. After a couple of hours he woke up and said, 'Sorry about that, I didn't get to bed until 4am.' We just laughed. I took him to my pal Barry Simpson's place just outside Pateley, overlooking Gouthwaite reservoir. Barry knew all the local gamekeepers and people from the shooting world. Barry's son, Paul, was a gamekeeper in Reeth in Swaledale, and he and Vinnie became good friends.

Vinnie spent a lot of time in our neck of the woods. He stayed with us on a few occasions. One time it was a bit unexpected. Late one Wednesday afternoon when Mick and I were in the office, the phone rang. A reporter from *The Sun* told us that Vinnie had been in a fight at Mr Craig's, the nightclub in Leeds. Mick got hold of the gaffer, who asked me to track Vinnie down, get him over to my place and wait for the lawyers to get in touch. As luck would have it, he had already made his way to Pateley Bridge. I found him at The Sportsman's Arms in Wath. I told Vinnie that he had to stay with me until Peter McCormick, the Leeds United lawyer, arrived to see him. He filled me in about the nightclub incident. Vinnie had been in Mr Craig's minding his own business when he noticed a guy eyeballing him. Vinnie said, 'So, I asked him if there was a problem, and when he said, "Yes," I knew he just wanted a fight. The manager of Mr Craig's told us that he did not want his place smashed up and said he had a room we could use at the back'. Vinnie said it was a good fight, and talking to me in The Sportsman's Arms, he did not look any the worse for wear. This guy had wanted to have a go at Vinnie so he could sell the story to a newspaper like *The Sun*.

Peter McCormick arrived at our place at around 10pm and took a statement from Vinnie. On the manager's orders, I had to get him to the club early the following day before the press arrived. I had a routine of giving my pal Matt Cockburn a lift from Pateley Bridge to the American base at Menwith Hill on my way into Leeds. The next morning, I saw Matt in his usual spot waiting for a lift. I waved and shook my head to say, 'Sorry mate, not this morning.' Halfway up the High Street, Vinnie wanted to call in the shop to get *The Sun*, so I stopped at the post office and nipped out of the car. Sure enough, there was Vinnie's photo on the front page. When I got back in the car, there was Matt sitting behind us in the back. He had legged it up the High Street and jumped in the car. He said, 'Now then, Alan, I thought you'd forgotten me there for a minute.' Vinnie looked at me and buried his head in the paper. When we got to the base, Matt got out, said his thanks and then added, 'Great to see you, Vinnie.' Matt was a good guy.

Vinnie became well known in the Dale. He even turned out for the Lofthouse and Middlesmoor cricket team, wearing his Yorkshire shirt and sweater that some of the Yorkshire players had swapped with him. He was only at Leeds for 15 months but he became a legend to many supporters in the Dale, and rightly so.

Early in 1990, rumours were circulating that Leeds were trying to sign Peter Beardsley from Liverpool. But instead, Howard Wilkinson sold Ian Baird to Middlesbrough for around £500,000 and brought in Lee Chapman from Nottingham Forest. Lee was another ex-Wednesday player whom the gaffer knew well. Lee's debut was away to Blackburn Rovers, and we won 2-1 with Chappy and Gordon Strachan both scoring. The manager must have been happy on the coach on the way back as he said to Bob, the driver, 'Pull up at the next pub to get a drink for the lads.' We stopped in a place called Ramsbottom, but before we could get off the coach the landlord came out and said, 'Sorry, we don't want you in here.' The gaffer said, 'We are the Leeds United team. We've just been playing at Blackburn Rovers.' But the answer was still the same, 'We don't want you lot in here,' so we went down the road and found another pub. This landlord had only been open for a couple of weeks, there was hardly anyone in the place, and he welcomed us with open arms.

At the end of January we had a trip to Ireland arranged and a visit to a health farm. We had been knocked out of the FA Cup earlier that month in the third round, so we did not have a game, but our last match before we went for Dublin was at home against Stoke City. The records say that we won 2-0 but they do not tell what happened behind the scenes. At half-time, David Batty came into the dressing room. I was in there with Dr Berridge. David said, 'I can't carry on. I've pulled my hamstring.' The gaffer told us to take him down to the treatment room and sort it out. He had looked great in the first half. We tested him out and reassured him that he should be okay to play. Early in the second half he had a penalty awarded against him by the referee, George Tyson, for a cynical tackle. Fortunately, Mervyn Day was on top form and saved it. George loved to give a penalty, and luckily for us the next one went our way. Chappy was brought down and Strach scored, followed by another goal from John Hendrie. A couple of days after the match, I asked Batts what had been wrong with him. He said, 'It was my dad.' 'How do you mean?' I asked. 'When I come off at half-time, I look up at my dad in the stand, and he gives me a thumbs up or thumbs down. He was giving me the thumbs down in a big way, and it pissed me off.'

Just before we left for our break, we made another signing, Chris Kamara from Stoke City. Chris was on his way to sign for his hometown team Middlesbrough but Bill Fotherby and the gaffer hijacked him, and he made the trip with us to Ireland.

On Thursday, 25 January 1990 we flew from Leeds Bradford Airport to Dublin during one of the worst storms in recent history. We posed for a photograph on the steps of the Capital Airways 27-seater plane, and I recall Gordon Strachan saying, 'Smile for the birdie; we might be doing it for the last time.' Shortly after we took off, they closed the airport and gale-force winds buffeted the plane and made it a flight to remember, but not in a good way. As we were tossed around like a feather, the drinks were flying everywhere, people were sick and some were even making their peace with God. When we arrived in Dublin they closed the airport there too. Mervyn Day knew our pilot, who had skilfully grappled with the terrible conditions. He told Merv that it was one of the worst flights he had experienced, which was better to know once we were safely back on the tarmac.

It had been around 20 years since Leeds had played in Ireland, and that evening the crowds were out in force for the game against Shelbourne at Landsdowne Road. There were about 12,000 fans in the ground and another three or four thousand outside. Only one police officer kept control.

After the match, which we won 2-0, we went out for a meal with the Shelbourne players, and in the Irish tradition we had a singalong. Vinnie and I sang 'Danny Boy' together, but the star of the evening was Chris Kamara with his rendition of 'Candle in the Wind'. He brought the house down and left many of us thinking that if he can play football as well as he can sing, we have got a great player. Fortunately the flight home was a lot calmer. As we left the plane, there was a priest behind me. I said to him, 'We could have done with you on the plane yesterday!' He smiled; we were back home in one piece.

We followed up the Ireland trip with a few days at a health farm near Luton. While there, I worked with Mel Sterland, who had injured his foot, but his rehab went slightly awry when he and Vinnie decided to have a drinking contest. After some lagers they moved on to the Southern Comfort. The next day I went looking for Mel. He was rooming with Mervyn Day, who was supposed to be watching him, but his eyes were like slits.

Before our next match at Swindon Town, we had made another signing, the forward Imre Varadi, again from Sheffield Wednesday. During the Swindon game, Micky Whitlow sustained a serious injury. Initially the referee, Paul Durkin, would not let me on to the pitch. Micky was in agony, hopping on one leg as Swindon got a free kick. Ross MacLaren hit a 25-yarder straight under Micky's foot and into the bottom corner. Then I was allowed on with a stretcher. If I had been able, I would have put a drip up. Micky was out for about three months.

Our next game was at home to Hull City; if you were a fan, it was probably one of the season's best fixtures. Imre made a good start and scored a goal in our 4-3 victory. Eddie Gray, the Hull manager, popped his head around the medical room door to say hello; our paths had almost crossed in my playing days in the 1960s, and it would not be long before we would be working and travelling the world together.

We continued without a win until we went to Oxford United. By half-time we were 2-0 down, then in the second half the class of the Leeds team came to the fore. We were winning 4-2, and close to full time we were awarded a penalty. Usually Gordon Strachan was our taker, but this time Lee Chapman got the ball and put it on the spot looking to score a hat-trick. He put it straight over the bar. In the dressing room afterwards, the gaffer had a go at him. The league table was so tight that promotion might have gone down to goal difference, and that penalty miss could have cost us dearly.

We won the next three games, during which time another player had come into the starting line-up, the former apprentice and my helper, Gary Speed. He was ready to show us all what an incredible talent he would be, particularly with his skill in heading the ball and his excellent jumping ability. He was going to be a nightmare for lots of full-backs when playing on the left-hand side.

We went to Wolverhampton Wanderers on a high but lost 1-0. David Batty gave the ball away and Andy Mutch scored for Wolves. Shortly afterwards, David walked off the pitch. The gaffer turned to me and asked, 'What's up with him?' I did not have a clue, so he told me to go and find out. Wolves were rebuilding their ground at that time, including a new stand and dressing rooms, and we were still using the old facilities. I caught up with Batts and said, 'David? What's up, pal?' I got an answer I did not expect, 'I need a s**t.' The dressing rooms were locked up, so along came this old guy with the biggest bunch of keys I had ever seen. But he did not know which one was for the dressing room, and by the time he had tried out several keys and eventually found the right one, David said, 'I don't need to go now,' and ran back on to the pitch. After the game, the gaffer said to him, 'I hope they don't find out about that when they are picking you to play for England.'

With three matches to go until the end of the season, we had a home game against Barnsley in midweek and needed two wins to get us up. But we suffered our first home defeat of the season, losing 2-1; Barnsley had done the double over us. I think the stress was starting to get to us all at that point. But everyone at the club had to stay positive and we knew that we had some great players to get us over the line.

During that game, Chris Fairclough sustained a nasty gash to his forehead and needed stitches, so I took him off the pitch and straight into the medical room where John Berridge, the doctor, waited. No sooner had he started on the stitches when Glynn Snodin was at the door; he was the sub that night. He asked me, 'How long are you going to be?' I told him my usual two minutes, wondering whether the gaffer was planning to put the sub on, but then Snods returned. 'How long?' He asked once more. I told the doc that what he had done so far would hold the bleeding until half-time, and then we would finish it off.

I got a pad and bandages and ran up the tunnel with Chris. A roar went up as he ran on the pitch, and of course, Chris being as brave as a lion, headed in the first goal. But late in the game, both the Barnsley substitutes scored and they won. I saw Glynn again after the match, and I asked him if the gaffer was going mad, thinking we were taking too long with Chris. 'No,' he said. 'It was me.' 'You? Why?' I asked him. 'Because Bobby Davison and I had £10 each on Chris to score the first goal at 8/1, so we are now £80 better off!' said Snods with a grin. I had to smile too, but we were all gutted with the result.

Our final home game was against Leicester City, and we had to win. There was an incredible atmosphere on the day, and my son Miles, a ball boy, was in awe. The stadium rocked with the singing, chanting and cheering; I had not experienced anything like it before either. Gary McAllister, who was playing for Leicester at the time, said that it was so loud he could not make himself heard by one of his team-mates just five yards away. Gary had a good game that day but luckily for us he failed to get a hat-trick, scoring one goal and having a couple of near misses, including a great shot saved by Mervyn. However, Mel 'Zico' Sterland gave us the lead with a shot that went through his brother-in-law Tony James's legs and into the bottom corner of the net. Gary equalised, and despite Leeds having the best of play, Martin Hodge was on top form too, and the goalmouth was almost impenetrable. But six minutes from time Gordon Strachan scored in the top corner with one of his best left-footed shots. It was probably one of the most important goals of his career. The crowd went crazy and the game was interrupted as fans ran on the pitch, but we held on to the lead and won 2-1.

Gary Mac said that Gordon had shown us why he was one of the greats on that day. The truly great players always step up at the most crucial games, and Strach had certainly done that for Leeds. Sometimes players freeze under pressure, but as a true leader we knew that Gordon would bring out the best in his team-mates. In the dressing room Vinnie came in to tell us that Newcastle and West Ham had drawn, and we were up to the First Division. Some of the lads had tears in their eyes. As I was walking down the corridor, I saw my friend John Helm and said, 'We've done it, John!' He replied, 'No, you haven't, Newcastle are still playing.' Our celebrations were premature and Newcastle scored a late winner, so someone had to break it to the lads. Going into the final weekend we had 82 points, as did Sheffield United, and Newcastle were not far behind us with 80 points. We had a better goal difference than Sheffield, but Newcastle's was better than ours.

I think every Leeds supporter has a story to tell about that last game of the season at Bournemouth. The week beforehand, a guy I had been treating asked if I fancied going to Anfield to watch Liverpool play their last match of the season and see them presented with the First Division championship trophy. It was a fantastic night; I was just hoping that we would be experiencing a similar feeling after our game on Saturday.

We were heading to Bournemouth on the Thursday, but a couple of days beforehand the gaffer decided a bit of light-hearted fun might relieve the pressure. He wanted to organise a game of baseball or rounders and said to me, 'Alan, you know a few Americans in your neck of the woods, have a word and find out how to mark out a pitch.' I went to see one of my neighbours, a Detroit Tigers fan, and he gave me the instructions.

On the Thursday morning I had it sorted, and the players were in two teams. Everything was going okay and it was good fun. When it was Vinnie's turn I should have guessed that, with his usual enthusiasm, things might not go according to plan. After missing the first couple of pitches he hit the ball, and in typical Vinnie style he now thought he was a Major League baseball player. As he set off to run to first base, he threw the bat behind him like he was in the Yankee Stadium, and hit poor Andy Williams in the face. It looked like Andy might have fractured his cheekbone, so we were headed to the hospital before the coach could depart. I felt for Andy and when we saw the surgeon, he confirmed my suspicions. I left Andy in the surgeon's capable hands and made my way back to Elland Road to travel south to Bournemouth. Everyone was gutted for Andy.

On the first night we stayed in the New Forest. We had a chilled-out meal in an Italian restaurant and tried to think about anything other than the game. The next day was sweltering as we headed for Poole and a hotel on the waterfront. Thankfully we heard that Andy's op had gone well. The gaffer, Mick and I headed up to Dean Court to look at the pitch, which was bone hard. We asked the groundsman if he would be watering it. There was just one sprinkler out in one of the penalty areas. He said that he would, but we knew it was a load of bull. Harry Redknapp, the manager, would not let us benefit from a decent surface; Bournemouth needed to win to have a chance to stay up. Their physio was John Dickens, whom I knew from his previous role at Portsmouth.

That evening I am sure we were all thinking about the other games that would influence our result; if Leicester were to play in the same way against Sheffield United as they had played against us then that would help. We had heard that Ian Baird had given his team-mates at Middlesbrough the hard word to make sure they put in a performance against Newcastle; he wanted a championship medal for the games he had played for Leeds that season. But the bottom line was that it was down to us.

It was a bank holiday weekend. Leeds supporters had travelled from all over the country to be part of the atmosphere, and hopefully, the celebrations. When Sean, the kit man, and I went to the ground to put the kit out, it was already 21°C. On paper, Bournemouth had a good team with a lot of experience. It was surprising that they were having such a poor season.

Back at the hotel, after the pre-match meal, the gaffer spoke to the players. He used a golfing analogy, 'This is it. You are on the final tee to win the championship; you just need four good hits, and you're home. Just put in the same amount as we have done all season and trust your mates on the pitch. Let's go!' We had a police escort with five or six outriders, and when we arrived there were thousands of people flocking around the entrance, so we got off the coach at the other end of the stadium and walked across the pitch to the dressing rooms. There were fewer than 10,000 supporters in the ground but the noise seemed like three times that number.

Apart from Chappy's great goal, I remember Batty, who was the sub that day, warming up at the side of the pitch and coming back with the news that Sheffield United were winning 4-1 at Leicester while we were still 0-0. I said, 'Batts, I just don't want to know.' What we did not know at the time was that Leicester's keeper Martin Hodge, who had been brilliant the week before, had been carried off on a stretcher. In the end we got over the line and beat Bournemouth 1-0. Sheffield United won 5-2 and Bairdy scored twice as Middlesbrough beat Newcastle 4-1. When Roger Gifford, the referee, blew the final whistle at the end of our game, instead of meeting the other officials in the centre circle as was the norm, he was already halfway down the tunnel. He had decided that whatever was going to happen on the pitch he would not be part of it.

After the game the dressing room was in chaos, packed with players, directors and the press. Vinnie was sat on the massage table while I stood behind him. He said to me, 'Sutts, you and me, we're the Pateley Bridge boys!' I put my arms around him and joked,

'You're not a Pateley boy just yet, Vinnie,' and the cameras started flashing. I still have the photograph of that moment from the *Sunday People* newspaper, signed by Vinnie.

I was chatting with Merv after the match. He had won the FA Cup in 1975 with West Ham United, so he had experienced something like this before. Merv knew that the gaffer was about to sign John Lukic, the goalkeeper from Arsenal. He said to me, 'I have got my medal, so they can do what they like.'

Thinking back over the season, I was also reminded of that penalty miss by Chappy at Oxford and how costly that could have been. We had won the title on goal difference by seven goals; beating Sheffield United 4-0 on Easter Monday was a big turnaround.

The journey home was one big party. After 15 minutes or so, Gordon said to Mr Fotherby, 'Can we stop and get some beers and lagers? Not all the players like champagne.' We stopped off at an off-licence in Winchester, and Vinnie, Sean Hardy and I went in and cleared out every beer and lager they had on the shelves. I think the owner was happy, but there was nothing left for his regular customers. It was interesting to hear Gordon say years afterwards that he was content to sit and watch the other players enjoy themselves while he took it all in. There was just a tremendous sense of relief at getting over the line after all the months of pressure.

On the way home, I reflected on the last 18 months under Howard Wilkinson's tenure as manager. When he arrived at the club there were two players the gaffer thought he might have to replace. One was Mervyn Day but by the end of his first season, Merv had surprised him with some outstanding performances. I recall Howard saying that Merv had saved him at least £400,000; he had not had to go out and buy another keeper. Even though John Lukic came to Leeds the following season, Mervyn stayed at the club for another three years. The other player was Peter 'Fish' Haddock, who had also won the manager over. Playing alongside Chris Fairclough, I don't think there was a better centre-half pairing in the league that season. They were both outstanding, especially in big games.

When we got back to Leeds I was a bit the worse for wear. I had already rung my nephew, Philip, who lived in Leeds, to ask him to pick me up, but not before I made sure I had my shirt, shorts and socks from the game. Back at Philip's place, I think the toilet was my best friend that night. The gloss was taken off our celebrations the following day when we got the news that the Leeds fans had caused a lot of trouble and damage in Bournemouth.

Many players and managers are well known for their pre-match routines and superstitions. We would believe anything if we thought it would get us over the line. I had a superstition of my own. I had a pair of 'lucky' underpants that I had got into the habit of wearing for every match that season. Don't get me wrong, they always had a good wash in between, but they must have done the trick. There were a couple of games where I didn't put them on, and we lost, so point proven – to me anyway. After the 1991/92 season, as the holes got bigger, I eventually threw them away.

The following Tuesday we played a game with the Italian team Genoa. After the match we were presented with the league trophy, followed by a dinner where the players received their medals. Dave Bassett, the Sheffield United manager, was there; he and Howard were good friends. Mick and I got our medals later as they needed a few extra ones for some of the players. I remember Jim Beglin telling me how different it was at Liverpool. They would go into the club at the start of the new season, and Ronnie Moran would just say, 'Well done for winning the league last season, lads. We have got to achieve the same this season, if not better. By the way, there is a box over there with your medals in it. If you feel you deserve one, then go get it.' Jim said that was the Liverpool way.

We had an end-of-season break just outside Magaluf in Spain so that the lads could chill out for a few days. Before we set off, the gaffer called Mick and me into the office. Because of what had happened after the game at Bournemouth, all eyes were on us. People would be looking for a story. He told us to make sure that there was no bad behaviour. Big Ian McFarlane, the chief scout, also went with us to help keep an eye on the players.

On the plane I sat with Gary Speed, who had been chosen for the Welsh national squad, and with the help of another Welsh lad, Ryan Nicholls, had been learning the Welsh national anthem. I remember Gary telling me a few weeks later at pre-season that he had made his debut as a substitute. He had a night out in Cardiff with the rest of the players, including Ian Rush and Mark Hughes. They went to one of their regular nightclubs and the guy on the door did not recognise them straight away. He asked them, 'Are you members, gentleman?' Rush said to him, smiling, 'Would you be able to get the manager for us?' The manager duly arrived, took one look at them, and said, 'Come on in, Rushie, and bring the boys with you.' Speedo said they were all laughing; as a young player, he just loved that thrill that fame brought.

The Spain trip went okay. We met the lads from Aston Villa one evening, and I caught up with Jim Walker, who I knew from Lilleshall and was now Villa's physio. Towards the end of our break Vinnie came into the hotel with two police officers, but whatever had happened he had sorted it out. We heard that the Sheffield United players had taken all the headlines with some of their antics while they were away, so that was a relief for Mick and me.

5

REACHING THE TOP

Pre-season training ahead of 1990/91 was at Trinity and All Saints College, part of Leeds University. Most of the lads had been doing plenty of running during the summer. We had some new players: John Lukic, the goalkeeper, returning to the club where he had started his career; Gary McAllister from Leicester and another centre-half, Chris Whyte from West Bromwich Albion. They would all have a big influence over the next two seasons.

Our first game in the First Division was away at Everton, and it was an excellent start for us. By half-time we were a couple of goals up and when Neville Southall came out for the second half and sat on the pitch with his back against the goal post, it was apparent that something had kicked off in their dressing room. Everton missed a penalty and we won 3-2. After the match, I spoke to Stuart McCall, who was now at Everton; he asked me, 'Did your keeper have glue on his gloves today? Everything he touched seemed to stick.'

On 8 September 1990 the day started well as it was Gary Speed's 21st birthday, the same day as my son Miles. But we played away at Luton Town where we lost 1-0 and it turned out to be Vinnie Jones's last game for the first team. We also got the dreadful news that David Longhurst, a player I had looked after as a physio at Halifax, had collapsed and died on the pitch while playing for York City against Lincoln. Chris Fairclough had played at Nottingham Forest at the same time as David, and we were both in shock. It was a tragic loss.

A few weeks after the Luton game, the news came that the gaffer had sold Vinnie. He had lost his place to our formidable new midfield of Strachan, McAllister, Batty and Speed, widely considered the best since the Revie era. As Vinnie once said to me, 'My image playing in the stiffs [reserves] did not fit too good.' He joined his old manager from Wimbledon, Dave Bassett, who was now at Sheffield United.

Every other Sunday, Hunslet Rugby League played at Elland Road; they also trained there on Tuesdays and Thursdays, unless there was a reserve game. I got to know Bob

Smith, their physio and kit man, and their coach David Ward, who had been a great player for Leeds RL and had played against Halifax when I had worked there. Many a time before training, we would all sit and have a chat. David had been a hooker for Great Britain and the formidable Leeds team that won the Challenge Cup at Wembley in 1977/78.

David talked about the games leading up to the final. He said the chairman would walk into the dressing room about 20 minutes before kick-off and say to the players, 'I've just spoken with the coach, and he tells me that we haven't sorted out what money you are on to win this game.' David continued, 'We would all nod our heads, and then he would ask, 'Who are we playing today, Coach?' and David would reply, 'St Helens, in the quarter-final of the cup, Mr Chairman.' Then he would begin, 'Well, Coach, I think £250 a win would sound about right.' The lads would nod again; then it would go to £350, and there would be more nods until the chairman would finally declare, 'St Helens are a strong side. Sod it! You are on £500 a man!' Then the dressing room would erupt with cheers. Most players were earning less than £100 a week in their day jobs. Then, as he walked away, he would say, 'By the way, lads, you know it is £20 for a loss, don't you?' David said, 'Alan, we went out there, and in the first 20 minutes, the other team was asking, "What the hell is going on?" We just ripped their heads off.'

David also told me another little story; one of his physios went on to the middle of the pitch to treat a winger. He turned to get something out of his bag and when he turned back, the player was nowhere to be seen. He had taken off when he had seen the opposing winger heading to score a try, so the poor physio was left adrift on the floor in the middle of the pitch. I knew the feeling; it had happened to me on a few occasions when I worked in rugby league.

Behind the scenes, both Gordon and the manager were having a good influence on the players. Gordon worked with a guy called Harold from Norway. He was not a traditional trainer but would test Gordon's fitness by trigger pointing weaknesses or lack of strength. Before games, Strach did a lot of work himself. There was still a big drinking culture in those days, but Gordon always put his fitness first. A lot of the other lads started to use Harold; his ideas were interesting.

I still laugh to myself about the time I came up with the bright idea of taking three injured players, Gordon Strachan, Chris Kamara and Dylan Kerr, to my home town of Bradford. For a change of scenery I took them to Peel Park. It is a large park with lots of hills; I knew it well from the years I had spent there visiting the fair at Whitsuntide. However, I had not reckoned on the number of people who would be there walking their dogs, so you can guess the stick I was about to get. Some of the dogs thought it was fair game to run with the players, but we managed a good session.

The game against Chelsea on Boxing Day 1990 was a great 4-1 win. One of our scorers that day was Micky Whitlow, who was starting to get some game time at left-back. After doing some running with him, he was a lot quicker than I had first thought. Like many others at the club, Micky was just another lad off the street and a down-to-earth character. Micky, Simon Grayson and Gary Speed bought houses in the same area of Leeds.

When Micky came to pre-season training, I asked him, 'Did you have a good holiday, Micky? Where did you go?' He said, 'Nowhere, I spent the summer digging out my fishpond.' 'Did you get it all done?' I asked. 'Yes,' he said, 'I fitted the plastic liner from the garden centre, and I've got the fish in. It's all set up.' As the weeks went on, I heard from Micky that some cats had taken a few of the fish, and then more had continued to disappear. One day he came to the club looking a real mess. I said, 'What have you done, pal?' He said, 'I got word that someone was coming into my garden to steal my fish, so I stayed up until 5am waiting for them, but nobody turned up.' A few weeks later, I heard on the grapevine that every bit of Mickey's prized pond was stolen, including the plastic lining. All that was left was a fishpond-shaped hole in the ground. Talking to Simon Grayson a few years later, he told me that it was not the end of poor Micky's bad luck; he had his washing stolen off the line too, but only the good stuff.

On New Year's Day we went to Anfield to play Liverpool and got a bit of a battering in a 3-0 defeat. We had a drink in the famous boot room afterwards. We asked the Liverpool staff if we could have a video of the game, as was common practice, and despite promising they would send one on it never arrived. But as the signs said, 'This is Anfield'. They did not like to give much away.

In the first few months of 1991 we played a lot of cup matches. We drew away at Barnsley in the third round of the FA Cup, and then three days later we beat them 4-0 at home. In the next round, we played Arsenal four times, first away and then three replays before losing 2-1 at home. I became friends with their physio, Gary Lewin. Whenever we met up we would run together around the track at Elland Road. After one of the replays, when we were travelling back up north, Strach asked me who we were playing on 6 April. I told him, 'I think we are away at Wimbledon. Why?' But he did not enlighten me then; I had to wait a bit longer.

The following month we played in the northern final of the Zenith Data Systems Cup against Everton, after beating Manchester City away in the semi-final. To fit this in with league games we played Arsenal away on the Sunday, Everton at home on the Tuesday and then Everton away on the Thursday, followed by Crystal Palace at home on the Saturday. We lost all but the home game with Everton, where we drew 3-3. It was just a crazy week. I think the manager said, 'Never again.'

A few days before our Wimbledon fixture, Strach asked me what my wife was doing on the evening of the game. 'Nothing, as far as I know,' was my reply. 'Great,' he said, 'Rod Stewart has given me 40 tickets for his concert at the NEC in Birmingham, and you and Shirley are coming.' Then the penny dropped as I remembered our conversation on the coach a few weeks earlier.

The club had done well with monies from the Arsenal games, so they provided coach travel for the wives and partners, including all-expenses-paid accommodation at the NEC hotel. The gaffer and Mick Hennigan were not going, so the gaffer told Alan Roberts and me that we were in charge. I thought to myself that only one person is running this show, and that's Gordon.

After a great 1-0 win at Wimbledon we arrived late but managed to see the second half of the show, followed by a party at the hotel, and a few hours later Rod Stewart, along with his brother, and his wife Rachel Hunter, joined us. After the concert, Rod had played in an England v Scotland five-a-side game with Bobby Moore, Eddie and Frank Gray, and John Hollins. Most people, me included, had bought a concert programme. Sean Hardy, our kit man, handed me half a dozen and said, 'Sutts, can you ask Rod to sign them?' Rod was chatting to Gordon, so I hung back and waited until Gordon introduced me. We shook hands and then Gordon said, 'Rod, do you know that you and Al are about the same age?' It was Gordon's sense of humour as Rod looked years younger than me, but it broke the ice. I said, 'Rod, do you see those people over there? Not one of them has the bollocks to come and ask you for your autograph. Would you mind signing these for me?' I gestured to the programmes. The answer was 'No problem,' and he signed them all. We had a good trip back home on the coach, I think it was a relief for Gordon that it had all gone well, and he had let his hair down with a drink for once. We offered him the money for the tickets, but it was all courtesy of Rod Stewart.

Our last game of the season was away at Nottingham Forest. We were beaten 4-3 and finished fourth in the table. It was a great season considering it was our first in the top division for eight years. Arsenal won the league with Liverpool and Crystal Palace second and third. The team and the staff had a few days away in Spain, this time in Marbella at the Don Carlos Hotel. It was a bit grand for some but the champagne breakfasts went down well, especially with the lads coming in from a night out. But at least we did not have the pressure of the year before following events at Bournemouth, and it was a good break.

There were a few new faces for pre-season training, including Tony Dorigo from Chelsea, Steve Hodge from Nottingham Forest and the Wallace twins, Rod and Ray from Southampton. There were also two young lads whom Mick Hennigan had worked with at Sheffield Wednesday, Jon Newsome and David Wetherall. We had signed Gary Kelly from Drogheda in Ireland the season before too.

Tony had an operation during the summer so he had to spend a few weeks with me before playing. There had also been some changes with the medical team. Tom O'Shea, the crowd doctor, took over as the new club doctor. Tom was a little bit reluctant to take on the role at first, but Howard Wilkinson was pleased with the appointment.

We had a pre-season trip to Ireland and played the final warm-up game in Cork. Tony was fit enough to be the sub. When he came on with 20 minutes to go, the Irish announcer cried over the tannoy, 'And now, ladies and gentlemen, Leeds United's new £1.2m signing, TOMMY DORIGO!' Everybody in the Leeds party just laughed. The name has stuck with some players to this day, and to make things worse for Tony, even the manager started calling him Tommy.

We also had a trip to Japan for four days to play in an exhibition match. Just before we set off, Gordon Strachan said to me, 'It looks like we'll be sitting together.' I said, 'Knowing you, Gordon, I will get battered for 12 hours!' He could be a funny guy. I knew Gordon had played in the World Cups of 1982 and 1986 for Scotland. In the previous season he had been the Football Writers' Association Player of the Year. He had also won the award with Aberdeen in 1979/80, so this meant he was the first player to win it in both England and Scotland. I didn't know until I was on this trip that Gordon was involved in two games billed by FIFA as World XI matches, comprising teams made up of players from various countries. The first was in the States after the Mexico World Cup in 1986, where he and Terry Butcher took part. Another was in Paris, where Strach started as a sub. I had to laugh at what he said next. He was on the bench with Zico from Brazil, Tardelli from Italy and Boniek from Poland. He said, 'Looking down the line, I thought what the f*** am I doing on this bench!'

We were in Japan to play against the Brazilian team, Botafogo. We trained indoors at the Big Egg in Tokyo, which was also the venue for our match. The gaffer wanted us to stay on UK time as much as possible so we trained at 1am, then went to bed at 5am, rising at 3pm. The day before the game, the Miami Dolphins and Oakland Raiders American football teams played in an exhibition contest in front of an audience of nearly 100,000. Some of the lads went to watch it.

As for our game, we lost 1-0. The dressing room laughter was all about the toilets, which operated by computer and did everything for you, including washing your nether regions. It was indeed a novelty. David Batty was messing around with the controls and could not turn it off so there was water everywhere. Back at home, Botafogo came to Elland Road to play us again, and this time we won 2-1.

At a reserve game I met Albert Phelan, one of the coaches from Sheffield Wednesday. He was going mad about Ron Atkinson who, just before he left them to join Aston Villa as manager, had sold David Wetherall and Jon Newsome to us for £250,000. Wethers always said it was £200,000 for Jon and £50,000 for him. At the time, David was doing a Chemistry degree in Sheffield and playing part-time football for Leeds until he completed his studies. In the end he got a first-class honours degree, which he accepted by saying, 'If I don't see the inside of a lab again, it will be too soon.' He went on to have a great career in football.

The season got off to a good start, only losing one of our first 12 games when we were beaten 1-0 in the last minute at Crystal Palace. I had to do a fitness test with Mel Sterland on the morning of the game. It was 1 October and both Mel's and my birthday. Gary McAllister went over on his ankle during the match. He was okay for the next game against Sheffield United, but he took a knock on it and had to come off. Gary was like Speedo and a few others; he hated to miss any games. So when it came to our next match against Oldham, I told the gaffer on Friday morning that he was okay to play, but Howard said, 'No chance.'

During training that morning, Steve Hodge had to pull out with an injury so when the gaffer came back in, he said, 'Tell me again about Gary McAllister.' I confirmed that Macca and I were happy and that he would not have a problem. Gary played the entire game and put in the cross that Brian Kilcline, Oldham's big centre-half, sliced into his own net. We won 1-0 and went to the top of the league for the first time in many years.

Two other games leading up to Christmas were especially memorable. The first was away at Chelsea where we won 1-0, Carl Shutt getting the only goal. In celebration he ran into the open space behind the goal and vaulted over the fence to the Leeds supporters. It was Shutty's first game of that season. During the summer he had been at a wedding, and being an ex-Wednesday player, he ended up in a fight with some Sheffield United supporters. He gashed his knee, which became infected, and he was in the hospital for a while. But it was a great way to come back into the side.

Our next game was Aston Villa away on Sunday, 24 November, live on television. The day before, I asked Gary Speed how his ankle was doing as he'd had a few problems. He told me, 'I will be fine.' I knew he would put up with a lot of discomfort but I had my doubts that he would be okay. I decided to take him for a run and told the gaffer what I was planning. We went on to the track at Elland Road. Gary got halfway round, facing the tunnel, when he indicated that his ankle was not right. He acknowledged that he would be struggling to play. I had to tell the Howard and Mick that one of their top players was out of the team; I expected there would be a reaction, but they were okay.

When we arrived in Birmingham and had our team meeting, the manager said, 'Speedo is not fit, so tomorrow we are going to play ten versus ten.' The lads were all looking at each other in confusion. Howard explained that Villa had a winger named Tony Daley, who'd been causing problems for other teams. 'So tomorrow, we are going to play Chris Fairclough, man-to-man on Daley,' he continued. 'Chris, this Tony Daley does not get a kick; even if he goes to the toilet, you will go with him.' The gaffer pushed Tony Dorigo further up the pitch and brought in John McClelland to play centre-back alongside Chris Whyte. We had a great result beating Villa, 4-1.

After the game Mick and I had a drink in the bar. We were joined by Brian Whitehouse, Villa's chief scout, who had worked with big Ron Atkinson for many years. He asked Mick and me, 'What would you have done if Gary Speed had been fit?' Mick said, 'Brian, I have not got a clue, but I am sure we would still have won.' The gaffer used that same system to stop top players a few times, and Chris Fairclough was always a great man marker.

We were still doing okay in the run-up to Christmas of 1991, but we drew 3-3 at home against Southampton on Boxing Day. I think Micky Adams was the happiest person on their team after getting a result against us; he had not been pleased when Leeds had let him go. A 21-year-old Alan Shearer scored against us that day. Years later, when I spoke to Alan, he told me that Leeds were one of his favourite teams to play against, probably because he scored more goals against us than against any other club.

Over the Christmas period and into the new year, we had to play Manchester United three times. We drew 1-1 in the league and then lost 3-1 in the League Cup. Our FA Cup fixture against them was postponed because of rain. None of us could understand why the pitch was not draining as it should. Then John, the groundsman, discovered that fat from the kitchen had blocked all the drains. The game was rearranged for after our Sheffield Wednesday match.

In our starting line-up at Hillsborough we had no Gordon Strachan or David Batty as both had picked up injuries. There was also a late fitness test for Tony Dorigo which, fortunately, he passed. My friend Alan Smith, their physio, said that when they saw the team sheet on the morning of the match Wednesday thought they had more than a good chance of winning.

As the game panned out, there were a few incidents that are well remembered today. We were winning 2-0 when Wednesday's striker, Gordon Watson, tripped himself up in their penalty area, and to everyone's disbelief, Phil Don, the referee, awarded a penalty. Our old player John Sheridan scored, making it 2-1. Then the gaffer was sent into the stand on the word of the linesman after an incident. As luck would have it, it was a televised game, so cameras were all around the ground. At the tribunal, it was proven that our manager had not done anything untoward. The TV footage showed that the linesman had got it wrong, and I am unsure whether he ever got to run the line again. As for the game, we had a fantastic win, 6-1; Chappy scored three, along with a free kick from Dorigo, one from Rod Wallace and another from Mike Whitlow, who came on as the sub. As for Gordon Watson, I met him years later and I asked him about the penalty. He said, 'Alan, I got battered by my own family, and I also got done by the FA.' I think he was fined £250 for gesturing to the crowd afterwards. He was honest enough to say that he had dropped a bollock.

In the Manchester United FA Cup match, we lost 1-0, but worse still Lee Chapman fell awkwardly and fractured his wrist. John Lawton took him straight to the hospital and operated that night. He rang me around midnight to let me know that everything had gone okay, and I let the gaffer know we had lost one of our top strikers for six weeks.

At the end of January 1992 Sheffield Wednesday were trialling a new French player, and things were not going well so he was about to go back home. Howard Wilkinson had heard what was going on and had spoken to Michel Platini, the French national team manager. He also talked to Glenn Hoddle, who had played in France, to find out more about the player who had a reputation for being temperamental. His name was Eric Cantona. Platini gave Howard the thumbs up and Eric came to Leeds with his agent.

I took Eric for his medical; a journalist friend of his from Switzerland sat in the back of my car to translate. When he had finished, he told the translator to thank me for being cordial and friendly towards him. I think he had a difficult time at Sheffield. Nobody knew more than me what it was like to be a foreigner in another country, after my experience working in the steel factory in Canada when I was 20 years old. On 8 February 1992, Eric played his first game for Leeds, against Oldham, when he came on as a sub for Steve Hodge who had picked up an injury. We lost 2-0. It was only our second defeat of that season.

Talking about Hodgie, one day he told me how he had acquired the shirt that Maradona had worn on that fateful day in 1986 when he scored that infamous goal with the help of the 'Hand of God'. Steve said that after the match he was the last player to leave the pitch, and with his head down in disappointment, he made his way down the tunnel. At the bottom, he saw Maradona at the other side of the fence separating the teams. Steve said, 'As I looked up, Maradona spotted me, so I tugged at my shirt, gesturing to ask if he wanted to swap. He took his shirt off and threw it over the fence, so I did the same.' I hid it down my shorts, and when I got into our dressing room, I kept quiet as I knew it would be sought after.' Steve brought the shirt into the club to show us and later loaned it to the National Football Museum in Manchester.

Lee Chapman only missed four games, and on his return against Luton Town, wearing a wrist protector, he and Eric both scored in our 2-0 victory. Chappy had worked hard with his rehabilitation.

Behind the scenes there was never a dull moment that season. The telephone in the corridor always seemed to be in use. It was usually Mel Sterland or Chris Kamara getting racing tips from their jockey friend, I think, in exchange for tickets. Listening to them, I don't think they ever won anything. Mel bought a share in a racehorse and I once asked him how it was doing. 'Don't ask,' was the reply, 'I think it's only got three legs the way it is running.' Mel picked up an injury that year that cut short his season, and he needed an operation.

After beating Luton, we won only two of our next seven games. At Spurs we won 3-1; Jon Newsome, who was filling in for Mel Sterland at right-back, scored a goal. At home against Wimbledon we had a 5-1 victory, and Chappy scored a hat-trick. We lost 4-1 at Queens Park Rangers and 4-0 at Manchester City. At that stage it looked like Manchester United were set to win the league for the first time in 26 years.

Eric Cantona was still waiting for his wife Isabelle and son Raphael to arrive from France. He lived in a semi-detached house off Street Lane in Leeds, and his dad Albert was staying with him. I found out that he liked to shoot, so I invited Eric and his dad to Pateley Bridge, just as I had done with Vinnie Jones. Everything was arranged for a Sunday when I did not have to go into the club. My friend Bobby Lee, a gamekeeper, had agreed to take Eric and Albert, along with Miles, my pal John O'Connor and me, up the Dale. Bobby was a Geordie and a big Newcastle supporter.

When Eric and Albert arrived at our house, Adele, who was learning French at the time, had a bit of a chat with them. Shirley worked in the community as a nurse and came home that day with one of her colleagues named Damaris. Damaris had lived in Eric's home town of Marseille, so she talked with Eric and his dad in their native dialect, which helped a lot.

When we arrived at our meeting place, Bobby was leaning on the gate. After the introductions, Bobby said to Eric, 'Before we get started, can you sign these for me? They are for the kids at my daughter's school, where she works as a teacher.' He pulled about 40 pieces of paper out of his pocket. We looked at Eric, wondering what he might do, but he was fine and signed the lot. Bobby gave Albert and Eric their guns, and off we went over the hills for some rabbiting. Eric was an excellent shot, and everyone had a good day. We finished off at my friend John O'Conner's house in Middlesmoor, which has a great view back down the valley.

Eric and his mum and dad came up to Pateley again a few weeks later. While Eric and his dad went shooting, Shirley and Adele took his mum around the local shops. I had to go to the club that Sunday but I joined them in the Crown pub in Middlesmoor afterwards. By the time I arrived, Eric, Albert, Bobby and John O'Conner had played snooker in the village hall. When Eric's wife and son came over from France, we also met with them quite a few times.

Negotiations had taken place for a year or so between the FA, the First Division clubs and the big TV channels to transform the First Division into a new league. BSkyB won the live television rights and the new Premier League was scheduled to start at the beginning of the 1992/93 season, but for now it was a matter of whether we could win the league. With five games to go we were two points behind Manchester United, who also had a game in hand.

On 11 April 1992 we were at home to Chelsea, and their assistant manager Stan Ternent, whom I knew well, was looking at me from their box. He kept placing his hand on his chest as if to say, 'How is your heart going, Sutts?' But we won the game 3-0. Eric came on as a sub and scored a tremendous goal, which could have been the goal of the season. He also made another for Chappy.

On Saturday of the Easter weekend we were away to Liverpool, and Manchester United were away at Luton, where Chris Kamara was now playing. I went with Sean, the kit man, to give him a hand and set up the medical table. I had a look at the pitch, which was always top class. Reggie, the groundsman at Anfield, was there, and we had our usual chat. He said, 'You know Al, I would not be too upset if you beat us if it means that mob up the road don't win the championship.'

Another job I had on matchdays was to measure the pitch for the gaffer. The differences in the size of some pitches were often surprising; Manchester United's was about ten yards longer than Highbury. Howard cut down the size of the Elland Road pitch when we signed John Lukic from Arsenal; John could drop-kick the ball three quarters the length of Highbury when he was there.

We had a 0-0 draw at Liverpool, and United, who were odds on to win at Luton, could only draw 2-2. Speaking to Kammy years later, I reminded him what a great result his team had got for us that day.

Going into Easter Monday, we had a 5pm start at home to Coventry. Manchester United kicked off at 3pm at home to Nottingham Forest. They were still two points ahead and their game in hand was to be played just 48 hours later, on the Wednesday at West Ham, who were already relegated. Before the Coventry match the news came through that Forest had won 2-1 at Old Trafford. It was a bit of a surprise as Forest had a lot of injuries that day. In the dressing room, the gaffer told our players to match Coventry with our pressing and closing, and our class would come through. It was 0-0 at half-time but we went on to win 2-0 with goals from Chris Fairclough and Gary McAllister.

On Wednesday, 22 April Manchester United went to West Ham, and to everyone's surprise, they lost 1-0. Kenny Brown, whose dad – also Kenny – had been a West Ham legend, scored a 20-yarder. We were now one point ahead of United and both teams had two games left to play.

On 26 April we had a midday kick-off away at Sheffield United, and Manchester United had a 3pm game at Liverpool. Gordon Strachan was struggling with his leg and it was 50/50 whether he would be fit to play. We went 1-0 down at Bramall Lane and then, just before half-time, Gordon took a quick free kick into their box. The ball ping-ponged around before Rod Wallace put it in the net. Rod had a great first season for us, chipping in with some vital goals.

Gordon did not play in the second half, so Eric Cantona came on as a sub. Gary Mac's free kick was met at the far post where Jon Newsome scored with a header. Mel Rees, their keeper, had picked up an injury and was not moving well. Then John Pemberton smashed the ball from a tight angle, and it hit Lee Chapman and went into our net for 2-2. A bizarre incident followed; Eric chased a long ball down the park along with Rod Wallace. Brian Gale, the Sheffield United centre-half, took control. He knocked the ball up into the air with his knee and headed it back to Rees. Unfortunately for Brian, Mel had come right off his line, and it sailed over his head and into their net. From our perspective it was just the break we needed and we went on to win 3-2. Mick and I hugged each other. The gaffer, with his usual coolheadedness, said to us both, 'We haven't won anything.' 'I know,' I replied, 'but what a great game.'

We needed just one more victory if Manchester United won at Anfield. We had a few drinks on the way back, so I asked my nephew Philip to pick me up and take me to our Joan's for a few hours. By this time the Manchester United game was in full swing, and Ian Rush had scored his first goal against Liverpool's deadly rivals to put his side 1-0 up. I was half asleep as Philip was driving around the roundabout at Pudsey. He suddenly shouted, 'Uncle Alan, I think you have just won the championship! Mark Walters has just scored a second goal for Liverpool with a few minutes to go!' I said, 'HAVE WE?!' as I jolted awake in disbelief. I was in shock; I did not think it would happen.

When the pressure was on, Manchester United had collapsed, whereas when Leeds had won the Second Division two years earlier we had held our nerve. However, unlike winning the Second Division, where we were one of the favourites, with all the associated pressure that went with that status, this time our success played out over eight days. Manchester United had always had their nose in front. But taking nothing away from us, we had only lost four games all season, none of them at home in the league, and scored more goals than they did.

At our Joan and Jack's, I did not have anything else to drink as I had to get home, but we had a good time. I spoke to my friend Norman Hunter on the phone; he was in the Radio Leeds studio. When I returned home, Jim Moore, our next-door neighbour, had hung a banner outside displaying in large letters 'Champions'. The only downside was that we could not celebrate as a club as everyone had gone their separate ways.

The next day, Monday, everything was beginning to sink in. It was great to see Mick Hennigan and the rest of the staff at Elland Road. We had a reserve game at Anfield against Liverpool on Tuesday. Just before we left, the gaffer said, 'Here, give these to Ronnie Moran or Roy Evans when you get there.' It was two cases of champagne to thank them for their help in our title win.

After Liverpool, we had to get ready for our final game of the season, at home to Norwich City on Saturday, 2 May. It was our Joan's birthday, so I got some tickets for her, my mum and Philip and his wife, Wendy. Miles was a ball boy again. It was the first and last time my mum would be at Elland Road, and it meant that she could watch us be presented with the championship trophy.

Gordon was on the bench and was going to come on later in the game, with Eric starting in his place, but Gordon did not want a sub shirt number – he wanted to wear his number seven shirt. Eric said that it was not a problem and he would wear the number 14 shirt. In those days the numbers were still one to 11. The referee that day was Roger Milford, who had officiated in the FA Cup semi-final against Coventry City in 1987. The week before, George Courtney had asked to be the referee at our game with Sheffield United as it was his last appointment before retirement. He had always been a lucky ref for us over the years.

On the day, Rod Wallace scored an early goal and we won 1-0, beating Manchester United in the end by four points. Afterwards, we celebrated with champagne in the dressing room and posed for photographs. It was great to have the family there.

The next day we toured in an open-top bus around the city and then went on to Leeds Town Hall, where we raised the trophy again to thousands of people. I saw some guys I knew who had travelled from Norway to join in the celebrations. The team went back to Elland Road with the trophy for official photographs on the pitch, and we had one taken as a family, which was a special moment.

After the excitement, I had a few bits and pieces to sort out before we went on our family holiday to America, including Gordon's operation. It was not looking good at this stage and, combined with his age, I think the gaffer was looking for someone to replace him. I was in the theatre while Mr Lawton performed the surgery. The operation would need to be followed by rehab, and then we would just have to wait and see.

* * *

Back at Leeds it was time to get Gordon and a couple of others fit for pre-season. After the usual pre-season training at Leeds University, we were on the road to Dublin to train and play a friendly. We had signed Scott Sellars from Blackburn Rovers; he had played for Leeds in the past. Glynn Snodin had left to go to Hearts and Bobby Davison had moved to Leicester City, so it was the second time I had to say goodbye to him.

Just as we were leaving Ireland, we made another signing, David Rocastle from Arsenal, I think as a planned replacement for Gordon Strachan. David and his agent Jerome Anderson came to Dublin to discuss the deal, and then I flew back with David the next day to make a start on his medical. David, who was known as 'Rocky' by the Arsenal fans, was a really nice guy and we had a good chat on the plane. Everything was hush hush. We travelled under the names of J. Anderson and G. Anderson. Those were the days when you only had to show your airline ticket to get back in the country, and at Manchester Airport the security guy looked at our tickets and asked, 'Are you brothers?' David was nearly 30 years younger than me, considerably taller, and black. We looked at each other as David said, 'Yes, something like that,' and we both laughed.

We were met by Jack 'The Rottweiler' Williamson, the gateman from Leeds United, who drove us to the club. It was a sweltering hot day and when we arrived at Elland Road a guy was sitting in the middle of the car park with a red handkerchief tied around his head. As the cars were driving around him, he was taking in the fumes. As we got closer, I realised who it was. I said to Rocky, 'Isn't that your agent sat there, pal?' We stopped the car and I said, 'Jerome, what are you doing?' He replied, 'I was hot and feverish, so your security guy,' he pointed at Jack, 'told me to wait out here to get some fresh air until he got back.' I took him inside to get checked out by the doctor. Jack just looked at me. I thought, 'What is he trying to do, kill him before we have done the deal?'

In August 1992 work was taking place on the new East Stand at Elland Road. That month we hosted the Makita Tournament, featuring Leeds, Nottingham Forest, Stuttgart and Sampdoria. The day before the competition, one of the lads said, 'I am spending the night in your village. Eric has been shooting up there and everyone says what a nice place it is.' He had booked into the hotel on the High Street, and as I only lived half a mile away, I said, 'Why don't you come round to my place for a bite to eat?'

When he arrived in the village, Shirley and I picked him up and on the way home, I called round to Frank Dean's, a friend of mine, to drop off some tickets for the game the next day. I was about to put them through the letterbox when Frank rolled up in a car with his boss. I had a quick word with Frank, and the Leeds player watched out of the car window and then asked Shirley, 'What's that black bag in the back of that guy's car?' My wife, being a nurse, replied, 'Oh, it's probably a body.' Frank was a part-time undertaker and had been up the Dale where someone had just died. Shirley said the reaction of the player was priceless. He was horrified that out in the sticks you could drive around with a body in the back of a car. It completely freaked him out.

As for the tournament, we beat Stuttgart in the first game and then played Sampdoria in the final the next day. They had two world-class players, Attilio Lombardo and Roberto Mancini. Mancini became the Manchester City manager years later. For most fans, the game's highlight was when David Batty decided to have some fun winding up the Italians, including a defender who he shoved over the advertising boards on to the track. All hell broke loose. The referee had a word with me and Mick Hennigan and suggested we take Batts off but the gaffer came down from the stand and told us he was staying on. It did not go down well with the ref.

The next stop pre-season was Norway, and I was both physio and kit man on the trip. Leeds had a large fan base in Norway. We played Drammen, based just outside of

Oslo, and won 2-0 in front of a packed house. Then it was straight to Wembley for the Charity Shield against Liverpool.

On the day of that match I went to put the kit out with Sean and set up my table. We were told we could take our pick of the North or South dressing rooms, so we chose the South. The occasion is played between the league champions and the FA Cup winners, and when Ronnie Moran and Roy Evans arrived they were not happy. Ronnie said Liverpool always chose the South dressing room because they considered it lucky for them. It was first come first served; we had already set everything out.

I saw Ronnie regularly as he helped with the kit before Liverpool games, and occasionally we had a chat. I remember talking to him about the European Cup semi-final when Liverpool played Bayern Munich in 1981. They drew the first leg at Anfield 0-0 and had to play in Munich a few weeks later. Ronnie said that between the two legs, Liverpool were receiving newspaper cuttings from Germany. Paul Breitner, the Bayern and Germany left-back, had said that Bayern already had the job done. There were lots of builders from Liverpool working on sites in Germany at the time, and they fed back the stories. Liverpool got the newspaper cuttings translated and pinned them up on the wall for the players to see. The second leg was another draw 1-1, so Liverpool went through to the final on the away goals rule and won the cup.

As for the Charity Shield game, there were 61,000 supporters at Wembley and a fantastic atmosphere. Eric Cantona scored a hat-trick and Tony Dorigo scored from a free kick to give us a 4-3 win. The good news was that Gordon Strachan's rehab had gone well. He came on as a substitute, and even if the ball got stuck between his feet and went in for an own goal, it was great that he was up and running again. I know that Gordon would be the first to thank John Lawton for the surgery. On the coach on the way back up north, we had the Charity Shield in the front window for everyone to see. It was a great day out.

Back at the club, there were a few changes to the backroom staff. Dick Bate had left to take up a job abroad and Paul Hart was appointed head coach for the youth team. Paul had played for the gaffer at Sheffield Wednesday. Howard had also brought in athletics coach Wilf Paish to help with fitness; I had done some work with Wilf at Halifax RL. Pete Gunby was still there, and it was great to have him around.

Our first match in the new Premier League was at home to Wimbledon on a beautiful sunny day. John Motson, the TV commentator, was there early for the game. Before lunch, the gaffer, Mick and I decided to do a 12-minute run around the pitch, so John asked if he could join us. I ran with him; it turned out he was a good runner and we had a chat at the same time. We won 2-1 with Lee Chapman scoring both goals, becoming the first player to score for Leeds in the Premier League.

In the European Cup we lost 3-0 away to Stuttgart. While in Germany, Leslie Silver, the chairman, and the directors went for a meal with their counterparts. Word came back that when they had asked Mr Silver if he had visited Germany before. He replied, 'No, but I saw it from a Lancaster bomber many years ago.' For the home leg, Bill Fotherby decided to put extra speakers around the ground to make the noise sound twice as loud; I think it did work on the night. It was a great game with lots of high balls into the box, and we won 4-1 but went out on the away goals rule.

The next day, while I was in the office with Mick, we received a telephone call asking if we had heard that Stuttgart had used an ineligible player. They were only allowed four foreign players but had used five. As a result, we had to play a third match at the Camp Nou in Barcelona on the following Friday, 9 October.

During the trip, the doctor was Steve Feldman, our number two medic at the club. On the evening before the game we were in the hotel reception ready to leave for a training session at the stadium, when Eric Cantona told me that he feared he might be starting with a throat infection. The gaffer asked me to find Steve. At that moment, Steve was leading the rest of the players on to the coach, wearing his football kit and carrying a ball under his arm. Eric came with us to the stadium, and Dr Feldman sorted him out.

The following day, Eric was declared fit. We trained on Barcelona's third training ground – they had another 15,000-seater capacity stadium next to the Camp Nou. After I got the players sorted out and they began their training session, I spotted a guy warming up on the adjacent pitch; he walked towards me. As he got closer, I realised that it was the legendary Johan Cruyff, the Barcelona coach. To my surprise he asked me if it was okay if the Barcelona first team trained next to us. I replied, 'Mr Cruyff, this is your training ground; I am sure our manager has no problem with that.' Michael Laudrup, the Danish international, was also training there that morning. The players spotted me talking to Cruyff, and as usual, I knew I would be in for some stick from them.

Before the game I gave Gordon Strachan a massage. He was very chilled out, singing 'The Northern Lights of Old Aberdeen'. On our way down to the dugout, I was amazed there was a chapel in the tunnel. As for the game, Gordon put us ahead but Golke equalised. Then Carl Shutt, who had come on for Eric, scored the winner. After the game, Shutty leaned against the wall with his head in his arms, muttering to himself.

Someone asked, 'Shutty, what's up?' He replied, 'I can't believe I just scored the winning goal at the Camp Nou, and it is my birthday in the morning.' The response he got was, 'Shut up, will you! You will have us all crying in a minute!'

One Sunday morning, I was at the club treating the injured lads. Eric came in to have a massage and a bit of extra work. He got changed in the main dressing room. Some of the juniors had been in for training, so after everyone had left, I locked up. As I was driving out of the car park, Old Sarge, one of the first aiders, waved me down. He said, 'Alan, I've got this watch from one of the young lads. He said he found it in the dressing room and was trying to claim it.' It was an expensive Rolex, with 'E. Cantona' engraved on the back. When I got home I rang Eric and with Adele's help, I told him I had his watch, assuming he would be panicking about losing such a valuable item. He said, 'Oh, very good. I will see you tomorrow.' I don't think he had even missed it.

On the playing side, I got the feeling that Eric was not too happy. A few times, he started a match and the manager would take him off, or he would be on the bench and not get on until nearly the end. At that time he had a big following with the fans and became the first person to score a hat-trick in the Premier League when we beat Tottenham 5-0. Things would come to a head before we played Queens Park Rangers, but first we had to play the first leg in the second round of the European Cup away against Glasgow Rangers.

On the night of the game, I got the ice from our hotel. The reception staff told me, 'The green ice is in that machine over there. Make sure you take that to Ibrox!' When we scored in the first minute you could have heard a pin drop; it was as if we had imagined the goal. But at the end of the game we had lost 2-1. We had to show every player's passport to UEFA, so on the way back home Eric asked if I could get him his passport back. I think Jack 'The Rottweiler' Williamson had them all, so I told Eric I would sort it out later. He was going back to France after the QPR game.

We flew from Leeds Bradford Airport to Heathrow that Friday ready to play QPR. When in London, we regularly trained at a private pitch next to St James' Palace; we were there so often that we had a key to get in. That evening we were having a drink in the gaffer's room when his phone rang. He ended the call and said to Mick and me, 'That was Eric Cantona; he wants to speak to me downstairs.'

Things were not right between the two of them. The next day at training, Eric found out that Howard had left him out of the team. He left the pitch without speaking to anyone. Back at the hotel, Eric walked in from the coach and the gaffer said to him, 'Eric, I need a word,' but Eric waved his hand dismissively as if to say, 'I don't want to talk to you,' and walked away to his room. I know at this point that Howard had his passport. I waited on the coach for the team meeting to finish, chatting to the director Peter Ridsdale, when Eric came out of the hotel with his bag and got into a waiting taxi. Peter looked at me and asked, 'What happened there?' All I could say was, 'I've no idea.' We lost the game 2-1. That evening on *Match of the Day*, Ray Wilkins said, 'Although QPR won the game, the most outstanding player on the pitch was Gordon Strachan; he was head and shoulders above anyone else in terms of performance and most likely, the oldest.'

On Monday, to everyone's surprise, Eric turned up for training. It seemed he had been to France and returned. The following day, we had the second leg of the League Cup away at Scunthorpe United. When the gaffer announced the team at training that morning, Eric was not in it. He came to see me and told me that he was having a problem with his leg. I had a look and strapped it up, and off he went. The day after, Eric came into my room again and said, 'Alan, I am just going out to do some running.' The gaffer was on the phone to see if Eric had come in, so I told him where he was. Shortly after that, Eric was in the squad again, and things seemed to settle down. He scored in the second leg of our European Cup game against Rangers, but we lost 2-1 and went out 4-2 on aggregate.

Around this time, Eric read a newspaper article the manager had written about him. He asked me, 'Alan, what does that mean – "will I last the test of time?"' I explained that many players came from abroad, and after a year or so, discovered that this league did not suit the way they played. He pondered on what I said but did not say anything.

On Saturday, 27 November we lost 4-0 at Manchester City. Two days later, I was in the manager's office with Bill Fotherby, the gaffer and Mick. While we were there, Mr Fotherby spoke to Martin Edwards, the Manchester United chairman, about their full-back Denis Irwin. I heard Martin Edwards say, 'I have heard all is not well with you and the Frenchman.' But nothing else was said at that point about Eric.

Leeds had laid out about £1m to buy Eric, which was a hefty sum in those days. They also knew that Eric could jump on the back of a motorbike, go back to France and never be seen again. In my opinion, even in those days, he had the money to do it. On Thursday evening I was at a function in Bradford when the news came through that Manchester United had signed Eric.

The next day, the gaffer said, 'Can you get Eric's X-rays and medical notes together? There's a taxi coming to pick them up.' When the taxi driver arrived, it was Russell Doig, an ex-Leeds player. He said, 'Sutts, I've come for some papers to take to Old Trafford for Mr Ferguson.' Eric continued living in Leeds for the next 18 months or so, and we still saw each other a few times.

In early 1993 my son Miles had been picked for the Harrogate Schoolboys squad to play against Doncaster Schools at Belle Vue, Doncaster Rovers' ground. Miles was the substitute, but playing up front was Andy Gray, Frank's son and the nephew of Eddie Gray. I had seen Andy play some years before when he had scored five goals against Pateley Bridge juniors. I knew his dad Frank slightly then, but years later we would become very good friends in Australia.

On the night, Miles said Andy was on fire and scored a hat-trick. The Doncaster coaches had shown interest in him after the game. The next day, I saw Eddie Beaglehole, who was in charge of recruitment of youth players for Leeds, and I told him what Miles had said. It turned out that Andy had been at the club once before but they had let him go. Eddie said, 'I will have a word with Paul Hart, and we will get him back.' He signed for the academy and with coaching from Paul and later his uncle Eddie, he played for Leeds in the 1996 League Cup Final.

Len Browning was another guy who became great friends with me and Tom O'Shea, the club doctor, when he came to work at Elland Road. Len had been a centre-forward for Leeds when John Charles was playing centre-half in the 1950s. I think Howard came across Len during pre-season when we were training at Leeds University's Trinity and All Saints College. He was doing some video work, and Howard employed him to video our games and those of our competitors. Over the coming weeks I got to know him. At the time he was in his late 60s or early 70s. He loved table tennis and was still playing in a league against the likes of Denis Neale, who had played table tennis for England. Despite his age, he was also a 15-handicap golf player and a great all-round sportsman.

Len told Tom and me about a famous amateur match, The North versus The South, held at Elland Road. Len said the first half was poor. The Northern committee members were in the stand, watching in frustration as the boring game limped to the end of the first half without a goal. One committee member spotted Len in the crowd and pointed him out to the others, 'You see him, down there, that's Browning? He'd do a better job than this lot!' They asked Len if he fancied putting some life into the match, and he agreed to play in the second half. They got him some kit and boots. I asked Len, 'How did you go on?' Len said, 'We won 1-0, and believe it or not, I scored the winning goal.' Who says there are no real-life fairy tales?

He also told us what it was like playing for Leeds as a professional in the 1950s, 'One of the things that players do not realise today is that we had to get a tram or trolleybus to the ground, like the fans. One time, I was waiting at the bus stop, but every bus that went past was full of supporters, so I had to run the three miles to Elland Road to get there in time for the game. When I arrived, I was a bit late, and the manager Major Buckley gave me a bollocking even though I tried to explain what had happened.' During his Leeds career, Len scored 43 goals in 97 games. He moved to Sheffield United for about £10,000, where he scored 25 goals in 65 games.

Before the end of 1992, Gordon Strachan asked me whether I thought I needed some help now that the club had moved into the Premier League. Deep down, I knew he was right; at this level, most other clubs had a chartered physiotherapist. We were now signing better players from clubs with better medical structures. The players I worked with were costly assets, and tens of millions of pounds in revenue depended on them being fit and at peak performance. Day to day, I got on with the job to the best of my ability. I did not think about the demands or the responsibility. I had known pressure when my building firm almost went bankrupt, and I worked flat out to ensure that I did not go under. I took the rigours of the job in my stride, and it helped that I loved what I was doing. However, I also knew some physios who had been under so much pressure that their health had suffered.

Our other Scottish player, Gary McAllister, had an injury, and Scotland had a game coming up. Macca loved playing for his country. He said, 'Sutty, get me fit and if I can play, there is a signed shirt in it for you.' He worked hard, and between the two of us, we got him fit, but the gaffer's priority, of course, was Leeds. Howard told the Scotland coach that Macca must not return with an injury, so the coach had him sat on the bench. When Gary came back, he opened the medical room door and threw me a signed Scotland shirt, saying, 'I could have played; I was fit enough.' I still have the shirt to this day.

Macca also told me a story about when he and Gordon were playing for Scotland at Hampden Park. The manager always made sure that the players came straight back and would have a car waiting, so they did not miss training the next day. Macca and Gordon met up with Rod Stewart at the end of the game, and when they went outside, the crowd went wild at the sight of them with Rod. Two vehicles were waiting, a stretch limousine and a car that looked like an old Ford Popular. Gary said, 'Gordon and I got into the limo that the gaffer had sent for us, and Rod got into the other one. The look on the crowd's faces was priceless!'

On Boxing Day 1992 we were away at Blackburn Rovers. It was the day when Alan Shearer suffered a knee injury that threatened his career. It was also one of the last games that Mel Sterland played for Leeds; he was still having problems with his ankle. Mel spent a lot of time with me in the gym. On one occasion he was late back to start our afternoon session. I asked him, 'Are you trying to get me the sack?' He said, 'Sorry Sutts, but I had a bit of business on.' I replied, 'Mel, I'm sorry, pal, but I've got to fine you.' 'Oh, come on,' he protested, 'I thought we were pals! How much then?' 'A pound a minute,' I told him. 'You were 20 minutes late, so £20.' Mel smiled, 'Well, I've just won £80 at the bookies, so I'm still £60 up.' By this time everybody was laughing, but that was Mel, he always made us smile.

Talking about Mel, I remember him telling me once that he was stopped for speeding while driving back to Sheffield after a game. The police officer asked him if he knew what speed he had been doing and when Mel tried to protest that he had not been speeding, the officer invited him to sit in the back of the police car so he could show Mel the recording. When Mel looked at the screen, he was over the speed limit. He said, 'My first thought was, I'm in s**t street here.' He thought he would get a fine or, even worse, a court appearance. To his relief the officer said to him, 'As it turns out, you were one of my heroes at Sheffield Wednesday, so if you can sign me a couple of autographs and cut down on your speed, I'll let you off with a warning.' As Mel said with a grin, 'I thought happy days are here again. I could not stop smiling at my luck.'

After a 4-0 loss away at Tottenham, the gaffer said to me, 'I need to have a word with you.' We went into the coach's room, and he said, 'I have decided to bring somebody else in as head physio, and it's going to be Geoff Ladley. I know that you know each other.' With Gordon mentioning it earlier, I should have known that it would happen at some point.

As with the Bob Dylan record of the 1960s, the times were a-changing in football, and being number one at a top division club realistically meant that you had to be a member of the Chartered Society of Physiotherapists. I was not bitter, although I realised that everyone would know that I had been demoted. However I was looking forward to working with Geoff; the manager could not have picked a better person to work with. Geoff was like a walking encyclopaedia when it came to anatomy and physiology. He told me that he left lecturing at Pinderfields Hospital because there was too much paperwork and insufficient teaching; he wanted to get back to the shop floor.

So Geoff and I would now sort out the first team together for home games. I would still do the reserves but would not travel with the first team to away games. I would also do the juniors on a Saturday, helping Paul Hart and Peter Gunby because Alan McIver, who had worked with Billy Bremner, had left. I knew I had to turn this change into a positive; I would have a better work-life balance, see the family more and improve my knowledge of new developments in the physio world. I would also be able to do more private work and have the chance to learn how to play golf, which I had always wanted to do.

As time went on, Geoff and I worked well together. We bounced off one another and he showed me some tricks of the trade. One day, Mel Sterland was sitting in the back of my car; we were on our way to Leeds University to see Mr Sefton, who had performed Mel's operation. I had forgotten that Adele had brought me back a plastic mobile phone from a day trip to Blackpool as a joke present. It was between the front seats, and I had forgotten it was there until Mel spotted it. 'New phone, Sutts? What's your number in case I need to get hold of you?' I said, 'Sorry pal, it's a phone that only the gaffer has the number for, in case of emergency. He does not want anyone else to have it.' I just left it at that and forgot all about it. Shortly afterwards, another player asked about the phone, and Mel told him what I had said – only the manager had the number. The other player picked it up, looked at it and exclaimed, 'This is just a piece of plastic!' Mel's face said it all. I laughed as he exclaimed, 'Very funny!' For once, I had got one over on them.

Just before the end of the 1992/93 season, the youth team qualified for the semi-final of the FA Youth Cup. They were drawn away to Norwich City in the first leg and won 4-1, without our three star young players Mark Tinkler, Jamie Forrester, and Kevin Sharp, whom the gaffer wanted in the first-team squad. They played the second leg at home, where we lost 2-0. We went through to the final 4-3 on aggregate and had to play against the holders, Manchester United, who had many up-and-coming young players. However, before this match we had to play the final first-team game of the season away at Coventry, and I was on the trip.

Manchester United had already won the league, the first club to win a Premier League title. After their game against Blackburn Rovers, who they beat 3-1, they were presented with the new trophy on Monday evening. The next day, Eric and Isabelle Cantona had kindly agreed to help Adele revise for her A-Level French oral exam. They had her answering calls from their French friends who were ringing to congratulate Eric on winning the league. Eric showed me his medal; it was like an egg cup, a smaller version of the full-sized trophy. It looked a bit like an award for an amateur league game. I also talked to Eric about the FA Youth Cup Final; the first leg was at Old Trafford two days after the end of the season, just under a week away. Eric said, 'Alan, there is no way Leeds United can beat the Manchester United youth team.'

Later in the day, when I went to collect Adele, I thanked Eric and Isabelle for their kindness; I always left their house saying the same thing, 'Eric, you're French/English, I'm Yorkshire/English!' He would say, 'Yes, but nobody knows that I understand some English.' One thing we had in common was that we had both lived abroad and knew how hard it could be living away from home. As for Adele, she passed her French exam with a Grade A.

At Coventry, we were still looking for our first away victory of the season. Despite only losing one game at home, we could not buy an away win. We were 2-0 down during the game but Rod Wallace made it 2-1. David Rocastle lost one of his contact lenses on the pitch. Fortunately he found it, but we had to rummage through the kitchen to find a mirror so he could put it back in. When we came outside, Coventry had scored again. Rod Wallace made it 3-2, and then in the last minute, Rocky charged down a kick out of the keeper's hands and the ball broke loose towards the goal. Rod and Chappy chased after it; Rod wanted his hat-trick, and for Lee, it would have been his 20th goal of the season. But Rod was too fast so he got his hat-trick, and we finished 3-3. We missed relegation by two points.

In the first leg of the FA Youth Cup Final, Manchester United's team contained some big names of the future, including David Beckham, Paul Scholes, the Neville brothers, Nicky Butt and even a young Robbie Savage. One of the lads in our team, Simon Oliver, was the son of my fellow full-back from Bradford Park Avenue, Jack Oliver. Simon's job was to mark a Northern Ireland lad, Keith Gillespie, an excellent player. The referee for both legs was Paul Durkin from Poole in Dorset. He was the ref who would not let me on the pitch at Swindon Town when Mike Whitlow was injured three years earlier. When I got on the field, he spotted me and came over. 'Before you say a word,' he said to me, 'I want to apologise to you for what happened at Swindon. When I found out how badly your player was injured, I have been waiting for three years to say sorry to you for what I did that day.' What could I say, apart from, 'Apology accepted.' After that, we got on well. There were many times I had to get him up out of a mine in Dorset, where he worked as an engineer, to check with him about kit colours before a match.

Leeds won the first leg 2-0 at Old Trafford in front of around 30,000 fans. Jamie Forrester and Noel Whelan scored. Mark Ford, the Leeds captain and a Manchester United fan, picked up a knee injury, but he was fit for the second leg three days later. As we agreed, when you step over the white line on to the pitch, there is no turning back; you get on with the game. He played a full 90 minutes and Leeds won 2-1, Jamie Forrester and Matthew Smithard both scored. We finished 4-1 on aggregate to take the cup.

After the game, I talked to Eric Harrison, the Manchester United youth coach. Eric told me that even at half-time he was convinced that United could still win. I think that the Leeds lads were just physically stronger over the two legs. My old pal David Brock was at the game. He had flown over from Canada to see his dad. When I spoke to Paul Durkin at the end of the match, he told me that his uncle from Bradford was there, so I ended up giving him and David a lift back home.

6

FROM HOWARD TO GEORGE

Back at the club, Howard Wilkinson may have been feeling the pressure after almost being relegated the year before. Behind the scenes, Wilf Paish had decided not to return. I think he found it hard at a football club; it was easier to plan in athletics. Some of the lads who left included Mervyn Day, Carl Shutt, Dylan Kerr, Chris Whyte, David Kerslake and Lee Chapman. Chappy's departure was a surprise, but I think he was given a good offer to go to Portsmouth, although he did not stay there long and moved on to West Ham United. Two new players to arrive at Elland Road were Brian Deane from Sheffield United for nearly £3m and David O'Leary from Arsenal. Deano was to replace Chappy. In David's third game against Norwich, he picked up a bad injury and had to spend a long time with Geoff and me.

His rehab was going well, and we had started some running sessions. We went to Roundhay Park and along the Leeds and Liverpool canal. It was safety in numbers on the canal because you often came across people hanging around, sniffing glue, or doing drugs, so Sean Hardy, the kit man, started running with us. We used to set off from the Dark Arches in the city centre and run up to Kirkstall Abbey, about two and a half miles out. It was every man for himself on the way back, jumping over a few fishing lines. Sean had never enjoyed running while he had been an apprentice at Sheffield Wednesday but had told himself that as everybody was into running at Leeds, he had better give it another go. He said, 'At first, all I saw was your backside because I was always running behind you, Sutts!' After a few years, he became a great runner.

At the end of the 1992/93 season I was doing a lot of rehab work with Tony Dorigo following an injury. We were trying to get him fit to play the last couple of games and give him the chance to be included in the England squad bound for the USA for a pre-World Cup tournament. David Batty was already on the team and by hook or by crook, Tony got in.

When he got back, during pre-season, I asked him how it went. 'Yes, it was good,' he told me, 'but when we were in Washington DC at our hotel, the FBI came to see us and gave us all a lecture about the city.' At that time, many places in the city were no-go areas because the crime rates were very high. Tony said, 'They told us that we were not to go out on our own, only in groups, and whatever happened we should not turn right outside the hotel as there was every chance we might not be seen again.' I asked him, 'What did you do?' He said that he had not left the hotel apart from when they went training. He gave me one of his signed shirts from the trip. But as it turned out, England did not make it to the World Cup finals the following year.

After we drew 3-3 at home to Blackburn Rovers in mid-October, Leeds accepted an offer from Rovers of around £3m for David Batty. I think it was up to David to decide if he wanted to go, which he did. I was told that the fee would help to pay for the new East Stand. So the great midfield of Strachan, McAllister, Batty and Speed was breaking up.

I was sorry to see Batts leave, but what I remember at the time was his great love of motorbikes. Also, no one would forget how David would be changed and ready for the game at least an hour before kick-off. To amuse himself he would start smashing footballs around the dressing room. The worst time for me was when we played away, and I had to use the table in the middle of the dressing room to work on the players. As the ball whizzed past my ears, I would be shouting, 'Batts! Can you give it a rest until I have got these strappings done!' He would eventually give me some peace so I could get on with my job.

Before the end of the year, there was another change when we let David Rocastle go to Manchester City in exchange for David White. The only thing I knew about David was that he was a strong right-winger and had been part of a successful youth team at City. Everyone was sorry to see Rocky go as he had been a great lad to have around.

Another surprise that season was a player who became a crucial part of the team. It was a young lad who had come over from Ireland as a pro in 1991; his name was Gary Kelly. He hailed from Drogheda, about 20 miles from Dublin. Gary came from a big family back in Ireland, and he came to Leeds with his dad and another young footballer named P.J. O'Connell, known as PJ. When he arrived, his dad pulled me to one side and said, 'Our Gary is a bit streetwise, and we have had trouble with him from time to time, so can you keep an eye on him?' 'We definitely will, Mr Kelly,' I replied. In time, I told Kells what his dad had said to me that day.

In the early years, when Gary went on away trips, the gaffer would room him with Gordon Strachan, and I think Gary learned a lot from him. Gary came over as a centre-forward or a right-winger. After a couple of seasons, it was 50/50 whether we kept him, but everything changed during the pre-season of 1993/94 when Mel Sterland and Jon

Newsome were injured. The gaffer tried Gary at right-back, and he was like a duck to water; he looked like he had played there all his life. He had a great pace as well.

Before the end of the season, big Jack Charlton had Gary in the Republic of Ireland squad, preparing for the World Cup in the USA. Kells went on to play as a right-back for both Leeds and the Republic of Ireland for many years.

On New Year's Day 1994 we were playing Manchester United at Old Trafford. I was there to give Geoff a hand in what turned out to be a 0-0 draw. The gaffer had Chris Fairclough man-to-man marking again, this time on Eric Cantona. Eric and Chris got on well at Leeds, but in this game Eric reacted to some of Chris's tackles. When I called in to see Eric and Isabelle a week or so later, Eric asked me to send his apologies to Chris for what had happened. When I told Chris, it was like water off a duck's back. He just said, 'No problem.' Eric had also said how much he had liked and respected Chris when they had played together.

I had arranged with Eric that I would go over to Old Trafford to see Manchester United's game against Everton on 22 January 1994. It was also the draw for the Euro '96 tournament that day in Manchester. I did a game for the juniors and then set off with Mark Ford, the youth team captain and a season ticket holder at Old Trafford.

Eric was always interested in what made sportspeople tick. Michael Jordan, the Chicago Bulls basketball player, was renowned as an all-time great and a hero of my son, Miles. Miles had lots of videotapes about Jordan, so I arranged to loan them to Eric after the game. Miles was with us but I did not tell him anything about what was happening. He thought we were going to a Huddersfield Town game. When we went sailing past the road sign for Huddersfield and saw that I had his Michael Jordan tapes, he guessed we were on our way to Old Trafford.

I had already spoken to Norman Davis, the Manchester United kit man, to make sure that Eric had passed on the tickets for us to collect. After the match, which Manchester United won 1-0, I made my way with Mark and Miles to see Eric. I knew Ned Kelly, the head of security, and at first he was only going to allow me into the coaches' room, but eventually, he let Mark and Miles in as well. Eric was there with his agent, Bernard, and a few other officials from France. I think Alex Ferguson was more than surprised when he saw the Leeds physio and Mark Ford, the captain when Leeds had beaten his youth team seven months earlier, as well as my son. Bernard smiled at us, and I gave Eric the tapes. When I got them back I put them all together and made Eric a compilation tape.

On Easter Sunday we were in training as there was an away game at QPR the next day. By now, I was travelling to more away matches to help Geoff out; Jack the Rottweiler used to drive me on matchday. But on this particular day Shirley called me at the club to say that Miles had a nasty ankle injury from playing football that morning. I was extremely grateful to John Lawton, who saw us on Easter Sunday and operated the same day. The next day, I went to London where we won 4-0.

Back in Leeds, I got Gary Kelly, Mark Tinkler and a few other lads to come with me to the hospital to cheer Miles up. When we arrived, he had still not had a wash after his football game. Miles had all the lads laughing. He said, 'You see that guy over there, he looks a bit dodgy. I have to sleep with one eye open.' Eventually we got Miles out of hospital and on to a rehab programme. As always, John Lawton had done a great job and helped me out again.

Big Ian McFarlane, the chief scout at Leeds, had left and was replaced by Geoff Sleight, who had been doing a bit of scouting and match reports for the gaffer. Speaking to Geoff recently, he told me about one of his first jobs for the club. Howard Wilkinson had a pal, Johnny Brookes, in South Africa. Everything was opening up after apartheid and Johnny had told Howard that there was a player he needed to check out. His name was Lucas Radebe. Geoff went out there to watch him play for South Africa, but Lucas was out with an ankle injury on the day. While he was there another player caught his eye, a striker named Phil Masinga. Lucas was still creating a lot of interest, so when South Africa played away to Australia Geoff flew out to watch him. Geoff had lived in Oz and had played football for Australia. When he arrived, Lucas had not travelled but Phil was there, so on his return Geoff suggested that Howard should bring Phil over and look to get Lucas once he was back playing.

When Phil arrived in England, there were a few problems with immigration. At first Phil told them that he had come to visit a girlfriend in Leeds, but they did not believe him. I think it was the first time Phil had been out of South Africa apart from when he travelled with the national team. When he told them he was there for a trial with Leeds United, they got in touch with the club, and Geoff sorted everything out. It took a few more weeks for Lucas's work permit to come through but he and Phil were both at Leeds for the 1994/95 pre-season tour of Germany.

We finished fifth in the league at the end of the season, a significant improvement from the previous year. Howard also brought a few of the youth players into the first-team squad, including Mark Ford.

Paul Hart, who led the youth team, not only had Peter Gunby working with him as a coach, but he engaged another coach called Robin Wray from Sheffield Wednesday. Paul also brought in his old manager from his playing days, Eddie Gray, to join the youth set up. You had the feeling that things could only get better if we were bringing more youth players through to the first team.

That year we holidayed in America. The World Cup had just started and while we were away, the news came through that the Republic of Ireland had beaten Italy 1-0 in Newark, New Jersey. When I met with Gary Kelly after the World Cup, I mentioned that we were in Washington when we heard the Ireland result. Kells was still a young guy, not yet 20. He told me that after the game the dressing room was euphoric. Larry Mullin, the drummer from the pop group U2, had joined them. Larry informed the players that he was sending two stretch limos to their hotel for anyone who wanted a night out with him in New York. Gary said that he was straight in there, along with the other two youngest players, Jason McAteer and Phil Babb, and they had a great night out.

A few weeks ago I asked John Sheridan, who was also in the squad, if he had gone out with them. Shez told me that he had celebrated with his wife and some other friends that night, but later in the tournament he and some of the other Irish lads had also had a great night out with Brendan O'Carroll of *Mrs Brown's Boys* fame.

* * *

I was back in the club before the start of pre-season, and Geoff and I worked out a rota so we stayed on top of things. We had brought some players in early to work on their fitness. We also did medicals for the new players. Bill Fotherby always had to have a big-name player to keep ticket sales buoyant and supporters on the edge of their seats about each season's new line-up. He announced that we were signing Tomas Skuhravy from Genoa, the Czech Republic international, and one of the leading scorers in the 1990 World Cup. It fell on my shift to do the medical. My first thoughts were, 'Well, at least it's not Maradona,' whom Mr Fotherby had tried to lure the fans with the year before. Skuhravy landed at Leeds Bradford Airport with his representatives in a private jet.

The medical process took several hours and included x-rays and heart traces, an assessment by the club doctor and the orthopaedic surgeon, John Lawton. There was an interpreter to help us, and I jokingly said that they might speak English but probably not Yorkshire. As the medical progressed, Skuhravy asked through the interpreter whether he would get an apartment with his own swimming pool. I thought, does he realise this is Leeds and not sunny Italy.

Late in the day, we went to the BUPA hospital. At this point Skuhravy began to get a bit nervous. He went outside for a cigarette a few times. When John started the examination, he suspected straight away that Skuhravy's hip and knee might be problematic, so he ordered an MRI scan. In the meantime the female interpreter was on the telephone, I presumed, to Skuhravy's team at Elland Road. The player had been in the MRI scanner for about five minutes when all hell broke loose. The interpreter barged into the room and, despite attempts by the staff to stop her, she dragged Skuhravy from the scanner. Then they both scarpered.

When I returned to Elland Road, the press were waiting to interview our new signing. I asked to speak to Mr Fotherby, told him that we could not sign Skuhravy and explained why. As the colour drained from his face, I thought he was going to have a heart attack. He said to me, 'Do you know who we are dealing with? Those people from Genoa are part of the Mafia. You had better tell them what has happened. If they are going to shoot anybody, it can be you!'

I went to tell Skuhravy's team, but they already knew the outcome. They were trying to get a player off their books and get what money they could for him. They got up and left. Mr Fotherby had to tell the waiting press that there had been a hitch over Skuhravy's personal terms, so the deal was off. I had to laugh on the way home; Mr Fotherby was a great guy, but he was always jumping the gun. He should have waited until we had completed the medical before announcing the deal. It was left to John Lawton to inform the gaffer.

During pre-season, we signed two other players from Sheffield Wednesday, Carlton Palmer and Nigel Worthington, while Jon Newsome left us to join Norwich City. After his trial we signed Phil Masinga from Mamelodi Sundowns in South Africa. We also secured Lucas Radebe from Kaizer Chiefs after the PFA sorted out his visa, and he came to us officially in early September. A couple of the youth team players moved up to the first team, including Noel Whelan, who got off to a good start. The guys called him 'Snowy' because he was so good at the time; when he got in the team, there was no shifting him. Someone remarked that he was like snow, and Noel loved the nickname so much he had it printed on to his boots.

David O'Leary once told me about the first time he came to Elland Road as a young player with Arsenal. He said, 'I remember sitting in the dressing room and the manager, Bertie Mee, spoke to every player. He got to Peter Storey, who was like the "enforcer" who sorted people out on the pitch. The manager said to him, "I don't want the mid-field running the show today for Leeds."' After 12 minutes they had to bring the stretcher on the pitch. David said, 'Unfortunately, the stretcher was for Peter Storey.'

By the end of 1994 we had sold Steve Hodge to QPR, and in early January 1995 we signed another striker, Tony Yeboah, from Eintracht Frankfurt. When he arrived his fitness levels were low, so Howard arranged some extra training around the Elland Road track in the afternoons. The gaffer, Mick and I took it in turns to run the length of the pitch with him. However, one thing was sure: he knew where to find the goal. In our remaining league matches he scored 12 goals, and we qualified for Europe.

On 25 January I was with Gordon Strachan at his home on the outskirts of Leeds. Our reserve game had been called off, and I had dropped him at home. Around 5pm it started snowing heavily, so I set off home. By the time I reached Harrogate town centre the roads were gridlocked entirely, and I was stuck for several hours. I sat in the car and listened to Crystal Palace v Manchester United on the radio. It was the notorious game when Eric Cantona was sent off after an altercation with a supporter.

The day after the incident, I remember running in the snow with Chris Fairclough and Tony Dorigo, and we were talking about what had happened the night before. Chris said that there had been many times that a supporter had been in his face during and after games, and sometimes it was very tempting to do what Eric had done, but of course, you just cannot do it.

The club banned Eric until the end of the season. The police also charged him with common assault. The FA then summoned him to a disciplinary hearing and extended the ban until the end of September.

A few weeks after the incident, Shirley rang me at the club to say that a guy from Manchester United wanted to talk to me; his name was Maurice Watkins. Mr Watkins was a director at Old Trafford as well as the club solicitor. I was taken aback when I found out why he had contacted me. He said, 'You know that Eric has a court case coming up?' When I replied, 'Of course,' he continued, 'The Cantonas have requested that I contact you to ask if you would provide a character reference for Eric.' I agreed but said that I would do it via my solicitor, Howard Walker, so that everything was in order. I met Howard at his office and gave him all the details. As I was leaving, Howard said to me, 'You better inform your manager, Howard Wilkinson, about this.'

I remember thinking that I was not sure about it, but I knew I had to do as Howard Walker had told me. Of course, the gaffer reacted in the way that I expected. He was not happy. 'How can you give that Frenchman a reference?' he asked me. 'It is easy,' I said, 'both Eric and his wife Isabelle have always been kind to my daughter, Adele, and my son, Miles. If the shoe were on the other foot, I know that he would not hesitate to do the same.' As well as helping Adele with her French studies, Eric had been generous to Miles on several occasions.

Of course, I had opened a can of worms; Peter McCormick, the Leeds United solicitor, rang me to say that there was no way that the club's name could be associated with anything

I had to say. I had another word with Mr Watkins, who reassured me that my reference would not be public. It would be laid in front of the judge for their consideration.

Howard Walker spoke with Mr Watkins, who informed him that Manchester United would pay my costs and that he should send his bill to them. Being a Bradford City fan, Howard said to Maurice, 'If you can get me some tickets for Manchester United, that will suffice.' 'No problem,' was the reply.

Five years later, Bradford City were away to Manchester United on Boxing Day. Howard rang me and asked, 'Do you think I would still be able to get those tickets?' 'Give them a call,' I said, so he rang Old Trafford, and of course, they upheld the agreement and gave him four tickets.

At the end of March 1995, Gordon Strachan moved on to Coventry City to join his old boss, Ron Atkinson. Gordon had been a fantastic asset for Leeds.

Behind the scenes at Elland Road, we had two new staff members in the laundry, Margaret Mitchell and Claire Sheard. They were great to work with and always happy to help. Sean Hardy was in charge but we were all there to help each other.

We were at Spurs for the last game of the season; the manager had people stationed at other grounds, ringing in with score updates. I had to keep running into the tunnel to hear what they were saying because it was so noisy. We drew 1-1 and finished fifth in the Premier League, just above Newcastle.

Around this time I started running a six-week basic treatment of injuries course on behalf of Bradford Council. I was following in Geoff's footsteps as he had been doing the same thing for a while. I mainly taught at Shipley library, but often I held the exams at Elland Road so the participants could see the place. I tried to make the course fun while still getting my teaching across. I knew I could never be a full-time lecturer, but as the people taking part were mainly running local football teams, I was on their wavelength and we had good results. Some of them went on to train as physiotherapists. On one of the courses, I met Harvey Sharman, who would become involved with Leeds United in years to come. I also ran cardiopulmonary resuscitation (CPR) courses set up by the FA in response to the Hillsborough disaster.

* * *

During pre-season in 1995, Chris Fairclough left us to join Bolton Wanderers. We were at Trinity and All Saints College once more for training and Howard Wilkinson discovered that Noel Whelan had only just arrived back at Leeds Bradford Airport from his holiday in

Spain an hour before our first training session began. The gaffer had his usual 400m track set out on the grass, and the top runners did eight laps in 12 minutes, a six-minute mile pace. At the end of the 12 minutes, when Noel had completed nine laps, none of us could believe it. He'd just had two weeks laying on a sunbed. The gaffer got everyone together and then said to Snowy, 'When I found out you'd only just arrived back, I was about to throw the book at you. But after watching you run, another two weeks on the beach might be in order.' Everyone just laughed.

Whenever Noel had an injury and ran on the canal with us, I always gave the other lads a five-minute start. It was like watching Forrest Gump run; he just ate up the ground with his effortless style. It wasn't easy to tell if he was a centre-forward or a midfielder with his running ability.

We acquired a new first-team coach, David Williams, for the start of the season, a man I knew from Norwich City and Bristol Rovers. He had also managed Wales for a couple of games.

Geoff and I had our hands full with injuries, mainly to Lucas Radebe, who had been having trouble with his knee since mid-March. It had given way while playing against Coventry. I felt for him as his career with us had only just started, and when he began his rehab after surgery he was pretty low. After a week or so, I sat him down in the office and said, 'Lucas, nobody has died. I know you think your career is over, and you will be heading back to Soweto, but it isn't, and you won't. Geoff and I are going to work non-stop to get you back on the pitch, so let's get out there and get started.' It was the start of a great friendship with 'The Chief'.

In our pre-season games, Tony Yeboah failed to perform, although he was the fittest he had been for a long time. I asked him, 'Yobo, why are you not trying to get your match fitness up?' Tony said, 'I once did my knee ligaments in a pre-season game, and I was out for a while, so I don't want to risk it. But once the season starts, I will start to play.'

He was not kidding. In our first eight games he scored seven goals, including two on the first day of the season at West Ham. Before the match, the gaffer had asked me to see if I could sneak a look at whose shirts were hanging on the pegs in the West Ham dressing room to give him an idea of who would be playing. While we were there, it was good to catch up with Eddie Gillam, their kit man, and of course, I had my usual cup of tea with Harry Redknapp. Yobo's goals secured us a good 2-1 win.

Years afterwards, I met up with Eddie when he was living in Devon, and those times came up in conversation. Eddie said to me, 'Alan, it was always great to see you and I loved your company, but when you came into our dressing room, of course, I knew what you

Bradford Park Avenue 1964/65. I am second from the left on the back row.

Halifax Town 1982/83. I am in the centre row, far left.

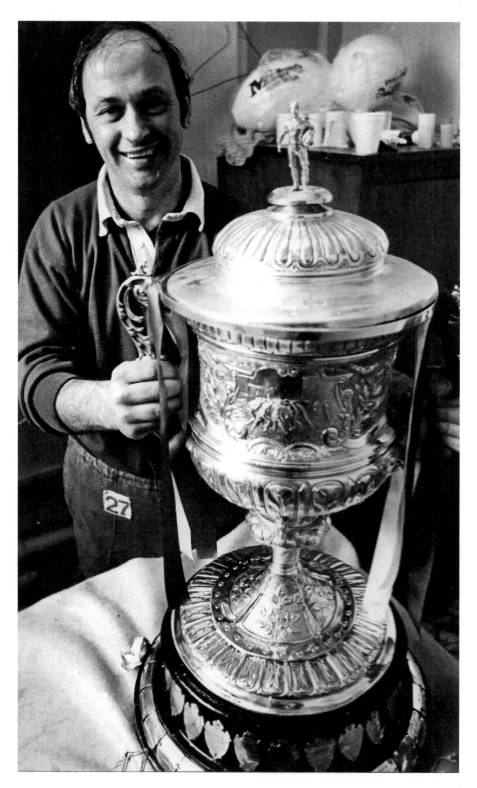

Leeds United in the 1987/88 Season.

Opposite: Winning the RL Championship with Halifax RL in 1986.

Appearing on the Gary Davis radio show in 1988.

With my son Miles and Billy Bremner.

In the dugout at Elland Road with Mick Hennigan.

With Vinnie Jones after winning the Second Division Championship at Bournemouth in 1990.

Howard Wilkinson, Mick Hennigan, Peter Gunby, David Batty and me in the dugout.

Receiving the Second Division Championship Trophy in 1990.

Treating Vinnie Jones.

Gordon Strachan is injured.

At Home in Pateley Bridge with Eric Cantona and his dad, Albert in 1992.

In the dressing room after winning the First Division Championship in 1992.

Receiving the First Divison Championship trophy at Elland Road in 1992.

With Geoff Ladley, helping an injured Tony Dorigo in 1994.

With Brad Fitler, Tony Ayoub and Billy Johnson of Australia RL at Thorp Arch, in 2001.

With Shirley and Lucas Radebe at his wedding in Sun City, South Africa in 2003.

With the Ausralian RL Team in 2004, with Dave Hancock, Harvey Sharman and Bruce Craven (on far right).

With Lucas Radebe and Adam McDougall at Thorp Arch in 2001.

The medical team, with me, Terry Crystal, Harvey Sharman, Dave Hancock and Lucas Radebe at Lucas's testimonial in 2005.

With Gordon Strachan, supporting Melanoma Awareness, in 2005.

Giving Steve Crainey some treatment.

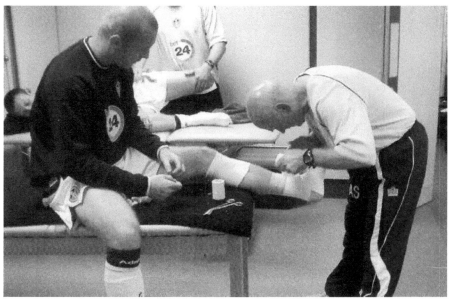

With Shirley, Miles and Adele at my surprise 60th birthday party in 2006.

With Gary Kelly at my 60th birthday party in 2006.

With Gary McAllister and Eddie Gray at my 60th birthday in 2006.

Receiving the 21 Club award from the FMA in 2014.

were up to.' Eddie, being a wily old bird, would hang random shirts on the pegs to catch me out. On a few occasions, when I looked at the team sheet it was nothing like the shirt numbers in the dressing room, but we weren't surprised; we used to do the same.

Two days later we beat Liverpool 1-0 at home and Tony scored a spectacular goal which won that year's *Match of the Day* Goal of the Season award. However, many people think it was eclipsed by his goal at Wimbledon a month later, when went on to score a hat-trick in our 4-2 win. Yobo was asked about the goals in his interview after the match. He said, 'My wife asked me if I would score a goal for her today, so I scored three.'

We also had a good early start in the League Cup. Players from the FA Youth Cup-winning team of 1993, such as Mark Tinkler, Andy Couzens, Rob Bowman and Mark Ford, had been given their chance in the first team, along with some of the younger players including Mark Jackson, Alan Maybury and Paul Sheppard. Two other players to break into the first team were Ian Harte, who was Gary Kelly's nephew, and Harry Kewell. Harry had come over from Australia aged 15 to join the youth team with another lad called Brett Emerton. Leeds wanted to sign them both but only Harry had a European passport as his dad was English. Harry was very single-minded and determined; nothing was going to stop him from playing in the Premier League. He reminded me of my other Australian friend, Chris Anderson.

Lee Matthews told me how he, Harry Kewell and some of the other young lads had been picked for the reserves. Harry was playing left-back at the time. At the last minute, Mick Hennigan told them, 'Sorry lads, you are on the subs' bench,' When Harry asked him why, Mick explained that an international match had been called off and another left-back was coming in to play, on the manager's orders. Harry looked at Mick and said, 'Well, I am a better player than him.' He had massive confidence in his ability and it was not long before he proved it. Lee also played in the first team a couple of years later.

David O'Leary decided to retire and David White had left for Sheffield United, then in November 1995 Swedish international Tomas Brolin joined us from Parma. He had a successful Euro '92 competition when Sweden reached the semi-finals. His medical prior to his signing took forever. He had a plane to catch and when we arrived at the airport, the gate had just closed. Brolin insisted on speaking to the airport manager, who, to be fair, came and sorted things out. After Brolin signed, he made it known that he thought Leeds was a bit of a s**t hole. Another change occurred in December 1995 when Gordon Strachan persuaded Coventry City to sign Noel Whelan for around £2m.

During our early Premier League fixtures we also had to play in the UEFA Cup, and our first game was away at Monaco. Geoff went on his own and we had a good win; Tony

Yeboah was on fire once more, scoring a hat-trick in our 3-0 victory. We were beaten 1-0 in the second leg at home but went through 3-1 on aggregate. We then played PSV Eindhoven, who beat us comprehensively 5-3 at home and 3-0 away in the next round. However, in the League Cup we were through to the fifth round.

Around this time, I caught up with the rugby league player after first meeting him at a rugby game at Elland Road. He was staying at a hotel in Brighouse with the England rugby league team. I was chatting with him and Karl Harrison, a big Leeds United fan; Phil played in Australia for Sydney Roosters. We were talking about the game in April 1986 when Halifax played Featherstone Rovers. Karl was a player that day for Featherstone, and I was the physio for Halifax. It was when the referee called time at the end of the match four minutes early, and we drew 13-13. The result helped Featherstone, who were struggling at the bottom of the league, to stay up. Phil told me that his dad got the sack at Wigan as head coach when they didn't win the Championship, so he was not happy when he found out about the missing four minutes.

I have always enjoyed quizzes, especially about football, and that year Gary McAllister asked me if I wanted to go to Manchester with him while he took part in the BBC TV sports quiz *A Question of Sport*. I went across to his house, and a car arrived to take Gary, his friend Richard Waring and me to the studios. In those days David Coleman was the quizmaster, and the captains were Ian Botham and Bill Beaumont. There was a three-course meal and a table full of drinks; you could have as much as you wanted. Rob Howley, at the time an international rugby union player with Wales, was one of the team members and Gary and I got chatting with him. Rob told us about the last time he had been in Manchester, when he and his team-mate Jonathan Davies got into a fight with some locals. I think they all ended up at the hospital.

Graeme Thorpe, the Surrey cricketer, was also there and then later, Ally McCoist and Niall Quinn arrived. We sat in the guest seats so that the cameraman could pan round to us during the programme. It was good fun to watch the filming, which took around an hour, and then afterwards we met everyone for a drink. I talked to Niall as I knew him slightly through David O'Leary. Niall loves his country and western music, and I recommended he pay a visit to Nashville. We had been there as a family in 1990. Ally was trying to persuade Gary to play for Rangers. Of course, Ally had helped knock us out of the European Cup a few years earlier. But Gary knew they only played four challenging games each season when they took on Celtic.

Leading up to Christmas we were still working hard with Lucas Radebe and by the end of November he was back running and feeling a lot more positive. In early 1996 South

Africa was due to host the Africa Cup of Nations tournament but Geoff had told Lucas that there was little chance that he would be fit enough.

As we moved into the new year we played in round five of the League Cup, at home to Reading, and Phil Masinga was in the team. However, he was due to join the South Africa squad for the AFCON before that game, as was Tony Yeboah with Ghana. The gaffer did a deal. If Phil could stay until after the Reading match then he would allow Lucas to join the squad, even if he had not made a competitive appearance after his injury. Geoff and I thought the risks were too great; the chance of re-injury for Lucas would be more than 50/50, but of course, it was the manager's decision and an agreement was reached. Phil played against Reading and scored a goal as we beat them 2-1. Lucas was simply happy to be going back home. So, for a month, we were without the three of them. In Yobo's last game before he went to Ghana, he scored at Derby County in the third round of the FA Cup, where we won 4-2.

In mid-February 1996 we were in the semi-final of the League Cup. The first leg was away at Birmingham City. Tony, Phil and Lucas had returned from South Africa. Lucas had played and, fortunately, was still in one piece. South Africa had beaten Ghana in the semi-final and then went on to win 2-0 against Tunisia in the final. Phil and Lucas were a bit late getting back; Lucas told me that Nelson Mandela had asked them to spend some time with him.

We won the first leg of the semi-final 2-1 in a hostile atmosphere, during which the Birmingham fans were trying to smash up our dugout. Yobo was on the score sheet, as was our old player Chris Whyte with an own goal. 'Huggy', as we called him, had been a great asset at the club and had helped us win the First Division. Between the two legs, we won at Bolton Wanderers in the FA Cup fourth round and then at Port Vale after a replay in the fifth round.

In the home leg against Birmingham we won 3-0, with all three strikers – Brian Deane, Yeboah and Masinga – on the scoresheet. We were in the League Cup Final, the first time since 1968, to play against Aston Villa, who had an impressive track record at Wembley. I knew their physio Jim Walker as we had been friends since our Lilleshall days. Villa's manager, Brian Little, was the older brother of Allan, who played at Halifax Town when I was there.

Before the final, Tony Dorigo picked up an injury. Around this time I had a phone call from David O'Leary, who was now living down south. His pal, the legendary goalkeeper Pat Jennings, was due to play in a charity golf match just outside Huddersfield and wanted to know how to get there. He was coming up by train. I told David that if Pat could get himself to Elland Road, either myself or Tony would run him across to Huddersfield.

On the day, I was free, so I gave him a lift. When we arrived at the golf course, there was a road crossing the first fairway. I was just about to drive across it when Pat's famous big hand swooped across my body and stopped me on the spot. He said, 'Alan, I have just seen Frank Carson [the Irish comedian]; he's just about to tee off and believe me, his ball could go anywhere. Watch out; this could end up through your car window!' Pat was excellent company, and I met him again a few times afterwards when David became the Leeds manager.

Another person I had a cup of tea with was double Olympic decathlon champion Daley Thompson. I think he did some training with Reading. Their manager Mark McGhee was a good friend of Gordon Strachan from their Aberdeen days. Gordon had arranged for Reading to use our training ground, Fullerton Park, a few times, and on this occasion they were playing at Sunderland the next day. Daley came up with them to stay with his great friend Steve Cram, the former GB Olympian and famed Sunderland supporter, Steve Cram. He was very likeable and easy to talk to; I could see why he was such a popular sportsperson.

Before the League Cup Final, we had the FA Cup quarter-final against Liverpool at home, where we drew 0-0. In the replay at Anfield we were beaten 3-0; that night, the best player on the pitch was Steve McManaman, who scored two goals, and I could see why he was one of the outstanding midfield players in the country at the time.

The day before the League Cup Final, I worked with some of the injured players at Elland Road. In London, Geoff worked on Tony Dorigo at the hotel, trying to get him fit for the match against his old team Aston Villa. I flew down later that evening while Shirley and Miles travelled on the day with the rest of the Leeds party of family and friends. When I arrived, Geoff told me that Tony had failed his fitness test. Understandably, when I saw him, he was very down. How often do you get to play in a Wembley final?

The next day I went to the stadium to put the kit out and set up the medical table. I remember chatting to Jim Paul, Villa's kit man, who I had known for a few years. The final was a 5pm kick-off, and it was forecast to be one of those 50/50 games. I was pleased to see that Andy Gray was playing as it had been just over three years since Miles came home to tell me what a great game Andy had played for Harrogate Schoolboys, and now he was playing at Wembley. It was also a big day for Mark Ford, who had come through the youth team, and of course for Lucas Radebe, who only a few years earlier had never thought he would get out of Soweto.

The players were in the dressing room 30 minutes before kick-off. Out of the blue, Tony Yeboah asked if he could have a word with me. 'Sure,' I replied. 'What's up, pal?'

Tony told me, 'My knee does not feel right. I am getting some pain from it.' We had already lost Tony Dorigo. I looked at Geoff and the gaffer. The easy thing to do would have been to tell Geoff and let him deal with it. Yobo had played many big games for his country so I was sure it could not be nerves, but I knew we had two strikers on the bench in Tomas Brolin and Brian Deane. I said to Tony, 'Just go out and give it ten or 15 minutes and let's see how it goes. If it's a problem, go down and just say you think you have twisted your knee. Geoff will understand.' I pulled Geoff to one side and told him what had happened with Yobo and what I had said, and he agreed with my suggestion to let him start. All I can say is he got through 90 minutes of the game, but it was a bad day at the office and we lost 3-0.

The supporters reacted badly, and the abuse the gaffer received at the end of the match was well and truly out of order. Howard Wilkinson had taken us from a club that had done nothing for years and built a team that, in the last six years, had won two championships and the Charity Shield, as well as twice qualifying for Europe. He had also established a great youth team with Paul Hart, Eddie Gray and the other coaches, bringing through the best young players the club had seen for years. But, at that moment, his success seemed to have been forgotten. It was hard to take. I thought we had done so well to get through to the final. But because of that one bad performance the supporters turned on the manager.

I sat behind the gaffer on the coach going to the railway station for the train home, and he looked like a broken man. It took a few hours before he picked himself up. I have always said I often wondered how I lasted working with Howard for eight years. I had my run-ins with him, but what he went through that day should not have happened, and I know that lots of people agree with me. We can all be happy when things are going well, but for me, if you are a supporter, it is all about how you also handle the bad times.

People have asked me how I handled some of those rollercoaster times of the championship years. Someone told me many years ago that the best way to cope was to enjoy the win but not to get too happy, or too sad when you have a terrible result. It's not always possible, but I think it did work for me.

Our captain Gary McAllister was so upset when he came down the steps at Wembley after receiving his loser's medal that he handed it to me saying, 'Here Sutts, that's for you.' He did not even want to look at it. A few days afterwards, I told him, 'When you are ready, let me know when you want your medal back.' It was Christmas before he got in touch to say that he was ready to take it back. He went on to win the League Cup with Liverpool and many more finals, but he knew the pain of that day.

After the League Cup Final, in the last nine games of the season, we won one, drew one and lost seven. We used portacabins outside the ground as they were renovating the dressing rooms in preparation for Euro '96, with Elland Road one of the host grounds. We moved our training facilities to Thorp Arch, near Wetherby, and Fullerton Park was used for parking. The manager was pleased because he had been asking for years to have a separate location for our training facilities; his theory was that going to Elland Road for home games made it more special when the players were not there every day.

In mid-April we were at Old Trafford playing Manchester United when, after 17 minutes, our goalkeeper Mark Beeney was sent off by the referee Keith Cooper. I knew Keith as we had a mutual friend in rugby league, Brian Juliff, who was at Halifax when we won the Championship. We did not have a keeper on the bench but Lucas Radebe had played in goal before becoming a centre-half, so he took over. He did brilliantly. The only shot that beat him was from Roy Keane six minutes from time, which went in the corner of the net from the edge of the penalty area. With Lucas around we did not need a sub keeper, and he also kept goal against Middlesbrough in another game.

Our loss against Newcastle was notable for David Batty returning to Leeds as a Newcastle player and for Kevin Keegan's famous interview after the match. Alex Ferguson had gotten under his skin. Newcastle had never had a better chance of winning the Premier League than that year, when they let their big lead slip, and Manchester United went on to take the title.

A month after the first team lost in the League Cup Final, we had another big game, which for me was just as important, as the youth team had to play in their own League Cup Final. We were playing Newcastle United at York City's ground, Bootham Crescent. The youth team had not won anything since the FA Youth Cup Final against Manchester United in 1993, so it was important to start picking up silverware again.

A few days before the final, Paul Hart decided to take the team to Blackpool for a bonding day; some of the players had to take the day off school. At the time, Lee Matthews had an ankle injury and was struggling to get fit. I went along to give him some treatment. Many of the players on the trip that day went on to play in the first team. Mark Jackson had already played one game; Paul used to call him 'Stonewall' Jackson, after the famous confederate general in the American Civil War. Paul Robinson and Jonathan Woodgate played the following season. Paul, Eddie and Robin's work with the squad was paying off, but they needed a cup win.

In Blackpool, Paul asked me whether Lee would be fit for Friday. I said, 'It is touch and go,' although I doubted his chances were that positive. Paul said, 'Let him run from this pier to the next one, and we will see.' Lee told me, 'No chance, Sutts,' but I said, 'Come on, let's try something,' and we went down to the beach. I made him stand in the sea for a few minutes, and then I got him to run to the next pier through the water. His ankle was so numb with the cold that he did not feel a thing. Harty said, 'He is in the team unless you tell me otherwise.' For the rest of the week we worked non-stop to get him fit.

Along with Tony Hackworth, Lee was our top striker in the youth team. At 16 or 17 years of age, he was 6ft 2in, a robust two-footed player, and a good header of the ball. On Friday morning we had a final fitness test, and we both agreed that he should be okay, but my last words to him were the same as to Mark Ford three years earlier, 'Once you cross that white line, there are no excuses, you get on with the game.' He said, 'Sutts, I won't let you down.'

Leeds won 2-0 with Lee making the first goal and scoring the second. The last time I talked with him, he said that he had never forgotten that game and how we had worked together to get him fit, despite my busy schedule with the pros. I told him that everyone was important at Leeds United, and at that time the youth team needed to win that game to show everybody what good young players were going to come through to the first team. In the following season, Lee scored again in the FA Youth Cup Final and we won 1-0, the second time we had won the competition in four years. Lee played a few games in the first team and then went on to play at Bristol City, Yeovil Town, and Port Vale. He and Jonathan Woodgate were big pals as they both came from Middlesbrough.

An essential member of the backroom staff at that time was a lad called Richard. He was the youth team physio at weekends while I was away with the first team on matchdays. I met him at Lilleshall at a medical meeting. He was in private practice in Bingley, not too far from Bradford, and did a few seasons at the club.

After a holiday in Australia and New Zealand to celebrate our silver wedding anniversary, I helped look after the dressing rooms and medical room for the Elland Road games at Euro '96. Alan Roberts, the club's general manager, was in charge of the Leeds and Newcastle grounds. He gave my daughter Adele a job working with the French press; she had just completed her second year at Birmingham University, studying Law with French. Wherever the French team went, she went with them. The Spanish national team was based at Elland Road for their three group matches. One of them was against France, so that worked out well for Adele.

After Spain played their first game against Bulgaria, which finished 1-1, the drug tests were in the medical room. Refreshments were provided, including beer, so the Spanish doctors started to get a taste for Tetley's Bitter. We all used sign language to communicate with each other. One of the coaches, Andoni Goikoetxea, had been a Spanish international, known as the 'Butcher of Bilbao' for his uncompromising style of play. He had been the subject of a ten-match ban for a cynical foul on Diego Maradona.

I got to know one of the players, Juan Antonio Pizzi; we had a bite to eat together a couple of times. He wore the number nine shirt and gave me one of them after their last game at Elland Road. He had been born in Argentina but played for Spain, mainly in Tenerife, and moved to Barcelona after the competition. I also became friendly with the Real Madrid captain Fernando Hierro, who I would see again about five years later at Elland Road in the Champions League. Spain got through the first round, and their next game was against England at Wembley. The day they left Leeds, Juan Antonio kindly signed the shirt he had given me, and then the doctors came into the treatment room at about 10am to ask if I had any Tetley's left so we could have a final drink together.

* * *

At the start of pre-season, Geoff and I were busy with medicals. We had signed Ian Rush and Lee Bowyer. We also paid a British record fee for a goalkeeper of over £2m for Nigel Martyn from Crystal Palace. Then, after a pre-season game at Grimsby, we signed Lee Sharpe from Manchester United. While these deals were taking place, the Caspian Group purchased the club from the shareholders Bill Fotherby, Leslie Silver and Peter Gilman. Leslie and Peter left the club, but Bill stayed on as chairman.

We had a new training ground at Thorp Arch for the start of the 1996/97 season. The only problem was the size of the medical room. When the gaffer first showed us around, everyone had been sorted out with rooms apart from the physio team and Sean, the kit man. All the gaffer said was, 'These are the only rooms left.' You could just about swing a cat in the space we were given, but we had to fit in an office and two treatment beds. At least it would prevent the players from hanging around if they were not having treatment. However, we did have a good area for rehab work. There was some new accommodation for the youth players, so they were living onsite. Peter and Maureen Gunby were looking after them, but Paul Hart had put Alan Maybury, the youth team captain, in charge overall.

A few players had left the club. Gary Speed, my first apprentice, had gone to Everton, his boyhood team, and John Lukic had re-joined Arsenal. Phil Masinga was sold to St Gallen in Switzerland as he had not played enough games to stay in the UK. Nigel Worthington also left on a free transfer.

Towards the end of July I was sitting on the coach with Eddie and Paul, ready to depart for a three-day tour of Scotland with the youth team, when Gary McAllister walked past the bus. I could see that he was upset. We got off the coach and Gary told us that the club had sold him to Coventry City. Gordon Strachan was there and was soon to take over as manager. Gary did not want to leave and loved playing for Leeds, but it had been made clear to him that the club were happy to let him go.

In Scotland with the youth team we played Hibernian in Edinburgh, and then the coach took us to Glasgow where we stayed at a B&B near the airport. We had a day off before playing Rangers' youth team. At 6.30am my phone rang; it was Eddie Gray, 'Alan, get up. We are going for a round of golf.' We had brought our clubs with us, so off we went to Renfrew Golf Club on the Clyde.

When we arrived there was not a soul around apart from the cleaner. She got us a card but said, 'I don't think you will be able to play. There is a members-only match today.' Eddie said, 'We'll have finished before they start.' The course was excellent and I will never forget the first hole. I was not feeling the best after the night before; Eddie teed off and the ball went out of bounds. I felt a bit better as the pressure was off. I got my five iron and hit my ball about 150 yards down the fairway, hoping that I would feel better over the next few holes. At the end of the round I had enjoyed myself, and it was great playing with Eddie. We walked back to the clubhouse to pay. The first thing the receptionist said was, 'I hope you do not want to play, gentlemen. It's closed to the public today.' Eddie told her we had just finished, so she asked us to wait while she brought Angus, the club captain. She explained the situation and then Angus looked at Eddie and said, 'Is it Eddie Gray?' When Eddie told him why we were in Scotland, Angus glanced around and said, 'Just give me £25, and I have never seen you.' We got a taxi back to the hotel.

While talking about Eddie Gray, I remember that he and Paul Hart loved to play head tennis, which involved heading a football over a net strung across a sports court. The two of them were a formidable team and rarely lost to their opponents. On one occasion they played against Jonathan Woodgate and Harry Kewell, and to Eddie and Paul's surprise, Woody and Kewell won. Unfortunately for the two younger lads, Eddie and Paul heard them bragging about their victory and they quickly convened another game. During the rematch, Paul and Woody jumped up at the same time to head the ball, and a 'stray' arm from Harty smacked Woody straight on the nose. With Woody holding his face, Paul joked, 'Now you're starting to look like a proper centre-half, son!' There was only ever going to be one winning team in that rematch.

We won seven points from our first four matches then, on 7 September, we played Manchester United at Elland Road. It was a bad day as we lost 4-0, and to make matters worse, Lee Bowyer sustained an injury. Nicky Butt, the Manchester United player, had his back to Lee when the ball hit Nicky's heel, rebounded, and hit Lee in the eye. It was a freak accident but Lee required surgery, so I went with him to the hospital.

On the following Monday, I was in the treatment room when I was told that the gaffer wanted to see me. At first I thought I had done something wrong, but most of the other staff were also there when I went into his office. Without any preamble, Howard told us that he was no longer the manager and that Paul Hart would be taking over as caretaker. When everything had settled down, Paul said to me, 'Can you ring Oldham and say that we will have to put the deal to sign Gunnar Halle on hold for now.'

When we eventually signed Gunnar a few months later, I asked him about that day. Gunnar said it was bizarre because he had already said goodbye to everyone and was just getting in his car to drive to the Leeds training ground when they told him that everything was off. Gunnar was a good player, and he turned out to be a great guy as well.

When we got back to work that day, I went out running with Tony Dorigo. He asked me, 'Has he gone?' The players had heard the rumours but had not been officially told of Howard Wilkinson's departure, so I told him the news. Alongside losing 4-0 to Manchester United, all in all, it had been a difficult weekend.

The next day the new manager walked in. It was the ex-Arsenal boss George Graham. Over the next few weeks, he brought David O'Leary back to the club as his assistant and moved Eddie Gray to work with the first team. Mick Hennigan left the club, and I was sorry to see him go. I think George liked Mick but he would always be Howard's man. Ian McNeil replaced Geoff Sleight as chief scout. In time, David Williams took a job with the Manchester United youth team. From day one the new manager worked on the defence, and I think the players benefitted from the new workouts brought in by George, especially Lucas Radebe.

Some months before Howard left we had signed another South African player, Paul Evans, the goalkeeper. The first game that Evo played was away at Preston in the reserves. It was raining heavily on the way over and I remember him saying, 'Well, this will be a first; I have never played in the rain before.' I wondered whether I should tell Mick Hennigan. Evo faced the first shot that came at him, it slid under him and into the back of the net, and we were 1-0 down, although we went on to win 5-1, so we got away with it.

During that season, Tony Yeboah was getting over a long-standing injury when Evo challenged him one day. He said, 'When you get fit, I bet you cannot score against me.'

Well, that was it; the challenge was on. Yobo said to me, 'Go get the footballs.' To Evo, he said, 'You and me, outside.' I found a place where no one could see them and got the goals set up. Yobo told me, 'You cross the ball, and I'll do the rest.' So off we went. I put the ball into the box and Yobo smashed it into the net, past Paul. Then he did a celebratory dance, singing, 'I am Tony, I am Tony Yeboah, I am the King!' You would have thought we were in front of thousands at the Kop end of Elland Road. After 15 minutes or so, some of the apprentices came to see what was happening. We could not help but laugh at Yobo's antics, but eventually I called time and said, 'Tony, you have made your point. Evo, you are going to get me shot, winding him up. We are trying to get him fit again.'

I went to the Newcastle United game on New Year's Day without Geoff Ladley, who had been ill for a few days. On that morning I had Tony running on the treadmill as we had to get him fit. But that afternoon, Alan Shearer scored twice and we lost 3-0. When we arrived back at Elland Road and were taking the kit off the coach, George Graham said to Sean and me, 'Thank you for all your help today.' We looked at each other in disbelief. We had never been thanked for anything during the eight years we had worked for the previous manager. But as Mick Hennigan used to say if the gaffer had not been pleased with us, we would not have been doing the job.

Early in 1997, the new management team brought in Ed Baranowski as a part-time fitness coach to join Eric Steele, the part-time goalkeeping coach.

In February I was hit by a bombshell when George Graham told Geoff Ladley that he was being replaced. I was gutted for him. He had been a loyal friend and had secured the job for me at Leeds in the first place. Geoff had initially intended to retire at the end of the season when he would be 65. I don't know why the club could not wait until then.

The guy taking over was David Swift. I knew Swifty through Geoff as they had been lecturers together at Pinderfields Hospital. I had to tell Geoff who had got his job. I also knew from the first week that Swifty would want me out too. For whatever reason, as much as he tried to get rid of me, in the time that he was there it never happened.

For the remainder of the season I worked with the first team, the reserves and the youth players during the week. Richard looked after the youth team on matchdays. In March 1997, the youth team was invited to play in the Dallas Cup in Texas, USA. The previous year Richard had accompanied the team, but this year he was unavailable so I went in his place. The competition was held for two weeks over Easter. It would allow me to get to know Paul Hart and Eddie Gray, and the youth players who would be playing in the first team in the not-too-distant future. On the outward journey my old friend Trevor Simpson, whom I had known from my Halifax Town days, was on the plane with us. He was part of the tournament's referee team.

National and club youth teams from all over the world took part, as well as the state champions from across America. We were knocked out by a team from California and the coaches were not happy; I think some of the lads thought they were on holiday.

When we arrived back in early April, I regularly worked with Ed Baranowski. He knew a lot about running drills and together we created more programmes for players recovering from injuries. I did the early running sessions, which enabled the injured players to get back to training quicker, then Ed took over when they could join in with the rest of the group. A lot of his drills came from America, where Ed was a frequent visitor.

On their return from the USA, the youth team got their heads down. They had a good win over two legs against Luton Town in the semi-final of the FA Youth Cup and played against Crystal Palace in the final, where they won 2-1 at home. We stayed overnight for the second leg, and on the night, Lee Matthews scored from Andy Wright's cross for a 1-0 victory.

At the end of the 1996/97 season the first team had only scored 28 goals, which was the fewest in the Premier League, but they had kept 20 clean sheets and finished 11th. The boss's work on defending was paying off, although not with all the supporters.

* * *

Just before pre-season, Chris Fairclough got in touch. He was now at Bolton Wanderers but I think he was looking for another club. He'd had an operation at the end of the season and asked if I could help him with some running, so he spent a few days with Sean Hardy and me. In the pre-season meeting, George Graham said, 'I understand one of the ex-players has been doing some training here?' He was not happy. I held my hands up and told him I had arranged it. I knew not to let it happen again,

The players who left that year included Carlton Palmer, who went to Southampton, Tomas Brolin to Crystal Palace, Ian Rush to Newcastle United and Tony Yeboah to Hamburg. Brian Deane went back to Sheffield United and Tony Dorigo signed for Torino in Italy; I think he was still learning to speak Italian. A lot of the youth players were given contracts and shirt numbers.

Among our new signings were Jimmy Floyd Hasselbaink and Bruno Ribeiro from Portugal, and Alf-Inge Håland joined his fellow Norwegian Gunnar Halle at the club. We also signed David Hopkin from Crystal Palace, Martin Hiden came to us from Rapid

Vienna and Clyde Wijnhard from Willem II. Pre-season was mainly in Roundhay Park; it was like going back to the old days with Billy Bremner.

In mid-August I went with the youth team, who had a trip to the Republic of Ireland to play three games. The most memorable match was in Sligo. It had been raining most of the day, and in the evening we played a combined team of players from around the Sligo area. Alan Smith had just got into the youth team and on that night he was unplayable with four goals as we won 6-2. It would not be long before he was scoring goals in the big stadiums. I left the lads early on the Saturday morning and travelled to Dublin and then on to Leeds Bradford Airport to be back for the first team's home game.

In the first 15 games Leeds scored 25 goals, just three short of the total for the entirety of the previous season. The big plus was that most of the youth team from the last couple of years were doing well in the reserves and getting plenty of experience playing against bigger teams. Players like Harry Kewell, Mark Jackson, Paul Shepherd and Andy Couzens were now in the first team.

One player who began to make an impression was Jimmy Floyd Hasselbaink. It took him a few matches to get his work rate up to Premier League levels, and to start with the boss regularly replaced him at half-time. George kept telling Jimmy that Rod Wallace was doing all his running for him. Rod was at Leeds for about seven years and had been an excellent buy, scoring a lot of important goals, but at times he was in the shadow of other players. Lee Bowyer was another player who had a good eye for goal and amazing stamina; he could cover ten to 14 kilometres each game.

Leeds played most of their home reserve matches that season at Halifax Town, where I first started my physio career. The Shay always had a great pitch; it was built on a tip and had good drainage. One cold night we were playing Wolves' reserves. Halfway through the first half the ball came to me, but it was a Wolves throw-in. Without warning, their physio grabbed the ball out of my hands. I thought, 'What the hell was that?' I found out his name was Dave Hancock; he knew Geoff Ladley from Pinderfields and while I was working with Geoff, Dave rang him a few times. Years afterwards I told him that I thought he was from another planet that night. I said he had only done it to impress their manager, Gordon Strachan's pal Mark McGhee, who was sitting behind him. I was to meet Dave again in the not-too-distant future.

Talking of Halifax Town, a few months later their groundsman, my old pal Norman Southernwood, took over the role of head groundsman at Elland Road. I remember telling George Graham that if he failed it would not be for lack of trying; he would work all the hours of the day or night to get things right.

At the beginning of 1997/98 there had been some changes to the backroom staff. Paul Hart left to take up the same coaching role at Nottingham Forest. Paul and the manager never really got on; it had been Howard who had brought Paul into the club. Eddie Gray moved up to work with George and was now the reserve team coach. They also brought in a guy called Clive Brown as a masseur for the first team squad. He had been in the Royal Air Force and was a very fit lad. Over time we got on well, but we were always winding each other up. He was a good guy.

One lad I got to know who had just signed for the academy was Alan Smith. I first met him on the Dallas trip the season before, but the first incident I was involved with was a junior game in Barnsley one midweek. I think it was a morning kick-off and Uriah Rennie was the referee. We knew each other quite well and he had just got on the Premier League circuit. Uriah did a lot of work for the community in Sheffield, and I had also heard that he was a black belt in karate.

Everything was going okay in the game until somebody went through Smithy; it looked like he was not happy. I went on the pitch to treat him and Uriah put his hand on my shoulder and said, 'Sutts, can you have a word with this young lad about how he has just spoken to me? If it had been a Saturday night in Sheffield he would be in the A&E department of the Northern General Hospital by now.' I looked at Smithy and pointed to the ref. 'You see him,' I said, 'he is on our side.' Then I whispered to him, 'You see him,' pointing to the offending player, 'that's the one that you need to sort out.'

It was the first time I would be involved in sorting things out with Smithy, but not the last time. Not everyone knows, but Alan was a late starter in football. Before that he was a BMX champion when, aged nine and despite fracturing his wrist, he won the British Championship. On the day of the final Alan had a pot on his arm, but it hindered using the brakes so he and his dad cut the pot off. I can't imagine how much pain he was in. His passion to succeed was also evident in football, especially when it looked like there might not be a Leeds United in the early 2000s.

By March 1998 we were doing okay in the Premier League. In the FA Cup we got to the quarter-final and had a home tie against Wolves. The physio from the reserve game at Halifax, Dave Hancock, showed up to see me. He asked if I could get our doctor for him as he needed some help with a player, which I did. On the day we lost 1-0 and Don Goodman scored against us, as he had for Bradford City on the day of the chip van fire at Odsal in 1986.

After the game we were in the coaches' room when Dave came in again. Almost immediately, Dave Swift got up and went home, so I knew then that there was some history between them, probably from Pinderfields Hospital where Swifty was Dave's lecturer.

I stayed a bit longer after the game as the Wolves staff were still in the coaches' room. A guy called Barry was their first team physio and Dave was his number two. While we were talking, Dave mentioned that he was meeting some friends in the city centre, so I offered to give him a lift. When I dropped him off I wished him all the best for the semi-finals. Little did I know then that in just over two years we would be working together. But before then he had a move to Blackburn Rovers.

With Eddie and the reserves we were doing very well in the Pontins League. All the top teams in the north participated, including from as far south as Aston Villa. It was getting towards the end of the season and we were in the top three.

On 30 March the first team flew to London to play West Ham. It was a televised match on a Monday evening. I was at Thorp Arch and after I had finished treatment I drove to Elland Road, parked my car and caught the train from Leeds to London with one of the players. We visited the hospital to get the player checked out by a surgeon, then we made our way to Upton Park, or the Boleyn Ground as Mervyn Day used to call it. As usual, the staff on the door just said, 'You know where to go.' If you go a few times to away grounds you see the same people all the time.

Sean had set up the medical room ready for the game, so I went to see my pal Eddie Gillam, the West Ham kit man. Then I called in on Harry Redknapp in his office to have a cup of tea, as usual. I remembered Adele had asked me to get his autograph for her friend at university, who was a West Ham fan. Harry's son Jamie came into the office. Harry introduced us, then Jamie kindly signed the West Ham programme for me. Then I went back to our dressing room for the game.

In the dressing room, Nigel Martyn came to me and said, 'Sutts, I have got a quiz question for you. Can you name six players who have played for England, who have the same surname, and one of them is white, and the other is black? I said, 'You mean like Mark Wright and Ian Wright?' He said, 'Yes. I'll be back at half-time to see who else you have come up with.'

During the match I sat behind the dugout with George Gavin, the reporter from Sky Sports. I asked George the same quiz question. 'I will think about it,' he said. We had a poor first half and Nigel did not have the best time; I think we were 2-0 down by then. In the dressing room, the boss had a go at everybody. We got through the game with a 3-0 defeat.

On the coach to Stansted for the flight back to Leeds Bradford, I sat with David Wetherall and Rod Wallace. The boss had stayed in London. The lads were saying that the outward flight had not been that good. They'd also had a bad experience flying a few years earlier, so I told them about the flight to Dublin with the Leeds team in 1990. As it turned out, it was not the best conversation to have just before this flight.

For once I was first on the plane; David O'Leary and Eddie Gray followed me. As they walked past I said, 'Why don't you sit behind me? It's the emergency exit door and has got more legroom.' So David sat next to the door with Eddie beside him. The director Peter Ridsdale and his son were also on board. My good friend Norman Hunter was across the aisle; it was great to see him again. He had been working with Bryn Law from Radio Leeds. I heard Nigel Martyn shout from behind me, 'Sutts, have you got the answer to my quiz question yet?' I called across to Norman, 'Hey, Norman, have there ever been any black players named Hunter who played for England?' He looked at me and asked, 'What are you talking about?' But before I could explain, our attention was diverted by the take-off.

We had started to taxi down the runway. It was pitch black, so I could not see anything from the window as we picked up speed. Suddenly there was a loud bang, and I saw that the engine on the opposite wing was on fire. Like everyone else, I thought we were still on the ground. In that split second the captain must not have been aware of the fire, as we were told later that no lights came on in his cabin. The air stewardess picked up the phone to let him know, and then we were told to brace ourselves for an emergency landing.

As one of the players said later, it was like we were on a Hollywood film set because everything seemed to be in slow motion. A few seconds later, as we hunched in the brace position, we heard another loud bang, which turned out to be the front wheel hitting something, and then the front of the plane nose-dived. We had landed in a field at the end of the runway, right next to the M11 motorway. Everyone started to leave their seats quickly, but there was no panic despite the engine still being on fire. David O'Leary put his shoulder against the door until someone instructed him to pull the lever above his head, and then the door opened. I thought I had better get my coat out of the locker above, but then David Wetherall said, 'Sutts! What are you doing? The engine is on fire. Just get out!' I still managed to grab my coat.

With Lee Matthews in front of me, I joined the line to exit the plane. I thought there would be a chute to slide down, but I must have seen too many movies. We jumped on to the wing and then jumped from there on to the ground. The plane was tilted upwards from the front, and at the back there must have been a 15-foot drop. At first I walked away, but then I went back when I saw people were still jumping out. The last person to leave the plane was the air stewardess; she landed on the ground but was okay.

We stood on the runway, watching the burning plane as the fire engines approached. Thankfully we had all got out safely. Eddie Gray said to me, 'If this is the only time it is going to happen, I hope I have taken one for the family.'

I spoke to the pilot, John Hackett, who stood with us on the tarmac. He told me we were 150ft up in the air when the engine caught fire; many of us thought we were still on the ground. What he said then surprised me. He had not followed protocol; he should have circled and come back down the runway. As it turned out, when the facts of the accident were established, it was fortunate for us that he didn't.

I borrowed a phone to ring home, put the family in the picture and told them that everyone was okay. We all went back into the terminal, and by this time Bryn Law was dealing with the press. At about 4am a coach arrived to take us back to Elland Road, where more reporters were waiting. The players who had parked their cars at Leeds Bradford Airport stayed on the coach, so it was down to me to speak to the press. I talked to a Radio Leeds presenter and told them we had been very lucky to be alive. I had been 11 years old at the time of the Munich air disaster, and their plane did not even get off the ground. As David O'Leary said later, 'Someone up there was looking out for us.'

After I had been up to the training ground to see Claire and Margaret in the laundry, I made my way home. The following lunchtime we all went to the local pub, and of course, the first thing that greeted me was, 'Did you have your parachute on, Al?' It was good to be at home and get some light relief.

Some weeks later there was an inquiry and we were all interviewed. The likely cause of the crash was a blockage in the fuel pipe from a disintegrated piece of metal. In the accident, the propeller had broken off. If it had gone sideways it would have sliced through the plane. But it was accepted that if the pilot had done as the rulebook had said, and shut the engine down before turning around, it was unlikely we would have survived. Two things worked in our favour. First, we were on a very long runway at over two miles, enabling the pilot to land there rather than on the motorway nearby. Secondly, it was a propeller plane; if it had been a jet engine we would have only had a few seconds before it blew up.

For about a year no one said anything much about the crash, apart from how relieved we were to have all escaped unscathed, but then one day in the treatment room I think maybe enough time had passed for some of us to recall the few funny moments within the panic. Lee Matthews said that Rod Wallace had tried to open the door on to the wing that was on fire, but he felt the door handle was hot. Lee said, 'Rod, what are you doing. It's the wrong door, pal?!' Also, one of the paying passengers would not jump out at the back of the plane. He just sat there until a size nine shoe helped him on his way. It took a lot of the lads a long time to fly again. For me, I had too many friends around the world to give it up.

As an aside, going back to the quiz question, I never explained to Norman why I needed to know if he knew a black player named Hunter. It may well have been the last quiz question I ever asked him if luck had not been on our side. In the drama, I forgot to give my answers to Nigel; however, I wouldn't want to leave this up in the air (excuse the pun), so these are the players I had thought of: Ian Wright and Mark Wright, Stan Anderson and Viv Anderson, John Barnes and Peter Barnes, Billy Walker and Des Walker. There may be several more.

Back to everyday life and Adele got in touch with me to see if I could send her word processor to her at Birmingham University. As it turned out, Lee Sharpe, who came from the Bromsgrove area, was going down there to see his mum and dad, so I gave him the address on Pershore Road. I think Lee had a Porsche at the time. According to Adele, when he arrived her housemates were waiting to greet him, still in their nightclothes.

With the first team, we had seven games to play until the end of the season. One of them was at home to Coventry, when Gordon Strachan and Gary McAllister would be returning to Elland Road. George Graham still could not believe that just before he arrived at Leeds, the club had let Gary move to Coventry and kept other players he did not think were good enough. On the day we drew 3-3; Darren Huckerby got a hat-trick for Coventry and joined us at Leeds a few years later.

At the end of the season, the first team finished fifth in the Premier League and qualified for the UEFA Cup. The reserves also won their league for the first time in 61 years. Eddie had promoted many of the youth players who had won the league and the FA Youth Cup the previous year.

As well as working with the first team and the reserves, that season I had spent a lot of time with the youth players, including treating injuries and covering games. Richard, the youth team physio, had moved on, so when the club announced that John Bilton was to take over as the youth team coach, I think a few people were surprised, as, on the coaching side, we already had John Dungworth working with the younger kids. John Dungworth was a great guy to have at the club. I first met him when he was a youth player at Huddersfield Town, and he went on to have a good career as a striker. John Bilton also appointed another guy named Gordon Staniforth as a coach to work with the youth players.

But by the end of the 1997/98 season things were not going well with the youth team, and the manager became aware of some issues through his number two, David O'Leary, and Eddie Gray. Gordon left the club, followed shortly afterwards by John Bilton. They were replaced by Alan Hill, who had worked with Brian Clough at Nottingham Forest, and Dave Merrington, who had been a coach at the club years before with Jimmy Adamson. The manager also appointed another coach, Steve Beaglehole, son of Eddie. Steve was great to work with, and he helped me with some running and coaching drills. After he left Leeds, Steve went to Leicester City, and he is still there over 20 years later.

7

A FORCE IN EUROPE

At the start of the 1998/99 season, Andy Gray had left us to go to Nottingham Forest, although in December 1998 we re-signed David Batty. From our first seven league games we had won two and drawn five. In Europe we had beaten Marítimo on penalties over two legs, but the big news was that George Graham had left us to take over at Tottenham Hotspur. David O'Leary was put in charge, and Peter Ridsdale was now the chairman. It was no secret that Peter wanted Martin O'Neill as his next manager.

I also did a medical for a lad called John Scales from Harrogate. He had been at Leeds when he was younger, but we had let him go. We were now signing him from Liverpool. I understood that everything had been agreed and he just needed a medical to finish the deal, which I sorted on a Sunday morning. But then I was told he had signed for Tottenham instead.

In the meantime, David's first job was to give Steve McPhail and Jonathan Woodgate their debuts in the first team. Ian Harte and Harry Kewell were already in the first 11 and were doing okay. It then became known that Martin O'Neill had turned down the Leeds job to stay at Leicester City so the chairman offered the job to David, who accepted it with Eddie Gray as his number two.

There was another newcomer as Ian Broomfield was appointed chief scout by George just before he left, and later in the season we brought in another Norwegian player, Eirik Bakke.

The month I particularly remember from that season was November. Before our away game at Liverpool, David O'Leary had said to me, 'I never lose at Anfield.' He had been in the Arsenal team that won the famous game at Anfield to take the First Division championship in 1989. By 14 November 1998 David had Alan Smith on the bench; Alan had maybe played one reserve game.

In the second half Robbie Fowler scored a penalty to put Liverpool 1-0 up. We were playing towards the Kop end and the boss put Smudger on. He had not been on the field long when he got a ball on the edge of the box. As cool as a cucumber, he put it in the bottom corner of the net, then Jimmy Floyd Hasselbaink scored twice to give us a 3-1 victory.

In the dressing room after the game, our Scottish international David Hopkin said about Smithy's goal, 'If that had been me in front of the Kop on my debut, my shot would have been up in the rafters.' There was much respect from the other players for the way Alan had kept a cool head.

The next away game was at Old Trafford against Manchester United, and we thought we would never have a better chance to win there since 1981 when Brian Flynn got the winner, but we lost 3-2. Eddie Gray and I were in the coaches' room after the game when Alex Ferguson walked in. He said, 'Well done, lads.' Eddie replied, 'We just got beat, Alex.' Ferguson nodded, 'Yes, but at least you came here this time and tried to win.' It would be almost 12 more years before we got a good result there.

On Boxing Day we were at Newcastle United. We had a friend, Jeff Robbins from Spokane in Washington State, staying with us over Christmas, so I arranged with my great pal John O'Conner that he would take Jeff to watch the game with him. We had a great 3-0 win. When I arrived home Jeff was bouncing off the walls with the thrill of our victory, and he thought I would be the same. He asked me why I was not as excited as he was. I told him, 'It's three points and I'm delighted, but the league is like a marathon.' Five weeks later we played Newcastle at home and lost 1-0, so our three points were gone.

After the Newcastle loss we were in mid-table, but then we went on a great run and finished fourth in the Premier League. The last match of the season was away at Coventry, managed by Gordon Strachan. Before the game Noel Whelan came into the dressing room to see Sean and me. I said, 'How's it going, Snowy?' He replied, 'Yes, I'm okay; I'm staying at the gaffer's house for a bit.' When I asked why he said, 'You know me, Sutts, when I go out, even I don't know what's going to happen.' In the old days I remember Noel falling through a pavement light on a night out. It was good to see Gary McAllister that day too, and we drew 2-2.

By the summer of 1999, I had spent a lot of time with Lucas Radebe working on his injuries, more often than not on Sunday mornings when we had a bit more time to have a chat. When there were other people in for treatment, Lucas's stories left us spellbound. I remember him telling me about his early years playing football. Lucas and his team-mates used bandages on their feet for football boots. I have been to Soweto and seen the pitches; there is not a single blade of grass.

Lucas started his career as a goalkeeper before becoming a centre-back. One Sunday morning at Leeds he came in wearing a stylish football top with writing on the front. I said, 'Chief, what's with the writing?' He pointed to his chest and said, 'This is my hero.' I asked him, 'Who is your hero?' He replied, 'Mr Mandela. He wrote that for me.' I said in amazement, 'Why are you wearing it?' If it had been me, I would have had it framed and stored away in pristine condition. 'I like to have him next to my heart,' he said.

On one occasion after Lucas had come back from a trip with the South African national team, I asked him how it had gone. He told me, 'It was okay. Nothing much happened, apart from one morning I was fast asleep in the hotel when I had a phone call. The hotel receptionist told me that President Mandela was downstairs having breakfast and had asked if I would like to join him.' He said he jumped out of bed and shot downstairs. I also remember Lucas telling me once that he and Mark Fish, who also played in England with Bolton and Charlton, had a meeting with Mr Mandela, who said to them that it would be sportspeople who would put South Africa on the map, not politicians.

One Sunday morning Lucas told us what South Africa was really like during apartheid. He said that early in his footballing career he watched a game with his young nephew. Lucas saw a group of policemen pointing towards him; he was a target for them simply because he was doing well as a black player. Lucas tried to make his way out of the stadium, but the police cornered and beat him. The next thing he remembered was staggering across a white person's land. It was 48 hours later when his parents eventually found him, but Lucas had been so severely beaten that at first they did not recognise him and had walked past him twice. But he was lucky; he could have been shot for trespassing on white man's land.

One day I was massaging his back and asked him, 'What's with the scar, Chief?' Lucas told me the story about the day he had been shot while driving in Soweto. He heard a bang and thought it was a car backfiring, but he started to lose the feeling in his leg and felt pain in his back. When Lucas touched his shirt, his hand was covered in blood. Someone had shot him through the car door from the side of the road. His brother took him to the hospital.

I always found that Lucas's attitude about those days was like Nelson Mandela's; these events were in the past. He had moved on and embraced the new South Africa.

While he was at Leeds, Phil Masinga had been a lot more reserved than Lucas. My impression was that it took Phil a while to trust white people, even when he was in England. In one match back home, Lucas and Phil were on opposing sides. I got the feeling that they kicked seven bells out of each other. Phil said, 'Afterwards, some friends and I thought about going to look for Lucas to continue the fight.' But when Lucas and Phil arrived in England, I think they were glad of each other's company, and by that time they were both in the national squad together.

During the summer of 1999 I went to Gary Kelly's wedding in Ireland. Gary and his fiancée, Julie Anne, had invited most of the lads from Leeds and a few of his Irish international pals. I landed at Dublin airport and Kells had organised a lift for me to a B&B about five miles outside the wedding venue near Drogheda. I met Ian Harte's mum and dad at the airport; they were waiting for Ian, who had decided to fly over by jet from Manchester because of the plane crash the year before.

We met in a pub next to the church for an hour or so before the wedding. The ceremony was a Catholic mass. Gary and Julie Anne had laid on buses to take us to the reception a few miles away, but I got a lift from a lad called Nick Colgan, a goalkeeper who had played for a few clubs in England. We arrived at the reception around 4pm. I did not realise that there would be five hours of drinking before we sat down to eat. It went down well, and to say I had a bit to drink is an understatement. Most of the time, I sat with Shay Given and his girlfriend Jane, and I had a chat with Hartey's dad Pat. It was a great day.

* * *

In the summer, three Leeds players transferred to Bradford City: Lee Sharpe, David Wetherall and Gunnar Halle. I was sorry to see all of them leave as it had been great to work with them. At the start of the season, Leeds had an offer for Jimmy Floyd Hasselbaink from Atlético Madrid for around £12m. It was too good to refuse.

There were a few lasting things I remember about Jimmy. There used to be a saying in the American Great Depression, 'Another day, another dollar,' when a dollar was the rate for a day's work. One Friday at training, Jimmy came into the treatment room after doing an hour outside and said, with his deadpan style, 'Well lads, that's it for me today. Another day, another £4,000,' and walked out with a big smile on his face. We all had to laugh.

On the day of the sale, Jimmy came into the club for his boots and some shirts from Sean. In the morning paper it had been said that the club had some issues with him. I saw Jimmy and could tell he was a bit on edge about the report. But at that moment David O'Leary came round the corner, put his hand out and with a big smile said, 'Jimmy, £12m for you! We have just won the lottery. You can come back and train here any time you want.' Jimmy was like a block of ice that just melted, and that was how it should have been. He had been a great asset for the club and had scored some superb goals for us.

The new players that summer included Danny Mills, Michael Duberry and Danny Hay. While the first team were away for a midweek match against Southampton, I stayed behind to await the arrival of another signing, Darren Huckerby from Coventry. I was a bit surprised that Gordon Strachan was letting him leave. As Darren and I drove from the training ground at Thorp Arch to Elland Road, we stopped at the top of the slip road coming off the A1. While we were waiting to join the traffic, the car behind us hit my vehicle. It was not a serious bump but Hucks's first reaction was to grab his neck like he had whiplash. Straight away I said, 'Daz, are you okay?' He groaned but then smiled and said, 'Yes, mate, only kidding!' Fortunately, there was no damage to my car. I eventually got Daz through his medical. On that evening, our other new signing Michael Bridges scored a hat-trick.

We had a good run-up to Christmas, and in mid-December we made another signing, Jason Wilcox, a left-winger from Blackburn Rovers. He was a regular member of the Blackburn team that won the Premier League in 1995. Over time he was a great lad to have at the club, and his impersonations and funny tales made him a popular character. Underneath all the jesting he was a smart guy. As well as playing football for England, Jason was a black belt in judo and had competed at a national level.

Another signing we made was Danny Milosevic from Perth Glory, after he had been with us on trial. I found out that his father-in-law came from Bradford, and his surname was Wynn. I said to Danny, 'Ask your wife if her dad knows a lad called Malcolm Wynn.' Danny came back a few days later and told me Malcolm was his wife's uncle. Mally and I had played together for the Floodlit League in the 1960s in Bradford. Small world.

Early in 2000, we had a reserve game away against Liverpool at the St Helens rugby league ground. When we arrived back in Leeds, Michael Duberry and some of the other lads decided to let their hair down and went out in the city centre. We should have played Manchester United that weekend but they were in Brazil for for the Club World Cup. Later that night there was an incident outside the Majestyk nightclub involving Jonathan Woodgate, Lee Bowyer and Jonathan's friends. Other people who were there that night, including some of the other Leeds players, got involved. It would be the start of two court cases that would last all year.

We were doing well in the UEFA Cup. We played Roma again in the fourth round and this time we won 1-0 over two legs; Harry Kewell scored the goal. In the quarter-finals we beat Slavia Prague 4-1 on aggregate and then had to play Galatasaray in the semi-final. In the run-up we played well in the Premier League and many of our younger players were now permanent fixtures in the team.

We got through to the FA Cup fifth round after a great 5-2 away win at Manchester City, followed by a match at Aston Villa. Midway through the second half, Michael

Duberry had to go off the field to have a wound stitched. We had no doctor that day, so a young doctor from Villa sorted him out. The doc was more focused on talking about Villa's two goals, so I politely asked him to get on with it so that I could get Michael back on the pitch. Then their senior doctor, Dr Smith, whom I had last met when we had been in San Francisco on holiday at the same time, said to me, 'Have you got a minute, Alan?' I replied politely, 'Doc, I really do need to get Dubes back on the pitch.' He said, 'It will only take a few seconds.' I went over, thinking it must be important. To my surprise, he got out the photographs I had taken of him and his wife while we were on the boat to Alcatraz Island. I said through gritted teeth, 'Doc, they're great, but if I don't get him back on the field I am going to be in the s**t.' Dr Smith is a really nice guy; he once helped us out when we were in Birmingham and one of our players was taken ill, but on that day my patience was sorely tested.

Thursday, 6 April 2000 was a terrible day in Leeds United's history. The team were in Turkey for the UEFA Cup semi-final first leg against Galatasaray but the evening beforehand, two supporters who had travelled to watch their club were fatally stabbed in Istanbul. Their names were Christopher Loftus and Kevin Speight. I was at Elland Road when the news came through. I remember going to see our new secretary Ian Silvester, who had taken over from Nigel Pleasants, but the news was very patchy. As the days went on, what had happened on that night would have lasting repercussions.

We lost 2-0 in Turkey, and for the home leg two weeks later Galatasaray supporters were banned from travelling to Leeds. On the night we drew 2-2 with Eirik Bakke scoring both our goals.

Our last league game of the season was against West Ham United, and it was the first time we had been back to the Boleyn Ground since the plane crash the previous year. It was good to see their kit man, Eddie, and the manager Harry Redknapp again. I had a chat with Trevor Sinclair, their midfield player; his old manager at Blackpool, Billy Ayre, was my pal at Halifax Town. On the day all we had to do was match Liverpool's score and we would finish third in the Premier League to qualify for the following season's Champions League. I kept nipping down the tunnel to where Neil 'Razor' Ruddock, the ex-Liverpool player, was watching the Reds play at my old club Bradford City on the TV screens. City won 1-0 thanks to a goal from former Leeds player David Wetherall. We drew our game 0-0 and were through to the preliminary round qualifier for the Champions League group stages.

Leading up to that match at West Ham, David Batty and Jason Wilcox had injuries. David Swift sent Batts to France for treatment and I think Jason sorted out his own care. Jason missed out on the England squad for the Euro 2000 tournament. The day after the game, we made a new signing ready for the next season in the shape of former Everton player Olivier Dacourt from French club RC Lens for over £7m. A few of the younger lads had moved on to get more first-team football experience and make way for incoming players.

* * *

David Swift had brought in two more physios, Mark Nile as his number two and Tim Williamson to work with the academy. I was there to chip in as needed. At the end of July, David O'Leary watched some of our injured players taking part in one of my running sessions. He asked me, 'Do you know David Fevre, the physio at Blackburn Rovers?' I told him that I did and thought nothing more of the conversation.

A week or so later while we were in the office, Swifty said, for the first time, he would take the outside session. I wasn't sure what the players might think. Shortly afterwards, I saw him walk past the treatment room with Eddie Gray following on behind. Five minutes later, Swifty passed the treatment room again. Then, while I was on my own in the treatment room, David O'Leary walked in and said, 'I want you to be the first to know that I have just sacked David Swift.'

The next day, the new head physio arrived; it was Dave Hancock from Blackburn Rovers. The last time I had seen Dave was after our FA Cup quarter-final against Wolves. The only way I can describe his arrival that first week in August 2000 was like being in a whirlwind crossed with a tornado. Dave brought the players in for treatment until at least 5pm and for many hours on Saturdays and Sundays to get them fit as quickly as possible. It was no problem for me, but I think some of the other lads found it hard at first. The players moaned, but it was the way things were going to be.

I remember Dave's first Saturday when we had a pre-season game away at Huddersfield Town. He said to me, 'I'll stay here with the injured players; you go with the team to do the game.' When I returned after the match, he was still there working. The next match was in midweek at Dave's old club, Blackburn. When we arrived Dave and I got everything sorted out. Then I spoke to Dave Fevre. He told me what had happened over the past few weeks. He said that he had met with the manager and Peter Ridsdale and had been offered the role as head physio. To my surprise, he also said that he had been told that if he took the job, I had to remain part of the physio team. Dave said that he had to turn it down, but instead he recommended Dave Hancock. I still think about those words even today; the club still wanted me there despite all the changes.

In addition to Olivier Dacourt, the other early signings were Mark Viduka from Celtic for £6m and Dominic Matteo from Liverpool for £5m. As the weeks went by we had some excellent results, and everyone got into the groove of the new setup. Mark had been injured at the end of the previous season while at Celtic. He had been on his boat in Croatia for the summer. When he arrived at Thorp Arch he had not done any rehab, so the boss said to me, 'I want you to take him for a run while we go with the rest of the guys to Roundhay Park.' After they had gone, I asked Mark if he had done any training at all, but he had not done a thing. I don't know if he managed one lap or two that day, but that was all. I told the boss, and he arranged with Ed Baranowski to set up some running programmes for Mark, who gradually improved as a result. After a few weeks, when he was back to fitness he proved that he would be a great player for the club.

In August the lads involved in the Leeds nightclub incident were sent for trial. I had provided a character reference for one of them, Tony Hackworth. Tony had major knee surgery a few months before the night concerned and I knew it would be hard for him to run after anyone. In the end, the judge decided he had no case to answer.

In pre-season another coach joined us, the former Celtic and Scotland captain Roy Aitken. Roy had played against us while at Newcastle United in the 1989/90 season when they just missed out on promotion, and we won the Second Division championship.

I travelled with Roy and the reserve team many times in the 2000/01 season. I remember Roy telling me about the day he made his debut for Celtic at the tender age of 16 years old, when he was still at school. The manager at the time was the legendary Jock Stein, who had spent 44 days at Leeds in 1978 before taking the Scotland job. Roy told me he had not been fazed when he was in the dressing room with the older guys, but his abiding memory had been the following Monday back at school. Roy said the pupils were in the hall for assembly and the headmaster announced at the end, 'I want to see Aitken in my study.' Roy continued, 'I went to his office with my heart in my mouth, wondering what I had done now. The headmaster told me to sit down. He looked at me and then asked, "Aitken, what was it like being in the dressing room with the Celtic team?" I realised then he must be a massive Celtic supporter, so I told him everything. At the end of the season Jock Stein told me, "You have two choices. You either come to this club full-time, or you get yourself another club." Roy said to me, "You don't turn down Celtic Football Club, so I signed up, and I had a great time there."' Roy became a legend at Celtic and became known to all the fans as 'The Bear'.

Before starting the season, we had to play 1860 Munich in a qualifying game over two legs to get into the Champions League group stages. Shortly before kick-off at the first leg, at home, one of their players came up to me and said, 'You don't remember me, do you?' When he introduced himself as Ned Zelic, I remembered immediately. He had been on trial at Leeds ten or so years earlier. He was a good player even then; Mick Hennigan had rung him every day in Australia in an attempt to persuade him to come to Leeds, but in the end he went to Germany. We had a quick chat. Ned was sent off that night in the first leg, so he didn't play in the return in Germany.

Talking of trials at Leeds, another player who came to us once was Sami Hyypiä, the Finnish centre-back who later played for Liverpool. He was in our treatment room waiting for drug testing after a game, and when I said hello he asked me, 'Do you recall when I was here as a young lad in the Howard Wilkinson days for a couple of weeks' trial?' What he went on to say tied in with everything about those days. He arrived on the day of a first-team game and watched the match with some of the other players in one of the boxes in the stand. They were serving fish and chips, so he thought 'so far so good'. After the game he was taken into the dressing room and introduced to everyone, and then somebody threw him a training kit. He said, 'I thought to myself, "What's happening now?"' But I knew what was coming, and by now, I was laughing as he continued to tell me his story. Sami went on, 'I was told we were going to do a 12-minute run around the track.' Then he pointed outside. 'If you look out of the tunnel to the far corner of the ground, that's where I was sick after the big plate of fish and chips I had just eaten.' When I spoke to Mick Hennigan he didn't remember Sami, but we had so many players coming in for trials in Wilko's day.

We beat 1860 Munich 2-1 in the first leg. Alan Smith and Ian Harte scored. In the second leg we won again 1-0 with another goal from Alan, and we were through to the group stages with Barcelona, AC Milan and Besiktas.

At our home league game against Liverpool in November 2000, it was good to see Gary McAllister back at Elland Road. At the end of the previous season Gary had popped into our coaches' room. He had told us then that he was leaving Coventry and had been offered a chance to be a squad player and help bring the young players through at a big club, but he did not reveal which club had made him the offer. At 35, Gary was still an excellent player and would be an asset to Liverpool. On the day we won 4-3, with Mark Viduka scoring all four goals.

In the Champions League, our first match was away against Barcelona. Dave Hancock and I went to do the game, but we got a bit of a hammering and lost 4-0. Lucas Radebe had to spend the night in hospital, so I went with him accompanied by a security guard. Barcelona sent one of their staff to make sure we were looked after.

Our next fixture was at home to AC Milan. By this time the Woodgate/Bowyer trial had started, so they came to the match straight from court. At 5pm I got them their pre-match meal, and they got on with the game. It had been raining most of the day. Dom Matteo, who was injured when he joined us from Liverpool during the summer, made his debut that night. A last-minute shot by Lee Bowyer was fumbled by their goalkeeper and rolled into the back of the net for our first win.

Then we were at home against Besiktas. We won 6-0; Mark Viduka got his first goal for the club and Lee Bowyer scored another two. Despite the trial, he was playing out of his skin. Three weeks later we drew 0-0 away to the Turkish side in what had been an excellent start to our Champions League run.

Our next game in the tournament was at home to Barcelona. The day beforehand, Nigel Martyn came to see me in the gym. He told me he had just had a call from Liz, who used to work at the club and was now working in PR with the Australian national rugby league team. They had just arrived in Leeds with my former coach at Halifax RL, Chris Anderson, who was now coaching the Australians. Liz asked me to call him at the Queen's Hotel. When I did he said, 'Hi Al, any chance of a couple of tickets for your game tomorrow night?' It was a sell-out, but I managed to get him two tickets at the front next to the track, not fantastic seats but the best I could do. When I told him he said, 'I don't care where they are. That's great.'

Chris was there with Brad Fittler, one of the world's best rugby players, known by his nickname Freddie. I had seen him on TV a few times. When I looked across at them both during the match, they were joining in with the Leeds supporters. We drew 1-1. Lee Bowyer scored again and the Brazilian Rivaldo got Barcelona's equaliser in the 90th minute. At our last game away at AC Milan we needed one point, and Dom Matteo delivered for us in another 1-1 draw. We were through to the second group stage along with AC Milan, and Barcelona missed out.

Later that week I went to see Chris and his backroom staff at the Queen's Hotel. I met their physio, Tony Ayoub. Over the years, Tony and I have remained great friends. With David O'Leary's permission, I invited the Australian team to our training ground at Thorp Arch. As well as Freddie Fittler, Australia had some great players, including Andrew Johns, Brett Kimmorley, Matt Rogers, Adam McDougall and Darren Lockyer. I think they enjoyed watching the boys training and meeting our Australian contingent at Leeds.

Nigel Martyn was recovering from injury, and on that day I took him out to do a bit of ball handling. As we walked towards our second pitch, carrying the bag of balls, I looked up to see that Nigel was walking along with Gordon Tallis, a prop for the Aussie team. That Friday was BBC Children in Need day and unbeknown to me, Gordon had offered £20 to the charity if he could score a penalty against Nigel. Of course, Nigel could not resist the challenge. As I was bending down to get the rest of the balls out of the bag, Gordon swiftly took the penalty, and Nigel flew across the goal like Peter Pan. The next moment, my **** of a goalkeeper said, 'Sutts, I think I have re-injured myself.' At first I thought he was kidding, but then I realised he was serious. My first thought was, 'What am I going to tell Dave Hancock?' I can't remember what 'we' said, but I think one person who may have had a sly smile was Paul Robinson. He got another run in the first team thanks to Nigel and the £20 bet.

It was good to spend some time with Chris Anderson, who was now in charge of one of the World Cup's best teams and the favourites to win the competition. A week before the Rugby League World Cup Final, Leeds invited the Australian squad to watch our home game against West Ham United, where we lost 1-0. A few days afterwards we signed Rio Ferdinand for around £18m, and later that year, Robbie Keane for £12m.

Going to Elland Road for home games seemed a bit strange at times as Leeds had taken on so many new staff. One day I asked someone in the corridor what her job was; her reply was something like, 'I am the secretary to the secretary's secretary.' It reminded me of the old days with Bradford Corporation when you had one man digging a hole and three men watching. I remember Gordon Strachan and Mervyn Day visiting the club around this time, and both of them said the same thing, 'Sutts, you're the first person I've seen that I know here.' The close-knit, family atmosphere I had known when I had first started at Leeds was long gone.

After the West Ham match we had our first game in the Champions League second group stage, at home to Real Madrid. The other teams in the group were Lazio and Anderlecht. At the Madrid fixture I was in the tunnel as their squad arrived. Their captain, Fernando Hierro, came across and, smiling broadly, shook my hand. He remembered me from Euro '96 when Spain had been based at Elland Road and I looked after the medical and dressing rooms. On the night we lost 2-0, and Fernando was one of the scorers.

That weekend was the Rugby League World Cup Final at Old Trafford, where Australia beat New Zealand 40-12. The day after, on my way to Elland Road for our game against Arsenal, I called in at the Queen's Hotel to congratulate Chris and the rest of the boys on their victory. As they had just done a drinking 'through', they were all a bit worse for wear. Adam McDougall and I exchanged telephone numbers and kept in touch over the next year or so. As for our match against Arsenal, we won 1-0.

A week or so later we were on our way to Rome to play Lazio in the Champions League. The club hired a private plane for the 90-minute flight. When Dave Hancock took over as head physio, he decided that all the other physios would take turns accompanying him to a game, and I had a reason for wanting to go on this trip. When we arrived we agreed that Dave would look after the players that afternoon, and I would cover the next day while he went to Lazio's training ground.

The Doc, Tom O'Shea, and I had arranged to go to St Peter's Square to visit the Basilica and the Vatican. Just as we were about to set off, Eddie Gray and Roy Aitken decided to join us. The taxi driver told us he was a Leeds fan and that his favourite player was Eddie Gray; he did not have a clue that Eddie was sitting next to me in the back of the car.

At St Peter's Square, I gave Shirley a call to tell her where I was; it had been my mum's dream to visit the Vatican. Eddie, Roy and Tom were gesturing at me not to use my mobile phone, so I nipped behind a pillar. When I caught them up, they chastised me, 'Alan, you're in St Peter's Square!'

Inside the Vatican it was a jubilee year when the Holy Door, or Porta Sancta, was open. It was a special time to be there. While we were in the queue the woman next to us took out her mobile phone. I protested to the guys, 'I thought you told me I couldn't use my phone!' and was swiftly silenced by one of the Swiss guards. When we eventually got inside, they said to me in exasperation, 'We can't take you anywhere!'

It was a fascinating tour. We went into the crypt at St Peter's Basilica, where the papal tombs are located. Years later, the Catholic priest Father Steve, who visited the club and had worked in the Vatican for a few years, explained all about the Holy Doors. Steve sometimes played football with us on a Tuesday afternoon. He wasn't a bad player.

That evening, we had a police escort as made our way to train at Roma's stadium. As we tried to negotiate one of the narrow streets, a car had blocked the road. The police officers jumped from their motorbikes and bounced the car out of the way. God knows how much damage there was to the vehicle.

On the day of the game, we had a walk around the city zoo for some relaxation. Lazio, under Sven-Göran Eriksson, were a formidable team. It was one of Sven's last games before he took over the England manager's job. We played out of our skin and won 1-0; Smithy scored. Mark Viduka was up against Alessandro Nesta, the Italian international. He had an outstanding game and there was a lot of interest in Mark after his display that night.

After the match we enjoyed a glass of wine back at the hotel, and I went to bed around 1.30pm. But my night was not over just yet. Around four hours later my phone rang and straight away I thought it was someone with a problem. It was, but not what I had anticipated. It was Ian Harte. He said, 'Sutts, who were the first two brothers to play for Manchester United?' After telling him I had not got a clue and slamming down the phone, I went to sleep for a couple of hours. The following day I met Kevin, our security man, getting out of the lift. He said to me, 'Al, did you get a call from Ian Harte early this morning?' I nodded and he continued, 'Sorry about that, he and Lee Bowyer wanted to go for something to eat at McDonald's, so I said if they could answer that quiz question, I would take them into town.'

Back in Leeds, one Saturday morning Nicky Byrne from Westlife came to the training ground to see the lads. Nicky had been an academy goalkeeper a few years earlier in his career. He said, 'Don't let Glado know I am here; I will call back on Monday and surprise her.' He meant Gladys Smith, who worked in the canteen with Isabelle. She had a soft spot for Nicky and looked after him when he first came over from Ireland as a homesick youngster. That morning he asked me, 'Sutts, any chance of getting me some kit and gloves?' As it turned out, his best pal Alan Maybury and one of the keepers were doing a shooting session, so Nicky came out to join us. He had arrived wearing his best gear and had left it in the changing room. After 15 minutes or so we heard a shout. It was Gary Kelly dressed in Nicky's clothes. Nicky put his head in his hands. He had an idea what was going to happen and could only watch helplessly, as Gary did a 'Klinsmann' dive straight through a large pool of water. There was never a dull moment with the Irish lads.

While talking about Kells, his mischievous side was a feature at our Christmas parties. Everyone at the club from the chairman down was invited to the festivities; hundreds of people were in attendance, and no expense was spared. One Christmas the theme was Hawaii so the room was decked out in palm trees and exotic flowers, complete with a stream that wound its way between the tables. Kells and Robby Keane both offered one of the young Irish academy lads £100 if he would dive into the water in front of everyone. It was a large sum of money for the young apprentice, and encouraged by his heroes, he found it hard to say no. We watched as he threw himself in the stream and was immediately and unceremoniously dragged out by his collar and marched outside by the security staff. I think the chairman saw the funny side, and the young player was soon allowed back at his table, wet through. I hope he got his money.

In February 2001 we played Anderlecht in the next group stage game. At home we won 2-1 after being a goal down; Lee Bowyer, who was still travelling to Hull for the court case, scored one of our goals. The Anderlecht supporters were quick to say that we had been lucky. They had not been beaten at home in Europe for more than 20 matches but over in Belgium we beat them 4-1. We lost 3-2 away at Real Madrid and drew 3-3 at home to Lazio, all of which was enough to get us through to the quarter-finals.

The Woodgate/Bowyer court case had almost finished when a tabloid newspaper printed a story that caused the trial to collapse. The newspaper was judged to be in contempt of court, and a retrial was arranged for later in the year.

In the quarter-finals of the Champions League we played the Spanish team Deportivo La Coruña and won 3-0 at home but lost 2-0 in the away leg, so we went through to the semi-final 3-2 on aggregate and then met a strong Valencia side at home. The referee was the world-class Pierluigi Collina. I was always asked to give the ref a massage before a game, and I enjoyed chatting with him. We drew 0-0 at Elland Road but when we arrived in Spain for the second leg, UEFA told us that Lee Bowyer had been suspended for an incident in the previous game. It was just not our night and we lost 3-0, ending our excellent cup run.

Despite winning nine of our last 11 Premier League matches we finished fourth and missed out on a Champions League place. However, we were in the UEFA Cup for the 2001/02 season.

Behind the scenes at Thorp Arch, Brian Kidd from Manchester United had been brought in to run the academy. Andy Welsh came with him along with Bryan 'Pop' Robson, the ex-Newcastle and West Ham player. He also brought Warren Joyce, the former Hull City manager, and Steve McGregor to do the fitness work. By the 2001 pre-season, Steve and Brian would be working with the first team.

As for Elland Road, the chairman Peter Ridsdale was going full steam ahead with many changes. There was always a new face whenever I went down there, but thankfully, some familiar faces like Katie Holmes, Mandy and Tracey were still in the ticket office.

8

DECLINE

Pre-season was nicely under way when I received a surprise telephone call. I'd had the afternoon off to play in a golf tournament organised by the Bradford Bulls rugby league club in Cookridge. As I was getting in my car to head home my mobile rang; it was Dave Hancock. He said, 'Sutts, the manager wants you to come with us tomorrow instead of Mark Nile on our ten-day tour of Sweden.' Mark was the number two at the club's physio department, and David O'Leary had asked Dave, 'Why are the number one and number two physios both going to Sweden? Surely Mark has to stay behind to look after the injured players?' My first thought was, 'Oh no! Shirley is going to kill me!' We had a party arranged that weekend for our 30th wedding anniversary. So I went to Sweden while Shirley had a great time at the party without me. We played three games and spent a day at a funfair in Gothenburg, and then it was back home to resume training.

We had a solid start to the season, losing only two of our first 21 games. We had signed Seth Johnson from Derby County and Robbie Fowler from Liverpool. The first time I had to deal with Robbie, I asked him if he was good at football quizzes. He was up for some questions, so I gave him a few of my middle-of-the-road ones to try out. I said to him, 'We will see if you are Premier League or Vauxhall Conference with your answers.' It was one way of breaking the ice with new players. I always got on well with Robbie, and he was not a bad quizzer either.

In early September, three days after our home match against Bolton, we were at Thorp Arch. Early that afternoon we heard that a plane had crashed into the North Tower of the World Trade Center in New York. We were unsure what was happening, but shortly afterwards when one of the young lads who worked in the office told us that a second plane had crashed into the other tower, we realised that it could not have been an accident. We gathered around the television and watched as the dreadful scenes unfolded.

Shortly afterwards, I travelled with Michael Bridges to Germany to see Hans-Wilhelm Müller-Wohlfahrt, the orthopaedic surgeon, about an injury problem. Michael also took his girlfriend Katie with him. Bridgey had been an excellent signing for Leeds but he was very unlucky with injuries. We flew via Copenhagen to Munich. At the airport, security was very tight and I could not carry my bag on the plane; the next time I saw it was ten days later, back home as it got lost somewhere in transit. When we met with Mr Müller-Wohlfahrt, he suggested that Michael see another orthopaedic surgeon, Richard Steadman, in Colorado, which eventually he did, accompanied by Mark Nile. We were there for a couple of days, and on the last day we had a quick drink in the Hofbräuhaus and then made our way to the airport, only to find our flight was cancelled until the next day. I was still wearing the same clothes I had travelled in. That evening I think my shirt just stood up on its own in the room. The next day, when I arrived back at Leeds Bradford, at least I had some luck; my car keys were still in my pocket and fortunately I had not left them in the missing bag.

In early November 2001 the Australian rugby league team were back in town to play three Tests against Great Britain. During the last year I had been in regular contact with Adam McDougall. He and a few others from the World Cup-winning team, such as Brad Fittler and Andrew Johns, were still in the squad, but a few had dropped out not wanting to fly after what had happened in America a couple of months before, so it was now a young team. A couple of other players I had got to know last time were Brett Kimmorley and Robbie Kearns. I talked to Adam one day; he told me that he and Andrew Johns had watched one of our games while they were in Australia. Adam said that when Alan Smith got the ball, 'Joey' Johns would say, 'Go on, Smithy, pal. Get yourself a goal!' I asked Smithy if he knew Andrew. He reminded me that he had met him a few times to say hello.

After a week in the UK, Australia played their first match at the John Smith's Stadium in Huddersfield, where they lost to Great Britain. Chris was still the coach and had given me six tickets, so my nephew Philip, Alan Smith and his friend Longman and two young Australians from Leeds United, Jamie McMaster and Shane Cansdell-Sherriff, went with me to watch the game. While we were there I met up with Chris and Tony Ayoub, their physio. After the game I managed to get us into the players' lounge. Andrew Johns walked in and came to join us. His first words to Alan Smith were, 'Smithy, get your mortgage on us to win our match next week.'

After each game Chris would let his players off the leash for a few days; they had all had a hard season back home, so Smithy and Johnsy met up most nights that week. Johnsy was rat-arsed every night, but Alan is a teetotaller. Every morning, Smithy came into the treatment room shaking his head and saying the same thing, 'What?! Put my mortgage on them to win? After the state of Johnsy last night, I don't think so!'

At the next game at Bolton's ground, Australia battered Great Britain 40-12 and Johnsy was the star player. Smithy was straight on the phone telling me what he thought of

Johnsy, 'Hey, what a great guy that Johnsy is, and he's a great player as well!' Smithy loved people who backed up what they said, even if they did like a drink.

In the final test at Wigan, Australia ran away with it again and won 28-8. It would be Brad Fittler and Andrew Johns's last tour with the Kangaroos. Adam McDougall did not tour again but he gave me a signed shirt which is now in Australia with my grandchildren, Alex and Seb. Adam visited Pateley Bridge and had his photograph taken with a few of the rugby league locals. The Australian team also had their usual day at our training ground at Thorp Arch; even Rio Ferdinand had his photo taken wearing an Australian shirt. Most of the Australian lads had Leeds United shirts on.

Also in November, the Woodgate/Bowyer retrial commenced. Jonathan Woodgate's defence team asked me if I would be a witness. The trial was in Hull so the club paid for me to stay in a hotel the night before and I remember watching a great game on TV, Charlton Athletic versus West Ham United, which finished 4-4. The next day at court I gave my testimony, and Lee Bowyer's lawyer also asked me a few questions. Weeks later, Lee was acquitted and Woody got 100 hours of community service. Despite the pressure, Lee played better than ever during the trials. It took Woody some time to get himself right again but he went on to play for some great clubs.

We had an away game over the Christmas period at Southampton, and on New Year's Day 2002 Leeds went to the top of the Premier League with a home win against West Ham. We then had the FA Cup third round away at Cardiff. Cardiff have always been a bogey team for Leeds and this game was no different. Alan Smith was sent off, and unsurprisingly for any Leeds fan, we lost 2-1.

In the UEFA Cup we got through the first three rounds, and in February 2002 we were up against PSV Eindhoven, drawing 0-0 in the Netherlands. In the return leg at Elland Road, I was surprised to discover that they still had the same kit man I had met at our previous home game in 1995. I had another great chat with him. On the night we lost 1-0, so that was the end of our European campaign for another season.

In March 2002 we found out that 'Mr Halifax Town', Tony Thwaites, had died. He was a lovely man and had raised a lot of money for his beloved club. Just a month after Tony died, Billy Ayre, who had been so good to me when I first went to Halifax Town, passed away after a long illness. He was just 49 years old. Bobby Davison and I met up and went to both funerals to pay our respects to two great guys.

It is still a surprise to many people that we finished fifth in the Premier League that season, especially as we were top of the table at the beginning of the year, but we did manage to qualify for the UEFA Cup once more.

One Friday lunchtime at the end of the season, Ian Broomfield, the chief scout, was sitting on a bike in sports gear pretending to do a workout. Don't get me wrong, Ian was a great guy to have around. He had quite a few of the academy lads with him and I could see that they were laughing and looking at me. I asked one of the lads what was going on. He told me that Ian had been taking the piss out of my swimming technique. We had recently installed a new gym and a 25m swimming pool for the academy, and I had been doing a lot of swimming with the injured players. Dave Hancock had a lot of input into improving the facilities; they'd had the same setup at his previous club, Blackburn Rovers. I went to Ian and said, 'Right! Off the bike. You and me in the pool, let's see what you're made of!' At the time I had no idea if he could swim, but he was still smiling and laughing as we got changed.

When we got to the water, some of the kids and staff came to watch us. Ian was a big lad, so I was banking on him not being too fit. I told him, 'We're going to race four lengths of the pool. We'll do the first length front crawl, the second breaststroke, the third backstroke and the last front crawl again.' I was surprised when he agreed to it.

For the first length I expected him to keep level with me. The breaststroke had been my speciality at school, so I started to pull away, and by the backstroke I was already half a length ahead of him. Then, when Ian turned for his third length, he sank and had to be fished out of the pool. I finished the last stretch on my own, to the cheers of those watching at the side. Steve McGregor, who was in charge of fitness at the time, and our new physio, Harvey Sharman, were also looking on. I knew better than to take them on in a challenge. I first met Harvey when I had run a Treatment of Injuries course at Shipley Library in 1994. He had since become a good physio and became even better as time went on.

As for Ian, I think he was sick in the toilets and blamed it on having a big lunch. The mickey-taking and the laughter afterwards were great. Years later, Ian went to work for Aston Villa. At one of our games, I was chatting with Doug Ellis, Villa's chairman, when Ian came walking towards us. Of course, I could not resist joking, 'Mr Chairman, I see you have got Captain Webb working for you now.' Ian just smiled and said, 'Thanks, Sutts.' It was always great to meet up with him, and we always remained great friends.

In the summer of 2002 Shirley and I went to South Africa for a holiday. Lucas Radebe had arranged for him and me to do some soccer coaching together in one of the townships, but at the last moment the Chief was called to South Africa's World Cup squad, so I met him briefly at his hotel before the team flew out to Japan.

During our time in Johannesburg I accompanied Glynn, Lucas's manager, to a local hospital while he visited one of the other players he looked after. While we were there I had a chat with Mr Ferguson, the orthopaedic surgeon. Then Glynn said, 'I've told Phil Masinga that you're over here, and he wants to see you.' Phil had travelled an hour and a half to catch up with me; it was great to meet him again.

Shirley and I also went with Glynn to one of the local townships. While we were on our way I shared my memories of Lucas's spell at Leeds and about the time he was sent off against Everton in April 1998. I told Glynn, 'It was one of the funniest things I had seen. The game was at Goodison Park and Uriah Rennie was the referee. After Lucas tackled one of the Everton players, they both ended up on the ground injured. We had to get the stretcher on for Lucas. As they carried him off the referee said to Lucas, "Just in case you are thinking about coming back on, don't bother!" and showed him the red card. It was the first and only time I had ever seen anyone sent off at the same time as they were carried off. I can still picture it today and laugh about it.' Glynn and I did some football coaching with some of the kids and had lunch with them; they put on a great spread.

On the way home we hit a patch of bad weather as we were flying out of Johannesburg. The back of the plane was struck by lightning, and although the cabin crew did not seem too worried, it was not helpful for my blood pressure.

* * *

Because Leeds finished fifth in the Premier League, the board decided to sack David O'Leary, so Brian Kidd and Eddie Gray took charge of the team for our ten-day pre-season tour of China, Melbourne and Bangkok. Our new manager, ex-Tottenham and England boss Terry Venables, joined us in Melbourne. Before we set off, Nigel Martyn, who had just returned from the World Cup in Japan and South Korea, decided he did not want to travel. David Batty did not fancy the long flight either, so he stayed behind.

The word was going around that Leeds United had a lot of debt. On our flight from London to Hong Kong I sat in business class with our club doctor, Tom O'Shea. The directors were in first class. As well as Tom and me, Dave Hancock, Clive Brown, Sean Hardy, Steve Sutton, the goalkeeping coach and Ian Silvester, the club secretary, were also on the trip.

After landing in Hong Kong we had a three-hour flight to China. We trained in 35°C heat and played a game against Greentown FC, managed by the British coach Bob Houghton. We moved on to Melbourne and with six Australian players on the trip, the press were keen to talk to us, especially Mark Viduka and Harry Kewell. We stayed at the Crown Casino on the Yarra River in the city centre; we were told that Will Smith and Tommy Lee Jones had been there the week before. It was a great hotel with a big shopping centre next door. Mark was in good form and happy to be back in his home town. We trained at the ground of his favourite Aussie Rules team, Collingwood. Mick Malthouse was the coach there and Gary Swan was the general manager; I had met them both a couple of years earlier at our training ground at Thorp Arch. It was the Australian winter and very cold, a shock to the system after the heat in China.

Later that day I was standing at the hotel reception when the new Leeds manager Terry Venables arrived. Lee Bowyer also joined us that day; I think he had been in talks with Liverpool about a possible move, but it did not come off. In Melbourne, Terry met with Australian football player Paul Okon. He had worked with him when he was in charge of Middlesbrough and Paul became Venables' first signing for Leeds.

After training the next day, Robbie Kearns, who had been on the last Kangaroos tour and played rugby league for Melbourne Storm, came to the hotel with his young son to meet Mark Viduka, Jacob Burns and Alan Smith. Later that day Adam McDougall and his girlfriend Belinda travelled from Sydney to watch our game against Colo-Colo from Chile on Saturday night. That evening, while everyone else watched an Aussie rules game at the Melbourne Cricket Ground, I had dinner with Adam and Belinda.

We beat Colo-Colo 1-0 at the Colonial Stadium with a goal from Harry Kewell. Afterwards we were straight to the airport for a flight to Bangkok, where we trained and played another match. On the trip, I felt that some of the directors lived in another world to the rest of us. At the airport I watched as one of them signed an autograph book as if he were one of the players.

Back at the training ground for the rest of pre-season, Rio had left for Manchester United; it had been great to have him around the place. I will never forget one Saturday when I had to treat him, Michael Duberry, Eirik Bakke and Wes Boyle. The week before when Dave Hancock was in charge, it had all kicked off, so I arranged a meeting the day before to let them know how the day would pan out, to make sure we were all singing from the same hymn sheet. We got through the day without too much hassle. I organised a quiz and some bacon sandwiches to relieve the monotony, and we had a bit of laughter along the way. The players were all brilliant doing their six-hour session of rehab work.

Another signing arrived alongside Paul Okon: Hull boy Nick Barmby from Liverpool. As time went on I found that Nick was a great professional with a fantastic work ethic. He had been part of the England team that had famously won 5-1 against Germany in Munich in 2001. In August we signed Swedish international Teddy Lučić from Aik

Solna. Teddy's dad was from Croatia, and his mum was from Finland, so he had a bit in common with Mark Viduka with his Croatian-Australian heritage.

Robbie Keane was on his way out of Elland Road to Tottenham. He would be the first of many players to leave over the next few months as the effects of overspending started to kick in, as someone said, not only with players but with overstaffing throughout the club.

At the start of the season, Venables had decided that David Batty would not be a part of his team, so he told Batts to keep himself fit and pop into the club from time to time. Venables also left Nigel Martyn out because he had not travelled with us for pre-season, and Paul Robinson became the first-choice goalkeeper.

We got off to a good start, winning four of our first six games. However, in the next 11 we lost eight, drew two and won only one, away to West Ham United. James Milner, just 16 years old, made his debut as a sub that day. I had first come across James when he was about 13 years old. After being 4-1 up we scraped over the line to win 4-3, and James was soon a bright spark in increasingly gloomy times at the club.

Into the new year, the club's debts were getting out of control so in January Leeds sold Lee Bowyer to West Ham and Jonathan Woodgate went to Bobby Robson's team, Newcastle United. Woody was gutted about his move and came to see me. I said to him, 'Make sure you get off to a good start at your new club. Remember, when you are doing your interviews, think about how you feel having to leave Leeds and the fans who have been great to you through thick and thin. Then say what a fantastic club you are going to and how great their fans are.' I knew if he had spoken to Batts or Speedo, they would have advised the same. In early February 2003 Robbie Fowler went to Manchester City and by then, Olivier Dacourt had already moved to Roma. Looking back, it was like watching a falling pack of cards.

I cast my mind back to the early days of the David O'Leary era. There had been some funny moments, like the time Jonathan Woodgate was in a pub in Middlesbrough and decided to buy a decrepit car parked outside for twice its value. It was a three-wheeler like the one in the comedy series *Only Fools and Horses*. Somehow Woody got it down to Elland Road and it became a tradition that on a Friday before a home game, whoever was awarded the yellow shirt for being the worst player that day had to drive the car into the club on matchday. The lads thought it helped foster the team spirit and they all chipped in £100 each. By now the press knew about it, and so did the fans. The players kept the car in a shed next to the ground. I think Ian Harte was the first to drive it to the club having parked his own car in the shed while plenty of fans waited to see who had got the vote.

In the UEFA Cup, our first match was against Metalurh Zaporizhya of Ukraine. We won 1-0 at home and drew 1-1 away. We stayed 20 miles or so outside of Chernobyl, where the nuclear disaster had taken place in 1986; the area still looked very bare. There were security guards on every floor of our very basic hotel.

In the next round we played Hapoel Tel Aviv and won 1-0 at home. The away game had to be held in Florence and we won 4-1 with Alan Smith scoring all four goals. But before the end of 2002 we played Malaga and drew 0-0 away then were beaten 1-0 at home. Other than pre-season friendlies, Leeds haven't played in European competition since that second leg. By now the fancy planes were long gone, but it had been a great few years.

After our mini-run of four wins and a draw over the Christmas period, we lost six of the next eight games, drew one and won one. After our home loss against Middlesbrough, Terry Venables left. We had sold a lot of our best players and he could not do much more.

In the treatment room we were trying to keep everyone's spirits up. My nickname at the club with some players was 'Sausage Fingers' because of my short, stubby hands, but I also have strong wrists from my days in the building trade, so when I massaged some of the players the others would say, 'Get those sausages in, Sutts.' Of course, it was only a matter of time before I would fall victim to a practical joke. One day, one of the other physios said, 'Sutts, if I were you, I would look at your car.' In those days I had a club car like just about everyone else who worked there. When I checked it, they had completely covered my car in sausages. After all the laughter, Dave Hancock made sure they cleaned it up. The lads at that time had so much money that they thought nothing of spending £55 on sausages. As Claire and Margaret in the laundry told me, 'I wish they would throw some of that money our way!' It was half a week's wages for them.

Within 24 hours of Venables leaving, in walked Peter Reid as the new manager. He had about eight games left to keep us in the Premier League. The first thing he asked was, 'Where is David Batty?' When Batts was back at the club, Peter told him, 'Right, we have got Liverpool at Anfield on Sunday, and you are in midfield.' As Batts told me later, his response was, 'Gaffer, I have not kicked a ball in months; there is no way I could play against Steven Gerrard and the Liverpool midfield.' The gaffer told Batts that he would be travelling to the game and could be on the bench. When David came to see us in the treatment room, his first words were, 'Who has appointed him? It means I have got to start playing football again!' At 34 years old, David had been seeing out his contract by having a relaxing time at his caravan in Filey on the east coast. We lost 3-1 but the new manager got into the team spirit going over to Liverpool. He asked me to do a quiz on the coach, which got a few laughs from everybody.

About a week later there was another bombshell as Peter Ridsdale, the chairman, resigned with his now infamous words, 'We lived the dream.' He forgot to say that the rest of us would have to live with the nightmare, not just us in the medical team but also the girls in the canteen, the office staff, the ticket office and all the people who had worked there for years before he had arrived.

It was now starting to look like we had a revolving door at the training ground at Thorp Arch. Tim Williamson, Jeff Clarke and Steve Kemp had all come and gone as academy physios in a few months. Clive Brown and Mark Nile also left our department and were replaced by Harvey Sharman, who moved into a senior role. Dave Hancock's friend Bruce Craven, who had a Sports Science degree, came in to do massaging. Bruce, or 'Bonus' as he was fondly named, turned out to be a great lad.

On the coaching side, Peter Reid brought in Kevin Blackwell, who had worked with Neil Warnock at Sheffield United, and a fitness coach, Dean Riddle. I knew Dean from back in Howard Wilkinson's era, when he would watch our pre-season training.

With seven matches to go our next task was away at Charlton Athletic. What I remember most was not just meeting up with the assistant manager Mervyn Day again, nor our 6-1 win when Mark Viduka scored a hat-trick, but the journey back home. The boss said to the staff, 'Right, let's get the wine and the beers out.' Sean Hardy said, 'Sorry, but we have not had any booze on the coach for years.' So while we were still driving through London, Peter said to the coach driver, 'Stop at the next supermarket.' Then he shouted for Dom Matteo, the captain. Peter said, 'Dom, there's my credit card; you and some of the other lads, go and get us something to drink. This club has got to be a happy club after that result.' He was right about that with everything else that was going on.

I was sitting with Alan Smith and some of the other lads for the long journey back home. While we were talking, they asked me about my life in the building trade. I said, 'I know you won't believe this,' and then I told them about the time in January 1981 when I was in a cafe having a pot of tea and a bacon sandwich with a plasterer friend, Jack Halliday. We ordered our breakfast and I had a look at the morning paper. The police had just announced that they had caught the Yorkshire Ripper. I said, 'Jack, the guy is called Sutcliffe, and they are saying that he once lived on your road in Bingley.' 'Do you mean Mick Sutcliffe?' he asked, looking puzzled. I said, 'No, Peter Sutcliffe.' 'Bloody hell!' he exclaimed, 'That's Mick's brother!' It was the talk of Bradford and the whole country.

Everybody in Bradford claimed to have had a connection with Sutcliffe in some way or another. Sometime afterwards I met up with Stuart Harris, one of my former workers. He told me that once we had been standing at Sutcliffe's garden gate when Sutcliffe nodded to us as he went by. Years after, Stuart asked me, 'Do you remember Trevor and Donald Sumner who worked with us years ago? Well, Trevor was married to Peter Sutcliffe's sister.' I heard that Trevor and his sister moved well away from Bradford after Sutcliffe was arrested. The lads loved to listen to my stories and the characters I worked with on the building sites.

We finished 15th in the Premier League and late on had an excellent 3-2 away win at Arsenal. Viduka was on fire throughout and completed the season with 20 league goals. I used to say, 'Big man, you have got to be the most laid-back Australian I have ever met.' One Sunday morning summed up his relaxed attitude. The players had to come in for a warm-down and everyone was outside getting ready for some running and stretching. Mark arrived in a tracksuit, jumped over the fence and joined in. When we had finished he hopped back over the fence and got straight into his car.

I knew that Mark loved his sleep, but when I discovered later that he had his pyjamas underneath his tracksuit and had gone straight back to bed when he got home, I had to laugh. I remember telling one of the coaches at Middlesbrough that story at a reserve game when Mark moved there. The coach said, 'I bet the other players were not impressed.' I replied, 'With the number of goals he was scoring at the time; frankly, no one gave a s**t.' I rang Mark later that evening and relayed what I had said. He told me, 'There's not the same banter at the 'Boro as there was with you guys.'

Off the field, by the end of the season, Professor John McKenzie had taken over as chairman. I think the club was still trying to work out how much debt they had.

We were going to Mauritius and then on to South Africa for our summer holidays that year to attend Lucas Radebe's wedding in Sun City. Dave Hancock, Dom Matteo and Nigel Martyn were there with their partners. A couple of days before the wedding Lucas held a barbecue out in the bush for all his European friends. Although we were safely enclosed by wire fencing, we could hear the sounds of wild animals outside the camp, no doubt attracted by the smell of the food. The wedding was held outdoors but the day was a bit chilly. We had a great time and Lucas received a message from Nelson Mandela, wishing him all the best and saying how much he thought of him.

* * *

I was back at the club for a few weeks and then I flew to the States to attend the Athletics Trainers Conference. That year it was in St Louis, Missouri, but first I went to Chicago to visit Eric Waters. I had met Eric through Dave Hancock and Harvey Sharman, who had attended the same conference a few years earlier and had invited him to Leeds United. Eric was a physio for the Chicago Bulls basketball team, so I spent a couple of days at their training ground before we travelled together to the conference. I also met a few of Eric's pals, including Paul Pease, the manager of a sports gear company named Under Armour. He gave me some kit to take back home for the players to try out. Alan Smith was one of the first to test the gear and in one early game, televised in the US, he swapped shirts with an opponent and was wearing it underneath. I rang Paul to see if he had seen the footage, and he had. He came over to the UK a few times over the next 12 months to meet other sportspeople.

At Leeds, the revolving door was working overtime as the club's financial difficulties deepened. However we still had a lot of good players, many of whom were internationals or ex-internationals and who had been with us since our Champions League days. But the mood at the training ground was tense as the players did not know what lay in store for them. It did not make for a comfortable working atmosphere. To make matters worse, during pre-season Mark Viduka and the boss, Peter Reid, had a falling out, which did not help things, but come the start of the season we just had to get on with it.

On the plus side, another young lad who was given a chance in the first team was the goalkeeper Scott Carson, who came from Workington. I had first met Scott when he helped me out at a training session; he was just 15 years old at the time and on trial with the club. He had saved every ball Robbie Keane tried to get past him. I told 'Pop' Robson what had taken place and I was pleased to see that it was not long afterwards when they signed him up to the academy. I think it is no coincidence that he roomed with James Milner, and they both went on to have great careers.

Medically speaking, it was full steam ahead working with Dave Hancock. I would never forget Monday teatimes when he would have the doctors, radiologists, physios and injured players together in the treatment rooms so that the doctors could review the injuries. Dave would lay on tea and sandwiches, but if there were a lot of players to be assessed the session would often run on late into the evening, and it would occasionally get a bit tasty when the players would be jostling about who was first and who was last.

At the beginning of the season I had to accompany Eirik Bakke to America for his surgery. Eirik generously paid for me to travel business class with him. We flew from Manchester to Denver and then a car took us on to Vail in Colorado; the journey took us almost 24 hours. Vail was 8,000ft above sea level and a popular skiing resort. On our first night I could not sleep, so I went for a run along the river at daybreak.

The following day we were at the Steadman-Hawkins clinic to see Dr Richard Steadman, the sports medicine orthopaedic surgeon. There was some embarrassment at the reception as I was still waiting on the club to give me the go-ahead with the credit card. In the waiting room there was a photo of the Denver Broncos NFL team displayed on the wall. When Dr Steadman and his staff arrived, we shook hands and I gestured to the picture and said, 'Dr Steadman, it says Denver Broncos are the world champions?' 'Yes,' he said. I continued, 'But the game is only played in America.' He said with a smile, 'Good point,' and everybody laughed. Dr Steadman's office was full of sporting memorabilia gifted by past patients. It was like a sporting museum. He assessed Eirik and the surgery was arranged for the next day. Fortunately, the credit card details came through in the middle of the night to pay for the treatment.

In the operating theatre, two doctors who had travelled from Germany to study Dr Steadman's technique watched as he worked. Dave Hancock had asked me to film the operation, so one of them helped me by providing a commentary throughout. Back on the ward, Eirik and I were chatting with one of the nurses. She told us about the time they had treated the Juventus and Italian player Alessandro Del Piero. The hospital was swarming with press and TV crews trying to get an interview; in the end, the police had to clear them out.

The next day I made a quick visit to Eirik, who was staying on for a couple of weeks for post-op rehab, and then I flew back to Manchester. I landed early morning and was back at the club for a full day's work.

In the early days of the season our newly appointed fitness coach, New Zealander Dean Riddle from Sheffield United, like all newcomers tried to put a marker down and assert his authority. Dean was fine with the other staff and me, but I don't think he had registered the mood in the dressing room. Unfortunately, he found out what it was like dealing with higher-level players who were feeling the pressure of the club's instability. Sometimes the way he spoke to people rubbed them up the wrong way. One day in the corridor it all kicked off when he shouted at a couple of established players about a minor issue. It was like putting a match to a stick of dynamite. In time everything settled down. I never had any problems with Dean and I got some great running drills from him.

From our first ten matches we lost six, won two and drew two. At the start of November we played Arsenal at home and suffered a heavy 4-1 defeat. That day I believe history was made when James Milner and Aaron Lennon came on as second-half substitutes to join Alan Smith and David Batty. It was the only time the club had four Leeds-born players playing for them on the pitch at the same time.

The following week we were away at Portsmouth. The day before the game we were invited to tour the aircraft carrier, *Ark Royal*, in Portsmouth harbour. After going up and down all the narrow stairs, some of the players must have been knackered. However, it was no excuse the next day when we lost 6-1. It did not help when their player Tim Sherwood came off the pitch and said to me, 'The only one who was trying for you lot today was Alan Smith.' That result cost Peter Reid his job as the manager, and he was sacked on Monday morning. The club brought back Eddie Gray as caretaker until the end of the season.

At the same time, Chris Anderson, Tony Ayoub and Steve Litvensky were back in town with the Australian rugby league team. On the day Reid was sacked they had come to the training ground to do a work-out. The happiest man to see Chris and the boys that Monday morning was Mark Viduka, who had been left out of the last few games by the old manager. With Mark's rugby player physique, when he was with the Australian players you were left wondering who were the props and who was the star footballer.

On 22 November 2003, England beat Australia in the Rugby Union World Cup Final in Sydney. I watched the game with Chris and the lads at their hotel in Leeds. I remember when Jonny Wilkinson drop-kicked the last goal, all the Australian guys got up and left me in the room on my own. Afterwards I made my way to Elland Road for Eddie's first game as manager, against Bolton, where we lost 2-0.

In early December, Professor John McKenzie resigned as the club's chairman and was replaced by Trevor Birch, who tried to secure new owners. Many players had gone and the ones who came in were mainly on loan from abroad, including Roque Júnior from AC Milan, who had been in Brazil's World Cup-winning team of 2002. I completed his medical at Leeds University. His running capacity was impressive and he was more like a midfield player than a centre-back. He was a great guy to work with, but the Premier League did not seem to suit him. He went back to Italy and then ended up playing in Germany.

In late 2003 Graham Parsons, one of the academy physios, left to join Tim Williamson at Celtic, so I covered his job until Dave appointed his replacement, Donna Gormley, our first full-time female physiotherapist. Donna had previously worked in rugby league at Wigan and Leigh, and in time she became a great asset to the club. At first, the academy coaches Pop Robson and Warren Joyce were unsure about having a female physio at the club. In the early weeks I think Donna found it challenging to deal with some of the young lads who always had plenty of opinions of their own. It was up to Dave, Harvey, Bruce and me to make sure that we gave her our support as part of the team.

One day I found Donna in the dressing room; things had been getting to her and she was feeling down. She looked at me and said, 'I can't do it.' I told her, 'Donna, when you are dealing with these kids, you have got to work out whether you are dealing with the injury or with the person.' For many of the lads, it was their first time away from home, and some of them found it hard to compete for a place in the team. Sometimes it was easier to be injured than be out on the training ground. I suggested that she speak to the coaches to determine how the players were doing at training, which might give her the answer. Donna went from strength to strength, as we all knew she would.

Early in the new year we were on a six-game losing streak until we eventually had a breakthrough, beating Wolves 4-1 at home. Two weeks later, on 21 February, we played Manchester United away. I always enjoyed my visits to Old Trafford. The night before the game I was working with the players in the hotel giving massages when Rio Ferdinand turned up to see us all. He was serving a ban for missing a drug test at the time, so he was not in the Manchester United team. Rio was a great guy to work with when he was at Leeds, and everyone was delighted to see him.

On the day of the game we were told that John Charles had died. John was one of the greatest players ever to play for Leeds United. I had been fortunate to have met him several times when Billy Bremner was the manager. The Old Trafford fans were very respectful of the minute's silence before the game, and you could have heard a pin drop. Scott Carson made his debut in goal and the match finished 1-1 with Smithy scoring our equaliser. At that point we looked as if we had turned the corner with results.

John Charles's funeral was on 1 March, St David's Day. I went with the staff from Thorp Arch, including Steve Agnew, who had recently joined us as a reserve team coach. When I arrived at Elland Road Gordon Strachan pulled up next to me in the car park, followed by a guy who had been one of my heroes since I had been 12 years old, Denis Law. Gordon introduced us; it was a great moment for me. Along with striker Joe Baker, Denis had played for Torino in Italy when John was playing for Juventus. The papers said that when Denis and Joe were injured in a car crash, John had been the first person to visit them.

There were many other great names there including Mark Hughes, John Toshack, Brian Flynn, Gary McAllister, Gary Speed and most of the Don Revie era players. Many Juventus officials came to pay their respects, including Giampiero Boniperti, the captain of Juventus when John played alongside Omar Sívori, who also flew over from Argentina to attend.

Speedo and John had been great friends during Gary's time at the club. I remember one day giving Speedo some treatment when a young apprentice came in and said, 'There is a big old guy outside waiting to speak to you Gary.' The shit hit the fan when Gaz got back. He found the kid and said, 'What do you mean, "big old guy"?' Do you know who that is?' The kid had no idea, but Gary soon let him know that it was the great John Charles.

John's old friend John Helm did a great job paying tribute to his life and a male voice choir from his hometown of Swansea sang 'Land of my Fathers'. After the service, Speedo said, 'I was there singing the national anthem for Wales, Sutts.' To everyone's surprise, Sir Alex Ferguson and Sir Bobby Charlton were on the team coach back to Elland Road. While we were waiting in the tunnel for the cortege to arrive to be driven around the ground in front of the supporters, Sir Alex said, 'There is no way that I will be able to sit in the stand with the Leeds supporters.' Eddie Gray said, 'Come on Alex; you will be okay,' and of course, everything was fine. At the ground Eddie gave a great speech in tribute to John. As I left the stadium, I saw Leslie Silver, my first chairman at the club, who was now walking with a stick. I had a chat with him; he was still ever the gentleman.

I went into the pavilion for something to eat and found Jack Charlton and Denis Law chatting away. I could still picture in my head the 1965 FA Cup semi-final when Leeds played Manchester United. Jack and Norman Hunter had been marking Denis, who walked off the pitch wearing only half a shirt at the end of the game. It was hard to believe it was nearly 40 years ago.

In mid-March the chairman, Trevor Birch, handed over the club's management to some of the supporters. Gerald Krasner took over as chairman with David Richmond, Simon Morris, Melvin Helm, Melvyn Levi and ex-Leeds player Peter Lorimer. David Richmond's dad, Geoffrey, was always around the club too. I felt for many office and canteen workers who were unsure whether they would be paid their wages.

Some of the new board appeared to be using the club as a private leisure facility, inviting their mates as well. One Monday morning we arrived at Thorp Arch and someone had tried to kick our office door in. We discovered that a group of guys had been using the indoor pitch for a game of five-a-side on Sunday. They had spotted our bag of footballs and had done their best to get at them.

For the rest of the season we were hit and miss, and it came to a head on 2 May 2004 when having lost our previous two games, we travelled to Bolton Wanderers. We started okay when Viduka scored a penalty but then he was sent off. In the second half we were battered, lost 4-1, and were relegated to the Championship, the new name for the second tier. It was a bitter blow, not only for the fans but for players such as James Milner and Alan Smith, who had supported Leeds as youngsters, and the other young players who had come up through the ranks like Gary Kelly, Ian Harte and Stephen McPhail. My mind went back to 14 years previously when we were on the coach heading back to Leeds after winning the Second Division championship. I got the feeling that the summer would not be a good one.

That year I applied to register with the Health Professions Council (HPC), the health professionals' regulatory body. I had to submit references and provide evidence of my work with the treatment of injuries. The process took almost 12 months, but eventually I received a letter to say that I had been accepted and placed on their register. I remember walking into our morning meeting at the training ground and telling the rest of the team. To my surprise, they swarmed around me with their congratulations and good wishes. Of course, I thanked them for all their help and advice.

I told Alan Hodson at Lilleshall, who had been a friend for years, that I was now on the HPC register, and he suggested that I get in touch with the Chartered Society of Physiotherapy. After another lot of form filling and confirmation that I had attended Continuous Personal Development lectures, I was also accepted as a CSP member. By this time I had been a physio for around 24 years, and I like to think I had learned a lot.

Tom O'Shea had decided to finish at the end of the season after 12 years at the club. Tom and I had become great friends. Following a disagreement with Dave Hancock after our away game at Arsenal in April, it was not long afterwards that Steve Feldman also left. There was never a dull moment, that's for sure.

On the way back from our summer holidays I had a telephone call from Alan Smith to say that Manchester United had come in with a bid for him. They were the only club to make an offer. It was around six or seven million pounds, and it had been pointed out to him by the club that they needed the money. I don't think many supporters realised how close the club was to going under that summer. Alan was not only a great player for Leeds, but he was a supporter too. He had been heartbroken that day at Bolton when we had gone down. Like every other Leeds supporter, Smithy knew that to play for Manchester United was regarded as an act of betrayal. But to help the club he had to go. Smithy told me that if another club had offered the same money, he would have gone there instead, no matter where it was.

Peter Lorimer went on record to level with the supporters about the board's position. They had heard that Manchester United were interested in buying Alan, and the rest of the board had asked Peter to have a word with Sir Alex Ferguson to see if they could do a deal and have all the money up front. Usually they would pay half in advance and then the rest in stages. Peter said afterwards that Manchester United agreed to help Leeds out.

During the summer and early pre-season, Paul Robinson went to Spurs, Mark Viduka to Middlesbrough, Stephen McPhail to Barnsley and Ian Harte to Levante. We also lost Nick Barmby to Hull, Dominic Matteo to Blackburn Rovers, Danny Mills to Manchester City and James Milner, whom I knew was gutted to be leaving, to Newcastle United. A few of the outgoing players were owed thousands of pounds in contract payments and, as a magnanimous gesture they let the club keep the money to help them out. I think the supporters would have been surprised to know who they were.

* * *

Everyone at the club, including the supporters, was still reeling from what had happened at the end of the previous season. We had a new manager, Kevin Blackwell, with ex-Blackpool boss Sam Ellis as his assistant. Aidy Boothroyd came in from West Brom to be our new coach and Dean Riddle was still the fitness coach.

Kevin signed Neil Sullivan from Chelsea; Neil is still a good friend of mine. Clarke Carlisle came to us on a free transfer from QPR and Clarke was at one point known as Britain's brainiest footballer after winning a quiz on TV. We also signed Steve Crainey from Southampton, Paul Butler who had helped Wolves achieve promotion, and David Healy from Preston North End. David did well for us, and also Northern Ireland, his national team. Michael Gray from Blackburn Rovers, Shaun Derry from Crystal Palace and Rob Hulse from West Brom also joined, while our club doctor Dr Tom O'Shea was replaced by Dr Terry Crystal, the former England rugby union team doctor.

In November 2004, the ongoing financial crisis at the club resulted in the sale of Elland Road; the training ground at Thorp Arch had been sold earlier in the year.

The backroom staff had our usual Christmas night out, this year at the Skyrack in Headingley. We'd all had a few drinks when Bruce Craven, the masseur and fitness trainer, asked me, 'Have you got a minute, Sutts?' 'Sure, what's up?' I replied. What happened next will stay with me for the rest of my life. He lifted his shirt and said, 'Just have a feel.' He had a large marble-sized lump in his armpit. Bruce told me he had seen a surgeon and was awaiting an operation in the new year. He said, 'The surgeon is a good friend of Tom O'Shea's, and I know you and Tom are friends too. Would you be able to have a word to see if I could be seen sooner?' I told him to remind me in the morning; we had all had quite a bit to drink.

The next day I did not need Bruce to remind me to get in touch with Tom. I told him the story and what I had seen. A few days later Bruce was in the hospital for surgery. I received a telephone call from Tom to say that it was not good news and that Bruce had advanced melanoma. Bruce and I had worked together and had sat opposite each other in the office for the past few years. He was just 32 years old.

As the weeks went by everyone was made aware of Bruce's illness, and Dave was talking about sending him to America for treatment. Over the next few weeks Bruce popped in to see us in between his treatment at the hospital. At the end of February, the England rugby union team played Ireland in Dublin, and Terry Crystal had got tickets for himself, Dave Hancock and Bruce. The day before, we were at home to West Ham and secured a good result, winning 2-1.

On the way home I rang Bruce, who had travelled to Ireland by boat, and wished him well for his trip and said we would speak on his return. The next day my phone rang; it was Dave Hancock. He told me that Bruce was in hospital in Dublin and that he had deteriorated during the night. Terry and Dave were with him at the hospital. Later that evening I received the sad news that Bruce had passed away. I rang a few of the players to let them know. Everyone was in shock.

After the funeral a few weeks later, we had a memorial service for Bruce at a church in Headingley. His mum and dad and his friends from Castleford RL and the Rugby Football Union world were there as, well as his friends from Leeds United. I was amazed when I met Bruce's mum and dad, and they told me that Bruce had talked a lot about me.

We finished the season 14th in the Championship table. More players left, including Scott Carson to Liverpool for £1m. Our young striker Andy Keogh was let go to Scunthorpe United, where he and Billy Sharp made a formidable partnership. Jason Wilcox went to Leicester; as well as being a good player, Jason was a great lad to have in the dressing room. On the plus side, two lads who had come through the academy, Simon Walton and Frazer Richardson, got some good game time.

Towards the end of the season we had a charity night in Bruce's memory. Dave Hancock who had a great input along with Mary Lally from the office helped us to organise the event. As well as a race night we had a casino and an auction of sporting memorabilia. Terry Crystal also performed his after-dinner comedy act. Vinnie Jones kindly provided an auction prize of a day on the set of his forthcoming film, with lunch included. All the old players were there, including Alan Smith and Mark Viduka, with his Australian friend, the goalkeeper Mark Schwarzer. At the end of the night we had raised around £70,000 to pay for a melanoma nurse in Leeds.

We all agreed that we needed to do something positive to help the training ground staff deal with Bruce's death as everyone was very down. Dave Hancock had taken a week off to cope with it all. Shirley and I did some research about melanoma and discovered that at the time, there was only one charity that raised funds for melanoma research. It was run by a guy called Harry Townsend who lived in East Grinstead in Sussex. I spoke to Harry and he told me that he had set up the charity in memory of his wife, who had died from melanoma. He had spent many years raising awareness of the disease. I had a long chat with him about

Bruce. Harry provided us with some ribbons, and I sent a photo to Harry of the players wearing them on their tracksuits to use on his website. He said that having Leeds United on board would help his campaign, and I don't think the club ever let him down.

Michael Gray also came up with the idea of a charity wristband, so we made some enquiries. We found a firm to make them for us and decided to make them in lime green, the same colour as Harry's ribbons. Shirley suggested that we have the wording 'Melanoma Awareness' printed on them, and everyone agreed. I wear mine to this day, and as far as I am aware, the club still sells them and sends the money to Harry's charity.

At the end of 2004 the Australian rugby league team were back in England to play in a Tri-Nations tournament against Great Britain and New Zealand. A couple of weeks before the end of the tour, Tony Ayoub said to me, 'Alan, if we get to the final at Elland Road, do you think Tom O'Shea would be able to help us, as our doctor is flying back to Australia for his daughter's wedding?' I asked Tom and he happily agreed, but we thought they were unlikely to get there as some of the round-robin results were not going in their favour.

But in the end they made it to the final to play against Great Britain. It was a packed house at Elland Road. Tom began to have some reservations and said, 'You know, Terry Crystal might be a better choice.' I said, 'Tom, you will be okay.' Just before kick-off I asked Tony, 'Have you got a tracksuit top for the doc for when he is sitting on the bench with you?' so he got him one. I said to Tom, 'You should be at home wearing this!' It was green, the colour of Ireland. Just as they were going out, Tom said, 'Come on, you're sitting with me on the bench.' Tony had no problem with me being there.

Tom had to deal with one or two injuries and in the dressing room he was unsure whether the injured players would be fit enough to go back on the pitch, especially as one had a head injury. With half-time approaching we left the player in the dressing room and went back to watch the game for the last five minutes. I said to Tom, pointing at the scoreboard, 'I don't think they will need him in the second half.' It was 38-0 to Australia. The game finished 44-4, and we had a few beers in the dressing room afterwards. I said my goodbyes to Tony and the lads.

Since Kevin Blackwell had been in charge at Leeds, there was a kangaroo court every Friday at the club for minor misdemeanours committed by players and the staff. You could be fined for leaving a top out on the training ground or doing something daft, often with the evidence presented on screen. Sam Ellis, the assistant manager, was the judge. In 'court' on the Friday after the Oz game, Sam announced, 'Right, next one up is our physio, Sutty!' 'On what charge?!' I asked, baffled. They told me I had been charged with treason and showed me on screen sitting on the Australian bench and then drinking a beer in the dressing room. It cost me £20 for the players' pool. Another 'take it on the chin' and the pocket moment.

In January 2005, the former Chelsea owner Ken Bates took over as chairman. Within weeks the club felt more stable, and many people behind the scenes could sleep at night knowing that they would be paid their wages. However, we were certainly not out of the woods.

At Thorp Arch, Shaun Harvey, who had come to the club through Geoffrey Richmond, was kept on by Bates, and we had another new face, Gwyn Williams, who had been at Chelsea with the chairman for 20-odd years. I knew Gwyn slightly, but the guy who was the most pleased with his arrival was Harvey Sharman. Harvey was a Chelsea supporter, but don't get me wrong, there is a world of difference between being a fan of one club and having a deep passion for the club you work for. Gwyn was at the training ground to be the eyes and ears of the chairman.

The 2004/05 season ended on a high when on 2 May we held a testimonial for Lucas Radebe. We had not had the best season, so it was brilliant to see 38,000 fans pack into the stadium to pay tribute to the Chief. The great midfield of Gordon Strachan, Gary McAllister, David Batty and Gary Speed came together again for part of the game. Vinnie Jones asked if I would check whether he could take part, and of course Lucas was delighted. I was only sure that Vinnie would turn up when he put it in the papers that he would be there. Howard Wilkinson was also present and told Vinnie how he would love to meet Robert Duvall, who had starred with Vinnie in some of his films. Chris Kamara, Ally McCoist, Nigel Martyn and Phil Masinga, who had flown over from South Africa, were also taking part, as well as Gary Kelly and the rest of the Leeds team. Lucy Ward, the Leeds and England ladies player, also took part. Some of the guys wore our melanoma ribbons so that we could send a photo to Harry for his charity's website.

As for the game, Jimmy Floyd Hasselbaink and Tony Yeboah played up front. Gunnar Halle, still as fit as ever, was doing penalty box to penalty box runs. Someone jokingly asked, 'Can somebody put some concrete in his boots?' Lucy also turned out to be a star player on the day, scoring one of the goals and getting a great cheer from the crowd. It was a great way to finish the season.

9

THE END

Back at the club for pre-season, Aidy Boothroyd had been given the manager's job at Watford, so John Carver from Newcastle United, whom I knew well as he was Peter Haddock's brother-in-law, came in to replace him as coach. I always got on fine with John. We had the usual changes in squad players and signed the American international Eddie Lewis plus striker Richard Cresswell from Preston North End, Jonathan Douglas on loan from Blackburn Rovers and Liam Miller was loaned from Manchester United. We still had Gary Kelly and Eirik Bakke at the club. Another lad who came through the youth programme into the first team that year was Matt Kilgallon. Later, in March 2006, we also signed non-league player Jermaine Beckford. He had been working for the RAC fitting car windows when I did his medical. I was still doing a lot of reserve games; Martin Hodge, the goalkeeping coach, was now the reserve team coach.

In pre-season we were away at Celtic. Dave Hancock and I covered the game. It was good to see Gordon Strachan, who was now the Celtic manager, and my old colleague Tim Williamson. The game finished 0-0.

We had a good start to the league season. In 27 games we won 15, lost six and drew six up to the new year. Our main strikers were Rob Hulse and David Healy, scoring eight goals apiece. Robbie Blake and Richard Cresswell also chipped in with a few.

The best win was away at Southampton, although I don't think I got a cup of tea with their manager Harry Redknapp this time. They had a player named Theo Walcott, and in the first half his pace killed us. At half-time we were 3-0 down. Before the manager arrived in the dressing room, Neil Sullivan, our keeper, came in and kicked a load of bottles all over the room in frustration. People were diving for cover.

In the second half I sat with Steve Crainey at the back of the dugout, next to the Southampton supporters. They were enjoying the game and the score. But we came back into the match with a goal from Paul Butler and then Robbie Blake made it 3-2. At that point I said to a couple of the supporters behind us, 'I bet your backsides are twitching a bit.' Shortly afterwards David Healy, who had come on as a sub, made it 3-3 when he scored from a penalty. Then, in the closing minutes, the impossible happened and Liam Miller scored our winner. It had been one of the best comebacks in all the time I had been at Leeds. We had done something similar in 1990 at Oxford when we came back from 2-0 down to win 4-2 away from home.

On 2 January 2006 we won 3-0 away at Plymouth with goals from Cresswell, Blake and Hulse. Things looked good going into new year and through to March, we were still doing well.

Around this time, we held a service at a local church to commemorate the first anniversary of Bruce Craven's death. We had a meal at the Dexter pub in Alwoodley. Gary Kelly, who has always been a generous person, picked up the bill.

Back in the medical room, there was never a dull moment when Kells was around. When he was receiving some treatment one day, one of the lads asked me if I could smell something. I had noticed that there had been an odour in the room for a while, and as the days went on, the smell got worse. We were looking all over the place until, at last, we found the source. Someone had put some dead fish above the ceiling tiles. We knew the likely culprits. One time, we went for a swimming session and were greeted with hundreds of yellow plastic ducks bobbing up and down in the pool.

As the season came to a close, we won only one of our last ten matches, our final home game against Crewe Alexandra, who had already been relegated. We finished fifth in the table and played Preston North End at home in the first leg of the play-offs, where we drew 1-1. From what they had said in the papers, as far as Preston's manager Billy Davies and some of his staff were concerned, they were already in the final in Cardiff. All our manager had to do was pin up the newspaper articles in our dressing room at the return leg at Deepdale, and the players did the rest. We won 2-0, Rob Hulse and Frazer Richardson scored, but we also had two players sent off. But in the play-off final against Watford to secure our return to the Premier League, there was disappointment once more for the supporters. Aidy Boothroyd's team were just too good on the day, and we lost 3-0, but we did have some chances. We were destined for another year in the Championship.

* * *

We had to pick ourselves up again after our defeat at Watford and get off to a good start. The early surprise was Rob Hulse leaving us to go to Sheffield United while some of the kids had moved up to the first team, including Jonny Howson, Danny Rose and a lad from my home town, Fabian Delph. It was good to have them coming through. David

Geddes also came in as the reserve team coach and everything looked promising for the forthcoming season.

But after eight matches, Kevin Blackwell was sacked and John Carver was put in charge as caretaker manager. John took us through five games and was then replaced by Dennis Wise, who brought Gus Poyet and the goalkeeping coach Andy Beasley. They had been at Swindon Town, but the chairman knew Dennis and Gus from his days at Chelsea.

They had just over 30 matches to turn things around. In their first 13 we won three, drew two and lost eight up to the end of the year. By then, the attendances for some games had dropped to below 20,000, and behind the scenes it was very tense. One player they were desperate to get off the wage bill was Gary Kelly. It was very unpleasant; the more that Wise tried to put pressure on Kells, the more Gary dug in his heels.

I had arranged a get-together for our family and friends at home to celebrate my 60th birthday on Sunday, 1 October. The evening before, we had been invited to a function at the Woodlands Hotel by Tom O'Shea, the former club doctor. His son Jamie was getting married there, and Tom and his wife Veronica had suggested we test out the catering by joining them for a meal. Shirley was really up for it.

On Saturday afternoon I saw a few people for treatment, and that evening we set off for Leeds. Shirley had suggested that I take an extra shirt just in case we decided to stay over. On the way Shirley's phone rang, but she would not tell me who had called. I was starting to wonder if she was plotting something. When her phone rang again, Tom said he was getting the drinks in and asked how long we would be. He was waiting for us when we pulled into the car park; he waved and went inside, gesturing for us to follow him. As we went in, I said to Shirley, 'It's a bit dark in here, isn't it?' Then out of nowhere the place lit up, and there were hundreds of people looking at me, shouting 'SURPRISE!'

They were right; I had been taken totally by surprise. I was in complete shock. My sister Joan was the first to hug me. To this day I cannot get my head around how they had kept it quiet; for the first time in my life, I was speechless. From when I was a little boy to the present day, just about everyone I knew was there; our relatives, Susan and Paul from America and our Norwegian friends Bjorn Erik and Mona from Norway, had flown in for the occasion. The Leeds team had played away at West Brom that day, but some of them arrived along with many other former players. I was overwhelmed to see everyone.

It was also brilliant to meet up with my family and all our friends from Bradford, and there was lots of mickey-taking and laughter about the old days. Our surgeons John Lawton and Doug Campbell and Doug's wife Kathy were also present. Later in the evening, Rob Hulse, Jonathan Woodgate and Mark Viduka arrived after Sheffield United had played Middlesbrough that evening. I remember asking Hulsey, 'What's with that cut under your eye?'. He replied with a wry smile, 'Ask Woody.' I just laughed. It was great to see my old pals.

A big screen at the front of the room showed a slideshow of photographs from my life. I was so busy talking to everyone I didn't have a drink until a few hours into the evening. Eddie Gray joked, 'I bet this is the biggest crowd you've ever performed in front of!' As the night went on I discovered that Shirley, Dave Hancock, Gary Kelly and Mary Lally had arranged it all. Adele and Shirley both gave speeches.

Shirley began, 'As everyone knows, for the past 20 years Alan has been married to the one love of his life, and that is Leeds United.' The room erupted into laughter. Miles started his speech but then asked Brendan Ormsby to take over. Brendan recalled my earlier days as the only physio at the club when my stock answer to the queue waiting for treatment was, 'Two minutes, two minutes.' He also said, 'And people, don't bother going to Thomas Cook if you want to go to America, just go and see Sutty!' We'd had a lot of holidays to America over the years.

Dave Hancock and Gary Kelly presented me with a bronze figure of me carrying my physio bag. It was a great present, although whenever our family visit they never let me become too grand when they see it proudly displayed on our bureau at home. They always say I look a bit like Gandhi about to embark on his holidays.

One person I very much appreciated being there that night was Lucas Radebe. His wife was very poorly at the time.

It must have been about 3am before we went to bed, and of course, we had another party the next day at home. I also received messages from the rugby league guys, Chris, Tony and Adam in Australia. We had another great day.

Back at Leeds United, into early 2007 we had a few more new faces: Tore André Flo, the ex-Chelsea player, Ian Westlake from Ipswich, Robbie Elliott on loan from Newcastle United and Alan Thompson from Celtic. A few other players had left, but Kells was still there.

In the first ten games of the new year we lost six, won three and drew two. At our home match against Crystal Palace the manager came into the dressing room with a security guard and said, 'I have just been told that one of our players has been telling a player at Crystal Palace who is on our team today.' He referred to Shaun Derry. Shaun had previously played for Palace but was not playing that day. He had met up with his friend at the hotel where Palace were staying, but it turned out later to be a load of bulls**t. Why the manager said what he did in the dressing room was beyond everybody. A private word with the player would have sufficed, but maybe it would be an excuse if we lost again. As it was, we won 2-1.

Another shock for us was that Dave Hancock had been offered a job with Chelsea as head physio; I think he wanted to be back in the Premier League, so he accepted the role. It was a real shame and the beginning of the break-up of our excellent medical team. There was never a dull moment; sometimes the medical meetings got very tasty with lots of differing opinions, but once we walked through the treatment room doors we were a solid unit, and everyone had each other's back. We always worked well together, and as well as colleagues, we were good friends.

Gwyn Williams had Harvey and me in the office and told us, 'I want you two to run the medical department.' I told Gwyn that Harvey should be given the head physio role as he had more than earned it. So it was agreed. Donna was also doing well and was ready to step up to help and travel with the first team.

There was a bad atmosphere around the club. Gary Kelly's contract was up at the end of the season and he was considering retirement. While with us, he had a testimonial in 2002 against Celtic. The monies raised had paid for the building of a cancer centre in his hometown of Drogheda. Gary's sister, Mandy, had died from the disease some years earlier. I felt we needed a tribute of some sort for Gary, who had been at the club for over 16 years and had played over 500 games. I thought it would be good to get a few people together and develop some ideas like we had done for Bruce Craven a couple of years earlier. I mentioned it to Gary and said that many people wanted to wish him farewell and that they would like to raise more funds for his cancer centre. With what was happening at the club, he was not sure if it would be allowed.

I had a word with one or two people to see what they thought. One of them was Mary Lally, who had been a great help raising funds for Bruce's charity. The word came back from the chairman, Ken Bates, and we knew that the manager had also had a say, that I could organise it in my own time, but none of the staff at Elland Road could be involved. I asked Steve Lewis, who worked on the commercial side at Elland Road, if I could have a word with Mr Bates. The chairman met with me and said, 'You know the situation between Dennis and Gary, but as the money you are raising is going to the cancer centre, I have no problem with that.' We were permitted to use the banqueting pavilion at Elland Road, so it was all systems go.

We set about organising the event. Mary and one or two other people, including Allan Hegarty in the restaurant at the club and Mel from Leeds United Ladies, helped us on the quiet. Mary got in touch with other clubs to source memorabilia, and I contacted people for the guest list. Gordon Strachan, whom Gary had roomed with when he was a young player, immediately accepted the invitation. When I rang Mick McCarthy he told me, 'I would walk up the M1 to Elland Road for Gary.' Eddie Gray arranged that Gary's first manager with the Republic of Ireland, Jack Charlton, would be the guest speaker.

We sold tables of ten and looked at other ways of raising money on the night. I had been to a few charity events with Richard Blakey, the Yorkshire cricketer, and had taken a few of the Leeds lads with me. He came up with some good ideas and offered to help in any way he could. Mattie Rice, whom I had met through Dave Hancock, came from Drogheda and was a fantastic help sorting out the Ireland side of things. Bryn Law from Sky Sports agreed to be the MC.

We had set a date of early May, and as we got closer everything fell into place. We found a lad who gave us an excellent price to frame the shirts that had been donated. We had sold 60 tables; Dennis Wise paid for a table for the Thorp Arch training ground staff.

Of course, we still had matches to play. After our poor performances at the start of the year, we then won three and drew two to take us up to the beginning of April. Behind the scenes we had a few injuries and Tore André Flo was going to be out for some weeks; we worked with him mostly in the swimming pool. At first he struggled to regulate his breathing, but once he got it right, at 6ft 4in he was superb in the water. Tore would do 50 lengths of the pool just as a warm-up.

Shaun Derry was another player who loved the pool when he was not training outside. He once told me that when he was at Palace, Ian Dowie, the manager, took the players to the local baths and made them swim 50 lengths in two lanes. Everyone would be smashing into each other to get past. It was Dowie's method of team bonding. But the best swimmer of them all at Leeds was Ian Westlake. As a kid he had played water polo for England and could do anything in the pool. Ian showed us some great swimming drills to increase fitness.

At our home match against Ipswich, our relegation to League One was just about confirmed. Before it started, I talked to their centre-half Alex Bruce, the son of Steve Bruce. I had met him before through Alan Smith and Dom Matteo at a reserve game in Manchester. There was a crowd of over 30,000 and we got off to a good start as Richard Cresswell put us in front, but late on Ipswich scored an equaliser. The supporters invaded the pitch in an attempt to have the game abandoned. The players came off, but it eventually restarted and finished 1-1.

The following day I received a phone call from Eddie Gray to say that Jack Charlton could not be at Gary Kelly's tribute night. He would be attending Alan Ball's funeral, along with the rest of the 1966 World Cup-winning England team. I asked Eddie if he fancied doing the speech, but he suggested that I approach Gordon Strachan. I spoke to Gordon before his game that day at Celtic, and he kindly agreed. Gordon said, 'Can you ask your committee if they could fly Lesley and me down to Leeds.' I replied, 'Gordon, Mary and I are the committee.' But it was no problem, and I was grateful that Gordon was able to step in.

On 2 May 2007, over 600 people came to the tribute night and fundraising event for Kells and his cancer centre in Drogheda. Gary's Irish friends and family were there in force along with some of the staff from the centre, including the manager, Ann Tracey. Ian Harte, Gary's nephew, flew in from Spain where he was playing for Levante.

There was a brilliant turn-out from the footballing world, including Mick McCarthy, Howard Wilkinson, Robbie Keane, Stephen McPhail, Gary Speed, Gary McAllister and Gordon Strachan. Gordon brought the house down with his after-dinner speech recounting his days at Manchester United and Aberdeen with Alex Ferguson. It was always a good topic for the Leeds fans.

We had some fantastic auction prizes; Paul Butler got his pal Ricky Hatton to donate a pair of signed boxing gloves. We also had boxing gloves from Jonathan Douglas's cousin, Barry McGuigan. Our full-back, Steve Crainey, had sorted a Celtic shirt, signed by the team, with '1' printed on the back, which we presented to Gary.

To their credit the club did help in the end by providing an excellent service in the banqueting pavilion and allowing us to use their credit card machine at the auction. I was informed that they had turned over about £25,000 on the night, which I was pleased about. At one time I had thought that we were going to have to use the Queen's Hotel in Leeds. I think everyone had a good night, and when everything had been settled we had raised around £42,000 for Gary's charity. Mary Lally, Mattie Rice and Richard Blakey had all been fantastic in making the night a success.

Two days later the club was placed into administration, and under Football League regulations were deducted ten points, which confirmed our relegation. Fortunately, we got the money we had raised out in time. We still had one more game to play at Derby County, where we lost 2-0. Leeds were penalised again at the start of the 2007/08 season.

A couple of weeks later I was at the training ground. I did a swimming session with Matt Heath and Paul Evans, who had been doing some massaging for us. Later that day I discovered that the kit man, Sean Hardy, and Vicky Walsh in the office had been made redundant, which was a big shock. Then, I was about three miles from my home in Pateley Bridge when my phone rang. A KPMG employee told me that they were acting on behalf of Leeds United. She said that with immediate effect, I was no longer employed by the club. After working there for 21 years, I had been sacked over the telephone.

10

LIFE AWAY FROM LEEDS

Being given the sack was a shock, but I should not have been surprised. I am sure that Dennis Wise would have seen what I had done for Gary Kelly as taking sides. There had also been a couple of incidents which I believe had tarnished my name in Dennis's eyes. One time, I was talking to Claire in the laundry about Kells's event when Dennis came in. We both immediately stopped speaking and I am sure he thought we were talking about him. Afterwards, I went to his office to see him and explain.

Another time we were in the coach's room and the team was having a tough time with results. I had voiced my concerns that many of our players seemed happy to come in to do some training and then go home as soon as they could. They had the same enthusiasm about playing as a guy having to 'clock on' in a factory every day. It did not go down well.

The next day, I had to go into Thorp Arch to collect my stuff. I threw everything into a black bin liner. Before I left Mary Lally came to see me. She said she was sorry on behalf of everyone. All I could say was that it had been great working with everyone at the training ground. She also told me that Shaun Harvey, Ken Bates' right-hand man, had tried to get hold of me. When I spoke to Shaun he apologised for the way I had been sacked. Shaun said it should have been dealt with while I was at the club. Later that day, my pal Eddie Gillam, the West Ham kit man, rang me to say that he had read in a London newspaper that the Leeds United physio of 21 years' service had been sacked while driving home. I said, 'Well Ed, at least I've got fame at last.'

My daughter Adele got in touch. As a solicitor working for the law firm DLA in London, she was concerned that Leeds had terminated my employment without reason. I had not been offered any redundancy payment nor pay in lieu of notice, and Harvey had told me that the club were not in a position to offer me anything, as they were in administration. My wife Shirley suggested that I get in touch with my union, the Chartered Society of Physiotherapy, who assigned me a solicitor from Thompsons in Sheffield. I had been informed that I could not work for 12 weeks after leaving, so I had to sign on as unemployed.

Someone who helped me with advice at Leeds during those early days after I was sacked was Aileen Johnson, who worked in the accounts office. She had been very kind, providing me with advice and information.

In July 2007 I contacted Richard Bent, the fitness centre manager at Menwith Hill, the Royal Air Force station, to ask if they needed any help with physio work. He invited me in for a chat. They had an excellent treatment room and a gym for rehab work. A few days later I was asked to attend the medical centre to meet one of the doctors at the base. They were interested in me doing some work to help get the personnel through their fitness tests, so over the next few weeks I took in my HPC and CSP documents and waited for the security checks and everything else to be sorted.

I did some work for my cousin, Joe Lambert, on the building sites. It felt like I had never been away. I also worked as a lifeguard at the local swimming pool. Most of the other employees were very young, and occasionally when there was only one swimmer in the pool it was like watching paint dry. Craven College employed me as a physio for their football matches on campus. I also got some physio work for the cast and crew of *Emmerdale* at Yorkshire Television Studios.

For the remainder of 2007 I picked up work wherever I could, including a little bit at the Marley Stadium in Keighley for my pal Mick Wood from my Bradford City, Halifax Town and Lilleshall days. Dave Penney, the Darlington FC manager, offered me a job as their physio, but it was a 150-mile round trip to their training ground at Chester-le-Street. If I was going to do the job right, it could mean working seven days a week, so the travelling ruled it out.

On 24 November 2007 I went to Newcastle. Mark Viduka and James Milner had invited me to watch their game against Liverpool; my good friend John O'Conner and his son-in-law Tom Davis came with me. Tom was a Liverpool season ticket holder. When we were in the players' lounge before the game, the first person to spot me was Alan Smith. Now at Newcastle, he was out that day with an injury. Smithy was standing with a few of the Newcastle backroom staff, and straight away he called me over. After the usual handshakes and hugs, the first words he said were, 'Sutts, I have been telling all the boys that Peter Sutcliffe, the Yorkshire Ripper's brother-in-law, used to work for you on the building sites.' They were all interested because, at the time of the crimes, everyone had thought the Ripper was a Geordie because of some hoax tapes.

The next person who came to see me was Mark Taylor, one of the physios I knew from his Blackburn Rovers days. He said to me, 'Come on, Sutts, there are a couple of people who want to meet you.' He took me into the Newcastle dressing room. Mark and James were there, along with Shay Given, whom I had sat with at Gary Kelly's wedding, and Joey Barton, whom I had met a few years before through Robbie Fowler. Also there was Steve Harper, the reserve goalkeeper; we knew each other through Gary Speed. Liverpool won 3-0 and Tom was a happy man on the drive home.

At the start of 2008 I got a call from Richard Bent to say that I could start work at Menwith Hill. I knew one of the guys in the fitness centre; his name was Anthony Burton. Ant was a local lad whom I had known since he was 15 years old as he'd been in the same class at school as Adele. He was a good cricketer and had played for the Yorkshire CCC second team. I also met Tony Walker, who had been at Scarborough College with my son Miles. As time went on, it was great working with them all.

Around this time I got a phone call from James Milner, who was about to leave Newcastle for Aston Villa. He asked if I would visit his grandad, who was having trouble with his shoulder. His name was Don Smith and he lived just down the road from us in Harrogate with his wife, Edna. From day one, we hit it off and became good friends. Although he was a bit older than me, Don was still working as a clerk of works on the building sites, and of course, like all the Milner family, he was a big Leeds supporter. Over the years we got to know most of the family, and Shirley and I often went out with Don and Edna for lunch. I once said to James, 'Thanks for introducing me to your grandparents.' We had so much in common.

Meanwhile, my legal proceedings were continuing with the club. Adele was supporting me, along with my solicitor at Thompsons. It was great to have someone I could trust in my corner.

In late February 2008, Leeds Rhinos played Melbourne Storm in the rugby league's World Club Challenge at Elland Road. One of the Australian players offered to get me a ticket for the game. When I arrived there was no ticket for me, but a couple of the security guys I knew from matchdays saw me and welcomed me with open arms. I explained what had happened, and one of them said, 'Leave it with me,' and went inside to see someone. When he came out he said, 'Come this way, Alan.' While he escorted me through the tunnel to my seat, I bumped into Shaun Harvey. We were pleased to see each other; my employment claim was now with our respective lawyers and I knew that nothing was personal.

That summer, while on holiday in Canada and America, I met up with the physio John Pendlebury from my old Halifax Town days. He now had a private practice in Toronto. While we had something to eat, we reminisced about his days in Yorkshire at the Elland rugby league club and the freezing hard pitches we both had to work on, with just a wet sponge in a plastic bag and a can of cold spray. John told me that at one game, the coach had forgotten to order some spray for his medical bag. John said, 'I looked around the dressing room and in all the cupboards, but the only thing I could find was a can of fly spray.' He thought, 'I'll have to have something in my hand,' so he took the fly spray with him. When one of the players went down, he ran on to the pitch holding the can with the label covered. I chuckled as John continued, 'I sprayed the injury with the fly spray, and the player got on with the game. When I asked him later how he was doing, he said, 'Great, thanks! Never better.' John said he couldn't resist a quip, 'That's good; there's definitely no flies on you.' Sometimes, just thinking you have received some treatment works wonders.

I also caught up with John Carver, who was now head coach of Toronto FC in the USA's Major League Soccer. I met him at the football ground during a training session.

A few days before we were due to fly home for the employment tribunal, I rang my solicitor to check if everything was still on schedule for my hearing on 14 July. When I spoke to her she told me that they had been trying to get in touch with me as Leeds had come in with an offer. She said, 'To our amazement, they want to reinstate you, along with monetary compensation for the way you had been dismissed.' I discussed the proposal with Shirley and Adele. My answer was that I would like to go back if they would consider employing me part-time, two or three days per week. The solicitor said that she would put it to them.

After leaving Leeds in 2007 I had promised Shirley that I would not go back to football again, or at least working seven days a week in the sport. When I had taken the job at Menwith Hill, Richard Bent had asked me what I would do if Leeds offered me my job back, and I had told him that I would only return part-time, so I could continue working there. I had kept in touch with Harvey, the head physio at Leeds, and a few weeks earlier I had told him the same after he had asked me that question. Since I had left, Dennis Wise had moved on to Newcastle United as director of football and Gary McAllister was now the manager at Leeds.

A few hours later I spoke with my solicitor again. The club was agreeable to take me back part-time and said that I could do whichever days I chose. We also settled on the compensation. Both Adele and my solicitor found it quite bizarre that they should offer me my job back, but I had learned never to be surprised about anything in football. Ken Bates and Shaun Harvey were both still at the club and had no objection to my return, so maybe my sacking had been down to Dennis Wise.

Back home, I completed the paperwork for my return to Leeds and agreed on my new working pattern with Richard at the base. It all fell into place. People have asked me if I had missed football having being away. The simple answer was I had not thought about it too much, but I knew that as soon as I walked through the changing room doors at Thorp Arch I would be buzzing again, and it would be great to be back.

11

BACK AT LEEDS

I went back to Leeds the week after the first game of the season. Eddie Gray rang me a few days before to ask me to pass on a message to their new signing, Robert Snodgrass. He had seen him play for 20 minutes in their match against Scunthorpe and thought he would be a great player.

It was great to see everyone. Gary McAllister introduced me to his coaches, Neil McDonald and Steve Staunton, whom I had met at Kells's event in Ireland the year before. In the physio department Harvey, the head physio, was still there with Paul Perkins, who had taken over when I was sacked. Donna was there too, but she had given her notice. She went on to do great things when she left Leeds, and we have always kept in touch.

There was also a new kit man, a young lad named Chris Beasley, who became a good friend. His dad, Andy, had been the goalkeeping coach under Dennis Wise and had stayed at the club. I went to see Andy and said that I hoped we would get along after what had happened. There was no problem; everyone had moved on.

Harvey and I agreed I would work two days a week. At home games, I gave Harvey a hand with the physio and helped out Chris because I loved being there. It also helped me get to know the players and watch them play. It was also great to catch up with the rest of the ground staff and the girls in the ticket office.

I already knew some of the players, such as Fabian Delph, Jonny Howson and Jermaine Beckford, but on the first day Harvey got me to work with Andy Hughes and Bradley Johnson, whom I had not met before. One day I did some exercises with Andy that Geoff Ladley, my old mentor, had taught me. Andy, who I think had a Sports Science degree, said, 'Are we going back to the Stone Age with this stuff?' In time, we became good friends and bounced off each other with different drills, especially runs.

It was payback time eventually when one day, Andy and I were in the gym doing some bike work. Andy was very competitive, but unbeknown to him, I was on a faulty bike. When you cycled, the screen doubled the calories earned. When Andy saw my score it was way more than his. He was pedalling as fast as he could to catch up with me. I kept saying,

'Come on Hughesy, you're not going to let your grandad beat you today, are you, pal?' Later I let him in on my secret, and like most of the lads he took it on the chin.

Over the next few weeks I got to know the rest of the players. As promised, I passed on the message from Eddie Gray to Robert Snodgrass, and he thanked me. Rob went to be a great player and, like Eddie, he played for Scotland.

Harvey agreed that I could have some time off the following January to visit Adele in Australia. In return, I would work some extra days in the summer to cover Harvey's and Paul's holidays. It worked out with Richard at Menwith Hill too. In the long run, Dennis Wise had done me a big favour.

Before we left for Australia in early 2009, I was saddened to hear that Gary McAllister had been sacked after a run of poor results. We had known each other for nearly 20 years. Gary and Harvey had been influential in getting me back to the club.

While I was away, Leeds appointed a new manager, their former player Simon Grayson, who had been the boss at Blackpool. I had known Simon from when he had been an apprentice at Leeds. Simon brought in Ian Miller as a coach, and later my old pal Glynn Snodin was given the role of assistant manager. Daral Pugh moved to look after the under-16s as assistant academy manager and Neil Redfearn came in to work with the under-18s.

Of the last 15 games we won 11, drew three and lost only one to finish fourth in League One. In the play-offs we played Millwall away in the first leg and lost 1-0, but in the return leg at home Luciano Becchio put us 1-0 up only for us to draw 1-1 in the end. Becchio had been a McAllister signing and, along with Beckford, had been one of the leading scorers that year. We had fallen short again and lost out on promotion for a further year, another bitter blow for the people at the club and the supporters.

* * *

During the close season I helped Harvey with medicals for the incoming players. A couple of Australians came to the club; Pat Kisnorbo from Leicester and then later in the season, Shane Lowry on loan from Villa. Shane played alongside another Australian, Neil 'Killer' Kilkenny. Another player who came to us from Leicester was Max Gradel, who became a valuable squad member. We were hoping that these new signings might help us to get over the line and back into the Championship.

I covered a pre-season game with Paul Perkins at Newcastle United. It was good to see their physio, my old pal Derek Wright, again, and also Thommo, their kit man.

Alan Smith was still playing for Newcastle. Just before the end of the 0-0 draw, Alan was substituted. As he came off, Simon Grayson said, 'I hope Smithy does not come over here.' Sure enough, Alan came over and shook Simon's hand; the Leeds supporters were vociferous in protest. Peter Lorimer wrote an article in the local newspaper after what happened that night. He wanted to remind the Leeds fans that if Alan had not gone to Manchester United when he did, Leeds may very well not have survived.

Before the season began Harvey arranged for us to attend the annual Athletics Trainers Conference, held that year in San Antonio, Texas. Harvey, Paul Perkins, Dave Scriven, our new academy physio, and I flew out together. After landing in Houston, over the next few days we made our way to San Antonio.

During the four-day conference we met up with Dave Hancock, who was now at the New York Knicks in the USA's NBA basketball league, and with Steve Kemp, our former academy physio, and his backroom staff from Wolves. We had some interesting lectures and I visited the famous Alamo battlefield site a few blocks down the road.

On our way back, I drove us to Houston for an overnight stay before our flight. The following day we fitted in a visit to the Houston Astros' baseball stadium. Little did he know, but ten years after our visit Harvey would be standing in the same stadium again, having just won baseball's World Series with the Washington Nationals. The Nationals would be Harvey's next move when he left Leeds.

Along with Snods and Ian Miller, the boss got the 2009/2010 season under way with real momentum. Having worked with Simon and Snods for many years, I knew that they were great motivators. We played 23 games to the end of December 2009, with 17 wins, five draws and only one loss, away at our bogey club Millwall.

As a League One team we had to compete in the first round in the FA Cup. I remember as a kid, when I followed Bradford City, how I loved to run home from school on a Monday lunchtime to listen to the draw on the radio at Nellie and Arthur's. This year we beat Oldham Athletic 2-0, and after a replay, beat Kettering Town at home 5-1. We were through to the third-round draw with the big teams.

When Manchester United's number was pulled out of the bag, followed by ours, it was the game of the round. We were due to play them on Sunday, 3 January 2010. I no longer travelled to away games and was not particularly bothered about going, but a few days beforehand Harvey told me that I was on the bench with them next to the dugout. Dave Scriven was also going to be there. Harvey said, 'You make your way over to Old Trafford on the morning of the game, and we'll see you in the dressing room. You know how to get in there, don't you?' We both laughed as I replied, 'I should think so by now, pal.'

On the day of the tie, I picked Dave up just outside Huddersfield. We parked in the players' car park and made our way to the dressing rooms. As the security guard waved us through, the first person I saw was Albert Morgan, their kit manager. He did not know I had returned to Leeds and was surprised to see me. We met Chris Beasley and Paul Perkins in the dressing room, and the first thing they said to me was, 'Sutts, you know everyone around here, is there any chance of getting us some tea and bacon butties?' As I went out of the door the first people I saw in the corridor were Sir Alex Ferguson and Ryan Giggs. Sir Alex took one look at me and exclaimed, 'Bloody hell! I thought you were dead!' All I could say in return was, 'Hello, Mr Ferguson, it's nice to see you.' I nodded to Ryan Giggs and went on my way for the tea and butties.

Before the Leeds players arrived I caught up with Rob Swires, the Manchester United physio. I had known him for many years. Rob lived in Halifax and had also worked at Halifax Town. While we were talking, Rio Ferdinand spotted me. He said, 'Hey Sutts, are you still doing those quizzes, mate?' I replied, 'Yes, but I can see some things never change with you either, Rio!' ' What's that?' he asked me. 'That gear you're wearing is the same style you had at Leeds,' I joked. Rob smiled at our banter as I said to Rio, 'Would you mind signing my programme, pal?' 'Well, some things obviously do not change with you!' Rio replied as he kindly obliged. He was not playing that day, but it was great to see him.

Back in the dressing room, as soon as the gaffer arrived the other lads said to him, 'Guess what? Alex Ferguson thought Sutty was dead!' Everyone roared with laughter, and as Harvey said afterwards, it helped relieve the pre-match nerves we were all feeling that day.

A goal from Jermaine Beckford in the 19th minute, followed by magnificent defending, gave us our first win at Old Trafford in nearly 30 years. After the game we gathered in the coaches' room for a drink and a bite to eat. In his book, Sir Alex mentions that he asked me what I was laughing about. I was not laughing, but I was undoubtedly smiling when I said, 'I just can't believe that after all these years of coming to Old Trafford with some of the great teams we've had at Leeds, that we have got a win today.' He was gracious in defeat, but we knew it would have been killing him inside to lose that day.

As we were leaving we shook hands with Sir Alex. Our gaffer Simon said, 'Alex, the next time we play here, Sutty might well be dead!' When I got outside and looked at my phone, I had a message from James Milner saying, 'Get in there! What a great result!' He had been at Old Trafford a few weeks earlier after his move to Aston Villa, and they had won 1-0.

A couple of weeks after our Manchester United win, I went with James's granddad and his cousin Simon to watch Aston Villa play. While we were in James's box with his mum and dad and his uncle, Gary, I just happened to say that the boys in the backroom at Manchester United had been telling me how much they liked James and fancied him to go there. His dad Peter replied, 'If our James ever signs for Manchester United, I won't be bloody going there!' It was like waving a red rag at a bull.

A few weeks later when I was back at Leeds, I talked to Paul Dickov, who had connections at Manchester City, and I recounted the story of James and Manchester United. Without batting an eyelid he said, 'James Milner is signing for Manchester City at the end of the season.' And that was exactly what happened.

Leeds drew their fourth-round match against Spurs 2-2, and at the replay at Elland Road I bumped into Jim Beglin in the car park. It was great to see him again; he was doing the commentary for one of the networks. It was also good to catch up with the Spurs manager Harry Redknapp and his assistant Joe Jordan. Spurs were just too good on the day; Jermaine Defoe scored a hat-trick and we lost 3-1.

Our fortunes changed in the new year in the league, and we only had one win up until April. In March, Pat Kisnorbo suffered a bad injury and was out of the team for the rest of the season. Pat, along with Richard Naylor, had been a rock at the back, so it was a huge loss, but it also seemed like some of the other lads had lost a bit of form. At that point we had lost four matches on the bounce. But then, with seven games to go, we won five and lost two. On the final day of the season we were at home to Bristol Rovers with a chance of promotion; it felt like another Bournemouth.

In front of a 38,000-strong crowd, Max Gradel was sent off after an incident with the Rovers player Daniel Jones. When we went 1-0 down, it was backs to the wall until Jonny Howson came off the bench and bent a 20-yarder into the top corner. Less than five minutes later, Jermaine Beckford scored our winner. It would be his last goal for Leeds but at long last, we were back in the Championship.

We celebrated into the night, first at the supporters' club and then in Leeds city centre. At one point I fell asleep in one of the bars, and as the evening wore on I realised I had no transport to get home and nowhere to stay. I tried out a couple of hotels, but they were all full. Thankfully I bumped into one of our former players, Tom Taiwo, and his girlfriend. Tom had been at the club as a youngster and had gone to Chelsea for a large sum. When I told him what had happened, he offered me his sofa for the night at his home in Horsforth. I was very grateful; he was a knight in shining armour. He jokingly said, 'It's like helping my grandad out.' I had to laugh, but he was right.

* * *

One of our first defeats of the new Championship season was at home to Preston in a crazy game at the end of September. At one point we were winning 4-1, but just before half-time Preston got one back. They blew us away in the second half and won 6-4. Their manager, Darren Ferguson, was scratching his head along with the rest of us at the result. We drew our matches over the Christmas period, so we were fourth in the table going into the new year, pretty respectable for our first season back.

In October I had to see the orthopaedic surgeon Mr Jon Conroy, as I had been having a lot of trouble with my right hip. I had met Jon before when I had attended a medical meeting, and he was one of the lecturers. I met him over lunch and he introduced himself. He said, 'You don't remember me, do you?' Jon and his dad were big Liverpool supporters, and he reminded me of the time I got them some tickets for a Leeds United versus Liverpool game for his dad's 60th birthday. He said that he had spoken to me in the medical room after the game to thank me.

Jon told me I needed a hip replacement. He had a long waiting list, and I had a couple of issues I needed to consider. There was no way that I could take time off during the football season, and we had just found out that Adele was expecting a baby in March, so we were planning a trip to Australia. He told me that the pain would only get worse. I said respectfully, 'With the help of my mates at the club, I'll try to keep going a bit longer.' We agreed that I would give him a call when I got back from Australia and he would sort a date out.

In Sydney, my daughter Adele had a baby boy on 24 March 2011, named Alexander Christian. A few days after Alex was born, Josh, Adele's partner, and I went to the Manley versus Newcastle Knights rugby league game at Brookvale. We walked past the players' tunnel and I spotted our ex-striker Michael Bridges, who was now living in New South Wales and playing for the Newcastle Jets. Andrew Johns, the Australian rugby league player, was also there. Michael looked at me in disbelief and said, 'Sutty! What are you doing here?' It was great to see him. When Andrew saw me, I could tell he recognised my face, so I said, 'Me and Alan Smith, Leeds United,' and straight away he remembered. I had last seen Andrew in 2001 on his tour with the Kangaroos when he and Smithy had some great nights out together.

I also knew another guy at Manley, a jeweller named Sam, who had connections with the club. I had met him before when Manley had played against the Leeds Rhinos at Elland Road in the World Club Challenge. He told me to find him after the game, and the next thing we knew, Josh and I were invited into the Manley dressing room. Josh, who had been a Manley supporter for more than 30 years, remarked, 'I can't believe a Yorkshireman has got me into the Manley dressing room!' I also managed to fit in a couple of visits to Chris Anderson and Tony Ayoub, and then we were on our way home for the rest of the season.

I got back for the last couple of matches. Our final home game was a 1-0 win against Burnley. The following Friday I was booked for my surgery; I was still managing to do 45 minutes on the cross trainer, but I was ready for the operation. Leeds finished the season with a 2-1 win away at QPR. We finished just outside the play-offs at seventh in the league, but it had been a good season.

The surgery went well, and I sorted out my rehab programme using some new exercises from Steve Megson, who had recently worked with a player after a hip operation. My friend Lynn Iveson, who was head of physiotherapy at Northallerton Hospital, also helped me. Mr Conroy permitted me to drive after a month, so I was all set for pre-season at the start of July 2011.

* * *

During those early months of the new season my good friend John Reynolds, who had been the groundsman at Leeds when I first started there, was not in the best of health. I visited him at home and we laughed about my early days when he only allowed me a corner of the pitch to work with the players. We had become good friends and regularly had a round of golf together.

In November, John moved into a hospice in Wakefield. It occurred to me that Gary Speed would want to know that John was ill. As fellow Welshmen, Gary and John had always been good friends while Gary was at Leeds. On Thursday, 24 November 2011, two days before our game against Barnsley on Saturday, I left Gary a message and told him about John.

On the day of the match I was on my way to the club when I saw that Gary had replied to my message. He always used the same name for me, 'Top Man, I'm at *Football Focus* with Gary Mac. What's all this about John? Give me a call when you can.' I tried him a few times, but he did not pick up. As usual, I arrived early at Elland Road to get everything set up.

Forty-five minutes before the game, while I was on my way to watch the players warm up, Gary rang me back, 'Top Man, tell me again what's going on with John?' I told him about John's illness and Gary said that he would try and get over to see him at the hospice. I said that we were playing Barnsley that day and I was going out on to the pitch, so I would speak to him again soon. We lost 2-1 to Barnsley.

The next day, at around 12.30pm, I heard Miles talking on his phone saying, 'No, I don't think he does.' Then he said to me, 'Dad, Gary Speed is dead.' My first response was, 'Piss off!' I could not grasp what he was saying. Then Harvey rang me and confirmed the awful news. The Welsh FA had also announced his death on TV. The shock did not hit me for a while.

At tea-time I spoke with Gary McAllister, and he told me that Speedo had been on great form both on and off the set when they had been together at the BBC's *Football Focus* studios. It was just so hard to understand.

A couple of days later at Elland Road we were all still in shock; the news that Gary had taken his own life had floored us all. He was a gifted and talented player and had been doing a great job as the Welsh national manager. During that week, Leeds played away at Nottingham Forest. Gary always wore the number 11 shirt, so on the 11th minute of the game the crowd sang in tribute to him for 11 minutes. It was a touching moment, made even more so when immediately afterwards, Robert Snodgrass, wearing the number 11 shirt scored the opening goal in our 4-0 win.

The following Saturday, Gary's wife Louise and his mum and dad, Carol and Roger, were at our home match against Millwall. Gary McAllister, Gordon Strachan and David Batty led the tributes to Gary before kick-off, and once again the fans sang for 11 minutes. I spoke with Louise, Carol and Roger and offered my condolences. Louise looked at me and smiled and said, 'When I see you, it always reminds me of when Gary would impersonate your Yorkshire accent.'

That week I spoke to LUFC TV about the real Gary who I knew and loved. He would give his time to help anybody. I would never forget his generosity when he came to Pateley Bridge in 1996 to help me and Dennis Audsley, the pub landlord at the Crown, raise funds to purchase a wheelchair for one of the local lads, Steve Houseman. At the time I could not tell Dennis who was coming. The pub was packed with people, and when Shirley and I walked in with Gary and Louise, there was such an almighty roar we thought the roof of the pub would lift off. I had got together some signed shirts from Leeds as well as from other clubs. The last shirt to be auctioned that night was a Liverpool one sent to me by Sammy Lee. Dennis asked Gary if he would be the auctioneer. When it got to £90, Gary said to the bidder, 'If you make it £100, I'll put £100 in as well.' Gary shook hands with Steve and wished him all the best. We managed to raise more than the amount required to buy the wheelchair. That is the Gary I remember, and no one who was there that night would ever forget his kindness.

Early in the new year I had a telephone call from Tony Ayoub, who was now at Canterbury Bulldogs, the Australian rugby league team. He asked if I could do him a favour; he wanted me to perform a medical on the St Helens and England rugby league captain James Graham. He'd had some issues with players arriving in Australia with existing unreported injuries. James came over to Thorp Arch and Harvey lent his expertise with the medical. James was fine and he went on to have a great career at the Bulldogs. The next time I saw him was in 2017 when I was with Chris Anderson and Brett Kimmorley in a café near the Bulldogs' training ground at Belmore in Sydney. Initially, James did not recognise me, but when Brett said, 'Leeds United,' he remembered me from that day five years earlier.

After the Millwall game in November, Leeds went through a poor run up to the end of the year, losing three and drawing one of their next four matches. In the new year we started with two wins and a draw, but when we played Birmingham at home on 31 January 2012 we lost 4-1, with Nikola Žigić scoring all four goals. The next day, Shirley and I were flying to Australia. While we were at Manchester Airport the news came through that Simon Grayson, Glynn Snodin and Ian Miller had been sacked. I managed to track them down and told them I was gutted for them. I had known Simon and Glynn for a long time. Neil Redfearn took over as caretaker manager.

While in Australia, we travelled down the Ocean Road and spent time with Donna Gormley in Melbourne, who was now the personal physio for Harry Kewell. I also hosted a quiz night for the Melbourne Leeds United Supporters' Club. They were complaining about our chairman, Ken Bates. Most of them wanted him out. I told them, 'Be careful what you wish for; not every club has an owner like Chelsea or Manchester City.' We would discover later that there were less attractive options than Ken Bates running the club.

Back in Sydney, I heard that Neil Warnock was our new manager. I knew Neil from when he visited Halifax Town in 1984. My old boss at Halifax Town, Mick Jones, was Neil's assistant and Ronnie Jepson was the coach.

Back at the club I met Chris Short, appointed as the new fitness coach, then of the final 14 games Leeds won four, drew four and lost six. They had been tenth in the league when Simon was sacked but finished 14th. I felt for Harvey; it does not always help when the manager continually changes, and you must prove yourself yet again.

12

THE END OF AN ERA

Neil Warnock had a home in the south-west so pre-season that year was held mainly in Devon and Cornwall. In the first 25 Championship games of the season, we won ten, drew five and lost ten, and we were ninth in the table. We got off to a great start in the League Cup, first beating Shrewsbury at home 4-0, and again at home we beat Oxford 3-0. We played Everton in the next round at Elland Road and had a good 2-1 win. Our record in front of our own fans was impressive. Our next home game was against Southampton; I had known their manager Nigel Adkins for years, first as a physio. His assistant, Andy Crosby, had been at our academy in his younger days.

We secured a good result on the night, winning 3-0, so we were through to the quarter-finals. Our next opponents were Harvey's team, Chelsea. We got off to a strong start and went 1-0 up with a goal from Luciano Becchio, but in the second half Chelsea went up a gear and beat us 5-1. But it had still been a great run.

Over the years, I've had the honour of working with many players from the Don Revie era. I spent a lot of time with Eddie Gray's brother, Frank, while I was in Australia, and I also got to know the strike partners Mick Jones and Allan Clarke when they came for treatment at the training ground at Thorp Arch.

I once asked Mick how he ended up at Leeds from Sheffield United. He told me, 'One day I had been to the supermarket, and as I was walking up the road I could see some people in my garden. They were reporters waiting for me. They told me that Don Revie was inside, and sure enough when I walked in, there was Mr Revie and Harry Reynolds, the chairman from Leeds United. Mr Revie said that they had been watching me and would like me to play for Leeds. When I asked if Sheffield United were aware they were talking to me, he said that everything was sorted. In the end they made me an offer I could not refuse. Of course, in those days there were no agents.'

Mick also told me that after the £100,000 deal went through, Leeds put him and his wife Glynis up in a hotel while they looked for a house. One day they were walking through the city centre when a group of girls ran across the road and, without warning, began to touch Mick. He said, 'I asked them what they were doing while Glynis was telling them to get off me. One of them laughed and said, "We just wanted to touch someone worth £100,000!"' Mick said, 'Alan, that's a week's wage for players nowadays.' I replied, 'Yes Mick, and a bit more!' I still keep in touch with Mick and Glynis.

On another occasion I was at Elland Road before a game when Allan Clarke came to see me. 'Alan, have you got a minute?' he asked. 'Sure, what's up?' I replied. 'It's not me,' he said, 'it's my son-in-law. He's had some surgery and needs to know what rehab he should do.' I was pleased to help, but I pointed out that Allan lived in Scunthorpe and my place was in Pateley Bridge. Allan said he was happy to drive his son-in-law over so that I could sort him out. I also gave Allan some treatment.

While I was working on him, we had a good chat. I asked Allan, 'Do you remember playing for Fulham against Bradford Park Avenue in January 1967 in the FA Cup third round?' I reminded him he had scored two great goals that day; one of them was a half volley into the top corner of the net. I had been standing behind the goal when it went in. I was a bit surprised he could not remember as most goalscorers can usually recall every one.

We went on to talk about his debut for England at the World Cup in Mexico in 1970 against Czechoslovakia. Allan said, 'As we were leaving the dressing room, Alf Ramsey asked who was on the penalties. Bobby Charlton, Bobby Moore and the other regulars were there, but no one put their hand up, so I volunteered. We were not long into the second half, when guess what? We got a penalty. Les Cocker, the trainer from Leeds United, was on the bench and told me afterwards that Alf had turned to him and asked if I was any good at penalties. I was the third-choice penalty taker behind Johnny Giles and Peter Lorimer at Leeds United. Les told Alf, "Don't worry boss, you can bet your mortgage on him." I sent the goalkeeper the wrong way, we won 1-0 and we were through to the next round.' It was a fantastic story, but had Allan missed the penalty then England, the reigning world champions, could have been eliminated.

We had a good couple of hours together, and the next day a large bunch of flowers arrived for Shirley with a thank you note. But it was thank you from me to Allan for all his great stories.

On New Year's Day we won at home against Bolton, but in the next five games we had three losses, one draw and one win. In the FA Cup we beat Birmingham City away in a replay and followed this up with a good 2-1 home win against Tottenham. In the fifth round, we drew the mighty Manchester City at their new Etihad Stadium.

One day in the dressing room, out of the blue, Neil Warnock had a chat with me; we had not spoken that much since he had arrived. 'Hey Suttie, when did I first meet you?'

he asked me. I replied, 'About 1984 at Halifax Town, gaffer, when the team used to play on a Friday night. You were there scouting players for Burton Albion and were usually in the bar after the match.'

But his bonhomie changed a few hours later. He had a couple of matchday routines; when the players went out for their warm-up, Neil liked to have some time on his own in the dressing room to collect his thoughts. Then after the game he always enjoyed a warm bath, which for some reason I got the job of preparing for him. As usual, just after half-time I filled the tub with hot water, and five minutes before full time I would go in to add the cold water. But on this day, Harvey asked me to sort out an injured player with some ice strapping. It completely slipped my mind about putting the cold water in the bath.

The final whistle went, and the next thing I heard was an almighty scream. The gaffer had jumped straight into the bath without testing it first. Of course, I went to see him later to apologise and explain. Even today, whenever I see the kit man Chris Beasley, or the fitness coach Tom Robinson, they laugh and say, 'Sutts, we can never forget that day with the bath,' but on a serious note, Neil could have been badly scalded. I am glad he was okay and he let me carry on doing the job for him.

In early 2013, Chris Beasley had an operation on his wrist. When he returned to work he struggled with lifting and carrying, so he asked if I could help him out. Harvey said it was okay; it meant I had to go into the club more often, but I still had a good work-life balance.

Soon afterwards, the fifth round FA Cup tie away at Manchester City arrived. On the day, one of the players asked if I could drive his car from the hotel to the ground. Big Martin Sykes, the security guard, said that he knew Manchester so we went together. Don't get me wrong, Martin is a great guy, but on this day we took a wrong turn at some traffic lights and we seemed to go all over Manchester, trying to find the right road to the stadium, and I could feel my stress levels rising. When we eventually arrived, there were some familiar faces. I knew Les Chapman, Manchester City's kit man, from when he played at Bradford City. I also spoke with James Milner, who was now playing for the club. When he saw me he asked, 'What are you doing here? I thought you only did home games?' I explained I was helping Chris. I also had a chat with Brian Kidd, who was working at the club. We lost 4-0 against a superb Manchester City team,

The next day I found out how much stress the job could bring when I had to go for my six-monthly general medical check-up. The nurse took my blood pressure and looked at me in disbelief. She told me to give it five minutes and she would repeat it. On the second attempt it still read a very high 190 over 110, so I had to see the doctor, who sorted out some medication. As luck would have it Chris's wrist was healing, so he did not need me any more. It had been great working with him, but I was glad to get back to just doing physio work.

Before we left the ground that Sunday, the gaffer, Harvey and I were in the dressing room together. Neil told us he thought he might not be at the club much longer. After another nine matches, with two wins, four draws and three losses, his prediction came true and following our defeat at home to Derby County on April Fool's Day, Neil Redfearn took over as caretaker manager. At the time, I think we'd had eight managers in the last ten years, compared with only two in my first ten years at the club.

At the end of the season we finished 13th in the table and the club appointed Brian McDermott as manager. He had previously taken Reading into the Premier League. His assistant, Nigel Gibbs, had been at Watford for many years as a player and then as a coach. Brian also brought Jon Goodman as his fitness coach; Jon was a good friend of our former goalkeeper Neil Sullivan.

During the summer of 2013, there were some changes in the medical room. Harvey had put Steve Megson, the academy head physio, forward for a first-team physio role at Bolton Wanderers, and he got the job. So Steve's number two Faith Atack, who had been at the club full-time since 2010, took over his role. During pre-season Paul Perkins decided to leave, so Harvey brought in Marc Czuczman. We all knew Marc from his spell of work experience with Dave Hancock and he had then gone on to work at Walsall and Oldham as a physio.

Shortly after Paul left, Chris Beasley and I talked one day about our away game at Manchester United three years earlier. Before the team came into the dressing room, Dave, Scrivs, Perks, Chris and I were with Albert Morgan, Manchester United's kit manager. Albert was okay so long as you did not ask him for any shirts. Perks had never met Albert before, so when he asked him, 'Have you got a shirt for me, or a hat or anything?' I thought that Perks was on dangerous territory. Albert looked at me as if to say, which planet have you got this physio from, and in no uncertain terms, told Perks where to go. As Chris said, it scuppered any chance we had of getting anything that day, as kit men always liked to exchange shirts with other kit men.

At the end of 2012, Ken Bates sold the club to Dubai-based GFH Capital and stepped down as chairman to become president. Salah Nooruddin took over his role and in July 2013 Mr Bates left altogether. However, another change of ownership would not end the financial difficulties that had plagued the club over recent years.

Under our new manager, player turnover had grown. Harvey and I regularly remarked that you had to be a particular kind of player to play in front of the Leeds supporters. I know Harvey tried to mention this to the new manager to try and help him. I remember what happened to our left-back Steve Crainey when he made a couple of mistakes and the crowd was never off his back. Dennis Wise left him out of the team, but Steve was a great professional; he even came in on Sundays to keep up his fitness. Steve went on to have a great career at Blackpool, where he did not have the sort of pressure he had put up with at Leeds and helped the club gain promotion to the Premier League, also winning their player of the year award.

We made an excellent signing that year, but this time it was a member of staff. The club decided that Chris Beasley, our kit man, needed a permanent assistant. Chris brought in his friend Richard Murray, who, like Chris, lived in Mansfield, and they worked well together. It made my life a bit easier as well. As time went on Richard became affectionately known to us all as 'Plan B'.

By the end of 2013 we had won ten games, lost eight, drawn five and looked for better things in 2014. But in the new year it started to get crazy at boardroom level. The board had been looking for new investment, and in late January 2014 a new guy appeared on the scene named Massimo Cellino.

On the evening of 31 January Mattie Rice, who knew Brian McDermott from his Reading days, rang to tell me that Brian had been sacked by Cellino, who claimed to be the club's new owner. At the time, GFH Capital had agreed to sell 75 per cent of the club to Eleonora Sports Ltd, owned by Cellino, but the deal had not gone through at that stage. The next day, Nigel Gibbs was in charge, and Neil Redfearn, now the first team coach, was helping Nigel. On the day we had our best result for some time, beating Huddersfield 5-1, and by Monday Brian was back at the club as manager. But for the rest of the season, the Football League tried their best to prevent Cellino from taking over the club.

That same month Harvey also told me that he had received a telephone call from Eamonn Salmon, the chief executive of the Football Medical and Performance Association (FMPA). Eamonn wanted to know how many years Harvey had worked in football. Harvey said to him, 'The person you really need to speak to is Alan Sutton.' Eamonn replied, 'I remember Alan; I met him a few times when I was at Manchester City. Tell him to give me a call.'

When I spoke with Eamonn he explained that the FMPA had recently been established as the representative body for medicine and performance practitioners working within professional football. They were setting up a '21 Club' of physiotherapists and other medical professionals who had worked in football for 21 years or more, equating to being involved in around 1,000 matches. The FMPA wanted to present awards at a conference in May to qualifying professionals in recognition of their service to the game. At the time, I had been at Leeds for 27 years and at Halifax Town for five years before that. It was an honour to be included. The conference was held at the Radisson Blu Hotel at East Midlands Airport, and on the night it was great to see many old friends, many of whom had retired but had spent their lives working in football.

In the remaining games until the end of the season, we won five, drew three and lost ten. There was only going to be one outcome. Cellino, who had successfully challenged the Football League and was now our new owner, sacked McDermott and hired David Hockaday as our new head coach on a two-year contract. I remembered David when he was the coach at Watford, and he had recently been sacked as manager of the non-league team Forest Green Rovers. His assistant was another unknown, Junior Lewis. Most people's reaction was, 'David Who?'

* * *

The new owner had cut the wage bill and got rid of many staff members. I was a bit surprised that I had not been part of the cull. It was well known that Massimo Cellino had a hire and fire approach and at his previous club in Italy he had sacked more managers than most people had eaten hot dinners. So it was no surprise when, four games into the season with three losses and one win, David Hockaday and his assistant Junior Lewis, were out of the door. Next to arrive was Darko Milanič, again on a two-year contract. He lasted just over a month, after six games, with three losses and three draws. After that, Neil Redfearn was appointed the manager on a one-year contract.

Neil Sullivan returned as our goalkeeping coach; it was good to see him again. One of our ex-players, Henry McStay, had come back to help Faith Atack in the academy. Henry came from Northern Ireland and had played for both Northern Ireland and the Republic of Ireland as a youth player. He had qualified as a physio and, with his footballing background, was an ideal addition to the team. Harvey also brought Paul Evans back as a masseur. There was now a solid team in the physio department; I came in a couple of days per week and floated between the two physio rooms as needed.

As well as club doctor Terry Crystal and Doug Campbell, the matchday orthopaedic surgeon, we now had an academy doctor, Jamie O'Shea, whose dad, Tom was my great friend. I had known Jamie since he was about ten years old. The medical team met on Thursdays when Harvey would run through the injuries.

By this time the new owner had brought in quite a few Italian players. I told a Leeds supporter friend to not put any money on Leeds that season; some of the new players lacked the quality for the Championship. Over the years, you had to scratch your head at some of the signings that various managers had made.

Around the time of my 68th birthday, Shirley and I decided that in December that year we would visit Australia to spend time with Adele, Josh and Alex for six weeks instead of the usual three weeks. I had a word with Harvey, but arrangements had changed at the club. I had to get the owner's permission via Steve Holmes at the training ground. I had a word with Steve and told him of my plans and asked if he could sort it out.

While working with Faith and Henry, I got to know some of the academy lads. One of them was Lewie Coyle. Lewie came from Hull and was good pals with Nick Barmby's son Jack at one point. I got to know Lewie when he was travelling from Hull to train and play matches at the weekend. He had long hair in his early days at the club.

Another was Kalvin Phillips. One day when I was giving him some treatment and we were having a chat, he said, 'Sutts, my mum works for a friend of yours.' 'Who's that, Kal?' I asked him. 'Bob Sadler at Harpo's pizza place on Street Lane. My mum told me about that shirt you got signed for him back in the 1990s.' Bob had asked if I could get him a shirt and told me he would pay £20 to charity for every signature I could get on it. Kalvin went on, 'Bob told my mum that he thought you might get a dozen, and when you brought it back with around 40 signatures on, it cost him £800.'

I did remember; I got all the top players to sign it and I think Bob still had the shirt in the shop. After that, whenever Kalvin came to me for treatment, I would say, 'I can see you have been eating those left-over pizzas your mum has been bringing home, Kalvin,' and he would laugh. I am pleased that Kalvin has done well. I eventually met his mum Lindsay in the players' lounge at Elland Road, and we had a laugh about Bob, who is a great guy, and that shirt which cost him more than he planned.

The day after our game against Fulham, I had booked my ticket to Australia to travel on Sunday, 14 December 2014, but neither Harvey nor Steve Holmes had confirmed if the owner had given me the go-ahead. A few days before I was due to fly, Cellino came to the training ground. I was outside doing the physio for a training session with Neil Redfearn and the first team.

An old friend, Clive Brown, turned up that morning to see everyone. Clive used to do massage for the team and warm-ups on matchdays. That day, I had a quick word with Clive and I could see Cellino watching me. Nothing was said afterwards, so when I went into the club a couple of days later I got on with my work and then had a word with Steve at lunchtime. I got the idea that he and Harvey had decided to leave it as late as possible before saying anything. Aileen Johnson, the head of payroll, who also worked in HR, was at the training ground that day. Aileen had helped me in 2007 when Leeds had terminated my employment. I had a word with her and explained my situation; I did not want to go to Australia without getting it sorted out. Aileen said she would get back to me. I was beginning to suspect something was going on.

On my way home Steve Holmes rang me and said that I needed to get in touch with Aileen the next morning. When I did, she said that she wanted to see me. We could not get a convenient time for both of us to get together that day, so I said, 'I will be there for the game tomorrow,' and we agreed to meet at 10am. I had a sense of foreboding about the meeting, so I spoke to Ian Taylor at the Chartered Society of Physiotherapy and my good friend Mattie Rice in Ireland. Shirley was already in Australia as she had gone a week earlier.

Saturday morning came and I went into the ground in my tracksuit, ready for the game that afternoon. Aileen was there waiting for me and asked me to follow her into the office. I said hello to a couple of people on the way, but I knew what was coming as soon as she shut the door. Aileen said, 'Alan, Massimo Cellino has said that you are not allowed to be at the game today, and I have got to sort out a deal for you to leave the club.' I could see it was hard for Aileen to deliver Cellino's message. She said that Harvey had been informed the night before that I would be leaving, but he had been instructed that under no circumstances should he get in touch with me.

When we sat down, I said to her, 'Aileen, this is about me and Leeds United, not me and Aileen Johnson. You have been and always will be a good friend and whatever happens next is nothing to do with you personally.' Ten minutes later we had done a deal. After the dispute in 2007, I had retained continuous employment from 1986, which was taken into account. As I walked out I said goodbye to a few people on my way. I got in the car and I rang Harvey. He said, 'I am sorry pal, that I could not ring you. When Aileen phoned me last night, she was in tears because she did not want to do this to you.' His words touched me. Aileen and I have remained great friends.

I had a lot of people to ring. Of course I rang Mattie to thank him for his advice and let him know about my deal. I left it until Monday when I was in Australia to ring Ian

Taylor at the Chartered Society of Physiotherapy to sort out the legalities. That evening, some friends kindly invited me for a meal, and the following day I was on my way to Manchester for my flight to Sydney via Dubai. Miles would be joining us in Australia, and I was looking forward to having some time together with all my family.

When you are on a long-haul flight, you have a lot of time to think. I went over in my mind what had happened that week and where it had all started, first at Halifax Town and then on 22 August 1986 when I walked through the doors at Elland Road.

I had committed that I would make the same effort and have the same enthusiasm every day I was there, as I did on that first day. I was always conscious that with the vagaries of football, any day might be my last day. I always kept that promise.

At Elland Road I soon got to know everybody. It did not take long for the club and its people to get under my skin and to understand that I was working somewhere special. Every morning on my journey from home I relished the anticipation of another day at the club, even during those first seven years when I was the only physio, working seven days a week. It was physically demanding work, and mentally it consumed me 24 hours a day. But I loved every minute.

From those early days when we were struggling in the bottom half of the Second Division with crowds of only 12,000, to the heights of the Premier League and the Champions League, my only aim was to do my best. As they do everywhere, the results dominated everything, but my way of thinking was to enjoy it and never get too happy with a great win, nor too sad with a loss. My job as a physio was to get the players in the best shape possible to deliver the best performance they could, physically and often, mentally. I had to get them over that white line and back on to the pitch for whichever manager was in charge.

Spending my working life doing something I loved with such great people was an enormous privilege. We all worked together and tried to help each other, and I liked to think that my colleagues were also my friends. It was the same in 1996 when we moved to Thorp Arch; I enjoyed working with the new people there. We had a lot of laughter, and there were occasionally some not-so-good times. But behind the scenes, whatever was taking place within the club, we got on with the job.

I also came to love the supporters, who are extraordinarily devoted and intensely passionate. Hours before the match, there were always thousands of fans milling around the ground as I drove into work. Even now, when I go in for the odd game, the buzz of anticipation from our supporters reminds me that they are the real life force of the club. It is also heartening to see the staff.

When I first started at Leeds, if someone had asked me, 'Alan, are you a Leeds United fan?' the answer would have been, 'No.' If they asked me now, over 30 years later, the answer would still be the same, because my involvement with the club went a lot deeper than just being a fan.

Often I have been asked if I miss being a physio at the club. At my age, the answer once again would be, 'No.' However, when I went back in 2008 after being away for 15 months, I thought I didn't miss it then either, but as soon I walked through the door the magic of the place consumed me all over again.

I can put my finger on the moment I realised what Leeds United meant to me. In November 2003 we were in a hotel in London before our game against West Ham, having a few drinks. Eddie Gray, whom I have always loved working with, and I disagreed about a well-known Leeds player. Afterwards, I was not happy about how our conversation ended, so I went to see Eddie in his room. He said, 'I know why you are here. It's because you are as passionate about the club as I am.' That was the first time that someone had seen that passion in me, and until then, I don't think I had acknowledged it myself.

13

HOME

We had a good time in Australia with the whole family. I met up with all the usual people, including Chris Anderson and Tony Ayoub. I usually scheduled my return so that I landed at Manchester Airport and went straight to Elland Road to help with a matchday, but my departure meant that this year I did not need to plan anything. However, a few days after my return, I went to Thorp Arch to collect the rest of my belongings and say goodbye to the friends I had made. Then I went back home to begin my new life, including doing a bit of work at Menwith Hill.

Later that summer, we were back in Australia for the birth of Adele and Josh's second son, Sebastian James, on 6 August 2015.

In early 2016, my friend Martin Atkinson, the Premier League referee, gave me a call. Martin was at the Dallas Cup in Texas, along with Trevor Simpson, a few years after I had been there with the youth team. Martin is a big Leeds United supporter. The previous year we had worked together during a tribute game for Brendan Ormsby, who was not in the best of health. John Sheridan and Neil Parsley organised the match. Simon Grayson's Leeds Legends XI took on John Sheridan's team at Farsley AFC, and on the day, I looked after both dressing rooms. As a Leeds fan, Martin was the first to step up to take charge of the match, and he brought Jon Moss, another Premier League referee who lives in Horsforth, to help. When Martin rang me he said he had picked up a couple of injuries and wanted a second opinion. He had been selected as a referee for the Euros 2016 in France and was trying to get himself as fit as possible. It is always good to see Martin, and I enjoy our chats.

On 21 May 2016, I attended the FMPA conference again at the usual venue. After watching the FA Cup Final on the big screen at the hotel in the afternoon, I went to the evening dinner and awards ceremony. I was only there because I enjoyed catching up with old friends, although many of the old faces were absent this year and there were lots of youngsters. It was a sign of the times.

I sat with David Muckle, the orthopaedic surgeon from Middlesbrough. I had worked with Mr Muckle in my Billy Bremner days. He was there to receive his '21 Club' award. On our table were two physios from Carlisle United who had been nominated for a team award. Just before the ceremony began, Adele rang me from Australia, so we had a quick chat. As the evening went on and we were down to the last few awards, I looked forward to moving into the bar for a few drinks.

Finally, the MC, Eamonn Salmon, rounded off the evening, 'Our final presentation this evening is for the Longstanding Services to Football Award.' He continued by mentioning the sponsors, and then a name flashed on the screen: ALAN SUTTON. I was taken entirely by surprise as we all watched a video montage of my time at Leeds United on the screen. Still stunned, I cannot remember my long walk to the stage, where Eamonn invited me to say a few words. I think I managed to say, 'Oh wow!' and that there were many other people in the room who were more worthy of the award, but it was a great honour to be recognised by my peers.

My life in football, culminating in being there that night and receiving the award, had been a journey I could not have imagined 50 years earlier when I had been a flagger and kerber in Bradford. I had been fortunate to make a career that encompassed my lifelong passion, and I had loved every single minute and especially the friends I had made along the way. After the ceremony, I rang Shirley and Adele to tell them what had occurred, and then I made my way to the bar and had a chat with Eamonn. I thanked him and said to him that night was one of the highlights of my career.

A week later, Shirley and I were on the bus into Leeds when it came to a standstill just outside Harrogate. There had been an accident; a car was on its side in the middle of the road. I asked the bus driver if he would let me off to check if everyone was okay. When I got to the scene I said, 'I'm a physio. Can I give anyone a hand?' Everyone seemed to stand back, and then I saw that there was a young woman, hanging half in and half out of the driver's window. She was conscious and an ambulance had been called. One thing you learn with trauma is not 'what to do', but rather 'what not to do.' Sometimes it is better to do nothing than risk making the situation worse, so I checked her over and stayed with her until the cavalry arrived. A first responder paramedic arrived, and I told her what I knew; she asked me to wait until the ambulance came and it was not long before we heard the sirens and the sound of the air ambulance.

I was reminded of the day almost 40 years before when we had been at Jenny and Steve's house and had witnessed the car accident. I had felt hopeless while the others rushed to help. This time, I was confident that I could be of some use, and it was a much better feeling. I had come full circle.

Later that year, Gordon and Lesley Strachan invited us to their ruby wedding anniversary party in La Manga in Spain. The celebrations lasted all weekend, and there were many famous names there. I played golf with Alex McLeish and my good friends Gary McAllister and Paul Telfer, who were there with many other ex-Scotland internationals. Gordon's friend Rod Stewart and his wife Penny were there too, and for the entertainment on the first night, Gordon arranged for Lulu to do a surprise performance for Lesley. We had a great four days.

We had some great holidays, but the highlight was my 70th birthday in October 2016 while we were in Australia. Adele arranged a party for me. The night before, she asked me to reach over the table to get something for Seb, and then suddenly she let out a scream and exclaimed, 'Dad! My cake!' I had accidentally stuck my hand in the cake Adele had baked for me in the shape of a suitcase. Luckily Adele was able to repair it, but now it looked more authentic, like the battered suitcase I usually used for travelling. On the night, Tony Ayoub and his wife Lillian were there along with Frank Gray and his wife Jane. Frank was now living in Sydney; he had played for Leeds United in the 1975 European Cup Final and then went on to win it with Nottingham Forest in 1980 against Kevin Keegan's Hamburg. While I was in Australia, Frank and I usually met up most weeks for a coffee and a chat about Leeds United. We also got involved with a football team through Frank's pal Maurice Springfield, who became a good friend of mine, along with his brother David. Maurice was also at my birthday party that night.

Before the evening ended, Adele said, 'Sit on the couch, Dad,' so I did with Alex next to me. Then she said, 'I have got something to show you.' To my surprise, she and Miles had put together a video of my life. Lots of people, including family and friends, had filmed their messages as well as many from Leeds. Even Vinnie Jones sent me his greetings from Hollywood. Miles had sorted out the interviews while Adele had spent hours putting it together. It was a thoughtful and unique gift, which I enjoy watching from time to time.

I have lived my dream life. I want to say it was because I had clear goals, and I knew how to get there, but it was mainly through going with the flow, learning from my experiences, both good and bad, and making the most of the chances that came my way. Years ago, I became friends with Howard Clark, the professional golfer. He had played in six Ryder Cups for Europe. He told me about a tournament where he had been heavily beaten by the American Tom Kite, losing by eight holes. He said that he felt destroyed by the loss, but an American coach had given him a mantra to follow: D.B.W.A.: Dream, Believe, Work, Achieve. He kept that in his mind and played well enough to qualify for the next Ryder Cup. After that, he was on the winning side of three Ryder Cups and one winning draw. The motivational appeal of D.B.W.A. stayed with me too. It has guided me through a lot of my life, but mainly I have benefitted through luck, a loving family and the kindness of people I have met over the years.

Like many other kids, my dream was to be a professional footballer. It was a harsh lesson to learn that passion and hard work are not always enough, and admit that I had gone as far as I could. But football was always going to be in my life. There are so many people to thank for their part in my good fortune, and I hope that I have let them know along the way. I will be forever grateful to the late David Sharp at Fielders' Builders Merchants for giving me the opportunity at Halifax Town. As he said at the time, 'I have opened the door for you; now it is up to you what you do with it.' That was when my life changed. Geoff Ladley then did the same for me at Leeds United, I have him to thank for my career there, and we have always remained great friends. Over the years, I worked with many other amazing people, including Dave, Harvey and Donna, who went on to work with other sports teams all over the world. Faith now works in Formula One, and Henry became the head physio at Leeds United, a role he still occupies today. And, of course, none of us will ever forget our dear friend and colleague, Bruce Craven.

These days, I would never have got through that door. Especially at the top level, football and other elite sports have an army of health and performance practitioners. Doctors, nutritionists, psychologists, sports scientists, performance analysts, musculoskeletal and soft tissue therapists, osteopaths and chiropractors are among the many roles considered an essential part of any club in the modern game. A football league physiotherapist must have a degree, often at Masters level, and a host of other competencies and affiliations.

When I began working at Halifax Town, the approach to the treatment of injuries was far more rudimentary, but I had a desire to learn on the job and a willingness to work hard. I had lived a life outside of the football world and my people skills came from working on building sites and coaching youngsters in my spare time. Canada transformed my work ethic, and I worked with people from all over the world.

Those experiences stood me in good stead when I was the only physio at top-division Leeds United, covering the first team, the reserves and the juniors, working seven days a week and with players of many nationalities. I could understand what it was like to be away from home. But the greatest gift has been a very understanding family. It is no exaggeration to say that my family life often had to take a back seat, and without Shirley's unwavering support, especially in the early days, when Adele and Miles were young, I would not have been able to do the job. I owe her and Adele and Miles a debt of gratitude for their encouragement, understanding and love. They are the best team of all.

ABOUT THE AUTHOR

Alan Sutton was born to a working-class family in post-war industrial Bradford. A schoolboy footballer, who realised he would never make the top-flight, he turned his sights on working behind the scenes instead. Working his way up to the role of physio at Leeds United, he was at the club for almost thirty years. His time there took him all over the world where he has met and worked with some of the greatest names in football. Now retired, he lives with his wife in Pateley Bridge, North Yorkshire.

BV - #0060 - 050923 - C0 - 234/156/12 - PB - 9781780916279 - Gloss Lamination